Moral Judgement

Moral Judgement

An Introduction through Anglo-American, German and French Philosophy

Étienne Brown

ROWMAN & LITTLEFIELD
Lanham • Boulder • New York • London

Published by Rowman & Littlefield
An imprint of The Rowman & Littlefield Publishing Group, Inc.
4501 Forbes Boulevard, Suite 200, Lanham, Maryland 20706
www.rowman.com

86-90 Paul Street, London EC2A 4NE

Copyright © 2023 by Étienne Brown

All rights reserved. No part of this book may be reproduced in any form or by any electronic or mechanical means, including information storage and retrieval systems, without written permission from the publisher, except by a reviewer who may quote passages in a review.

British Library Cataloguing in Publication Information available

Library of Congress Cataloging-in-Publication Data

Names: Brown, Étienne, 1988- author.
Title: Moral judgement : an introduction through Anglo-American, German and French philosophy / Étienne Brown.
Description: Lanham : Rowman & Littlefield, [2023] | Includes bibliographical references and index.
Identifiers: LCCN 2022026465 (print) | LCCN 2022026466 (ebook) | ISBN 9781786615169 (hardcover) | ISBN 9781786615176 (epub) | ISBN 9781538173602 (paperback)
Subjects: LCSH: Judgment (Ethics) | Aristotle. | Kant, Immanuel, 1724-1804.
Classification: LCC BJ1408.5 .B76 2023 (print) | LCC BJ1408.5 (ebook) | DDC 170—dc23/eng/20220819
LC record available at https://lccn.loc.gov/2022026465
LC ebook record available at https://lccn.loc.gov/2022026466

To my mother, Louise, who raised three moral agents on her own.

Contents

Introduction ... 1

PART I: THE NEO-ARISTOTELIAN CRITIQUE OF KANTIAN JUDGEMENT

Chapter 1: Moral Judgement in an Aristotelian Communitarian Perspective ... 17

Chapter 2: German Neo-Aristotelianism and the Normativity of *Ethos* ... 39

Chapter 3: A French Aristotelian Perspective on Deliberation ... 57

PART II: THREE PERSPECTIVES ON THE FOUNDATIONS OF MORAL JUDGEMENT

Chapter 4: Habermassian Discourse Ethics and the Grounds of Moral Judgement ... 75

Chapter 5: Kantian Constructivism and the Normativity of Practical Identities ... 97

Chapter 6: Contemporary Aristotelianism and the Normativity of Nature ... 121

PART III: PRINCIPLES, SKILLS AND ACTIONS

Chapter 7: From Principles to Actions ... 147

Chapter 8: Kantian Virtues ... 173

(A Merleau-Pontian) Conclusion ... 193

Notes	205
References	215
Index	221

Introduction

At first sight, moral judgement is not very mysterious. Some would even say that they know it when they see it. At the very least, there are cases in which we can all agree that a person *lacks* judgement. Consider the following example which is taken from the television adaptation of Sally Rooney's novel *Normal People*. In the televised series, teenager Connell informs his mother Lorraine that he will not be taking his lover Marianne to the Debs.[1] This is because Marianne is a social outcast and Connell fears that his friends would mock him if they discovered that he has become intimate with her. Connell is driving his mother home when he breaks the news to her. "Pull over," Lorraine exclaims after hearing it. In this moment, she feels the need to have her son's full attention while explaining to him that refusing to be seen with your lover in public because of her lack of popularity at school is a significant moral failure. "What are you afraid of?" she then asks Connell. Without giving him an opportunity to answer, Lorraine expresses her disappointment by telling her son that she is ashamed of him. She then exits the car, looks Connell right in the eyes, and finally announces that she will be taking the bus home. As she makes clear, staying in the car could only make her say things that she would later regret.

I find it hard not to side with Lorraine in this dispute. To me, her anger is easily understandable. Not only did Connell hurt Marianne's feelings by not inviting her to the Debs, but he also degraded her by refusing to publicly acknowledge the nature of their relationship. He acted like a coward and emotionally harmed his lover as a result. Most importantly for the present discussion, Lorraine's ire reveals that moral judgement is not only a topic of interest for philosophers, but something that normal people wish to possess as well as teach to their children. Arguably, most people can lead good lives without reflecting upon complex philosophical concepts such as "metaethical constructivism," "epistemic infallibilism" and "metaphysical supervenience." In fact, very few people discuss these concepts in their daily lives. However, moral judgement is something about which people talk all the time, and this is a good thing. If they did not, the world would probably be in an even worse state than it currently is.

If we engage in philosophical reflection upon moral judgement, we soon realize that it is more enigmatic than it first appears. Although we often recognize good judgement when we see someone exercising it, it remains difficult to explain what moral judgement is precisely. Some consider that it is essentially a matter of following principles. After all, when we insist on doing something that is important to us, we often say that it is "a matter of principle." Interestingly, the principles that we believe we ought to follow often relate to our social identity. When I think about the moral faults I have committed in the past, for instance, I often consider that I failed to fulfill my obligations as a son, brother, husband, friend or philosophy professor. "This is not how good sons behave," I think, "for good sons do not ignore the phone calls of their mother just because answering them would disturb an especially productive writing day." Other times, I look back at the classes I could have taught better and compare my teaching style to that of my colleagues. Joseph would have taken more time to present the fundamental rules of inference before asking his undergraduate students to write a philosophy paper. Meghan would not have jumped right into a discussion of structural racism without providing hers with the conceptual tools they need to tackle this important yet delicate topic beforehand. My colleagues share many dimensions of my identity. For this very reason, I often judge that we must fulfill similar duties to lead good lives. For example, the three of us ought to create the best educational experience we can for our students regardless of whether we feel like it on a specific day (or anytime, really).

Does exercising moral judgement essentially amount to following principles that relate to the multiple dimensions of our social identity? In the second part of this book, I will defend a very similar conclusion. At this stage, however, this conclusion remains hasty. Consider the following objection. One of my students who is also a soldier—Anthony—once explained to me that he generally avoids relying on moral principles when he is deployed. This certainly sounds scary, but Anthony's point is a subtle one. Certainly, morality has an important role to play in warfare, and he would not deny this. Furthermore, moral principles are useful to the extent that they tell us which actions are permissible and impermissible. Yet they are often too general to help soldiers determine the best course of action in a particular situation. This is because claims about permissibility and impermissibility leave many courses of action open and, as a result, do not spare moral agents from the task which amounts to deciding which precise course of action they ought to follow in the case at hand. For instance, we all know that soldiers should never target civilians, but such a moral principle does not tell them how, precisely, they ought to behave when they encounter civilians behind enemy lines. What kind of relationship is appropriate between soldiers and civilians? Is friendship acceptable? Should the protection of one's fellow countrymen and women always trump the protection of foreign civilians? Even soldiers who are deeply familiar with the central tenets of just war theory will encounter moral questions that have not been pre-answered for them over the course of their career. This is why Anthony likes to say that soldiers should not bank too much on moral principles, but rely instead on their own personal judgement. As he once explained to me, "In combat, the situation will often dictate the action to be taken."

This last sentence is one that you can read *verbatim* in the U.S. Marine Corps training manual. Unfortunately, there is an obvious problem with this claim. If situations always dictated the action to be taken, soldiers would never make moral mistakes and all agents who are motivated to act ethically would behave in an exemplary manner. In fact, they would act in basically the same way when they find themselves in similar situations. This is not the case. Arguably, all human adults have found themselves at least once in a situation in which they desired to do the right thing, but were unsure what this right thing was. Realistically speaking, our moral lives are rife with difficult decisions. Often, the best way to act is not obvious at all.

The idea according to which all well-intentioned agents act in the same way when they find themselves in similar situations is also not very plausible. Some people are better at exercising moral judgement and tend to act very differently than others when they find themselves in comparable situations. When Lorraine explains to Connell that he lacks moral judgement, her speech implies that some people *do not* lack moral judgement, and that such people would have taken an entirely different course of action than the one her son chose himself when he refused to invite Marianne to the Debs. Interestingly, the person to which Lorraine is comparing Connell in this situation is not a different human being, but a *better version of himself*. Considering that Connell is in fact a good person—this is at least what the complete portrait of him drawn by Rooney in *Normal People* suggests—it even makes sense to claim that Lorraine is comparing her son to *his true self*—the one whom she has known for years and usually does not make such ugly moral mistakes.

My comments on Irish teens, bad sons who do not take their mother's calls and U.S. Marines are meant to introduce readers to two rival conceptions of moral judgement. According to the first, exercising judgement essentially amounts to identifying and following universally valid moral principles. If one reliably follows a set of true moral rules, then one can be said to possess moral judgement. By way of contrast, the second model portrays moral judgement as a *skill* which allows those who possess it to know what they ought to do in particular situations without *merely* relying on principles. As we have seen, the need to possess such skill comes from the fact that moral principles rarely help us determine which precise course of action is best among a list of permissible ones. What is more, such principles sometimes conflict with one another. For instance, it might be the case that the two following moral principles are true: (i) I ought to help my elderly relatives when they need me and (ii) I ought to comfort my friends when they are going through a difficult period. Yet we can easily conceive of a situation in which I must choose between taking my grandmother to her hospital appointment and spending an afternoon with my best friend, who just learned that her father died. In situations of this kind, it seems that we must navigate the moral landscape on our own, that is, by relying on our own judgement to find a reasonable compromise between two actions that we cannot perform simultaneously.

As Lorraine's behaviour suggests, we usually consider that the acquisition of moral judgement is the result of moral education. After all, if Lorraine did not hope that her reprimand would incite Connell to treat Marianne better, why would she bother explaining to him that he wronged her? The idea that people can develop moral skills through moral education also provides us with an explanation of why some of them appear to lack judgement. If a person has not been taught to pay attention to the needs of others, then it might be hard for them to understand that morality requires them to do so. Initially, we might be puzzled by this person's selfish actions. "Why in the world would they treat others like this?" we wonder. However, when we learn that they have had a difficult life—for instance, one without role models to which they could turn—then our puzzlement vanishes.

The tension between these two models of moral judgement—one which portrays it as rule-following and another which depicts it as an acquired skill—is the subject of this book. At this stage of my reflection, such models are very rough sketches. In what follows, my objective will be to turn these sketches into detailed pictures. Before I do so, however, I must stress that my primary objective will not be to proclaim a victor, that is, to argue that we should prefer one model of moral judgement over the other. Although I will end my reflection by presenting a conception of moral judgement which draws elements from *both* these models, I still find it necessary to point out that many questions I will attempt to answer go beyond the one which consists of knowing which model of moral judgement is best. Such questions include the following: are these two models of moral judgement truly incompatible; how did the proponents of each model react to the objections advanced by defenders of the other and—most importantly for this book—how has this debate shaped contemporary moral philosophy across the Analytic and Continental divide? To answer such interrogations, I propose to tell a story the main characters of which are French, German and Anglo-American philosophers whose proposed theories of moral judgement have been heavily influenced by two canonical philosophers: Aristotle and Kant.[2]

KANTIANS AND ARISTOTELIANS

Many contemporary philosophers who primarily conceive of moral judgement as a matter of *acting on principle* have been influenced by Kant's practical philosophy.[3] This is hardly surprising. Not only did Kant (1996) conceive of several moral duties that fall upon all rational beings—all of which can be expressed in the forms of rules—but he also attempted to justify such rules by grounding them in a universal principle—the categorical imperative—from which they all derive.[4] This suggests that moral reasoning primarily consists in wondering whether the courses of action we contemplate in our daily lives are compatible with rules of duty. To know that I am morally permitted to φ, for instance, I would need to ensure that φ-ing does not lead me to breach any of my duties. These simple claims already raise complex philosophical questions. First, can philosophers truly reach a universal standpoint from which they can identify rules that all moral agents ought to respect? Second, even if we accept that they can, will such rules be sufficiently precise to guide action? While the first question focuses on the grounding of moral rules, the second pertains to the function that these rules can or cannot play in moral judgement.

Several philosophers who raise such questions—often to criticize Kantians—have been influenced by Aristotle's practical philosophy. According to many neo-Aristotelians, grounding universal moral principles that all human beings ought to respect is quite simply an impossible philosophical task. Moreover, such philosophers typically draw on Aristotle's *Nicomachean Ethics* (1984) to argue that moral principles are not precise enough to help agents single out the best way to act in concrete situations. To do so, Aristotle argues, they need to possess practical wisdom (or *phronesis*), an intellectual virtue which allows agents to perceive what the best thing to do in the case at hand is. In other words, practical wisdom involves a form of moral sensation (*aisthesis*) which enables agents to detect the morally salient features of particular situations. To see this, consider that there are an infinite number of facts to which we can pay attention in our daily lives. Yet only some of these facts are morally significant. Let us say that an injured woman crosses my path while I walk to the office. Certainly, this is not a fact that I can ignore if I want to act rightly. If I did, then I would breach my Samaritan duty to help people in distress.[5] In contrast, the fact that the injured woman is currently wearing a purple sweater is one that I can safely ignore from a moral point of view. Put simply, the colour of the woman's sweater changes nothing about how I ought to act here and now. Morally speaking, it is probably better for me not to think about the sweater's colour for there are more important facts to consider (how badly injured the woman is, whether anyone else in my surroundings can help me assist her, etc.). Now, according to Aristotle and many of his contemporary followers, not everyone is equally good at identifying morally salient facts. Those that have not received an appropriate moral education and acquired a set of virtues (including practical wisdom) will not be able to do so as well as those who have and, as a result, possess moral judgement.

My tendency to speak of contemporary Kantians and neo-Aristotelians should not obscure the fact that Kant and Aristotle's practical philosophies are subject to myriad interpretations not all of which are compatible with one another. Nevertheless, neo-Aristotelians often join forces to undertake a general critique of the Kantian model of moral judgement. Indeed, in twentieth and early twenty-first-century philosophy, we can easily identify neo-Aristotelian critiques of Kantian approaches to moral reasoning and judgement. Before I explain how such critiques unfolded in France, Germany and the Anglo-American world—this will be the object of the first part of this book—let me point out that Kantian and Aristotelian models of moral judgement share many important features. First, contemporary Kantians and neo-Aristotelians agree that human reason has the power to determine how one ought to act morally speaking. When the latter criticize the former, they are neither claiming that the knowledge required to behave in a rightful manner will forever elude us nor that there is no such thing as the right way to act. In other words, neo-Aristotelian discourses on the insufficiencies of moral principles in the exercise of moral judgement do not pave the way towards moral relativism. Second, contemporary Kantians and neo-Aristotelians typically consider that a moral agent can have reasons to φ even if she does not desire to φ. For instance, they are both likely to agree that you have a reason to help the purple sweater–wearing injured woman whether or not you feel like it. Importantly, this means that the debate between Kantians and neo-Aristotelians on the nature of moral judgement which this book retraces is undergirded by a shared agreement that (i) that there are right and wrong ways to act; (ii) that moral agents can know what these are; and (ii) that our reasons to behave in such a way do not all depend on our subjective desires.[6]

Of course, other theories of moral judgement have been defended in contemporary moral philosophy. For instance, utilitarians influenced by Jeremy Bentham and John Stuart Mill defend a different account of moral judgement.[7] If this is so, why did I choose to focus on contemporary Kantianism and neo-Aristotelianism specifically? One reason relates to the way Kantians reacted to Aristotelian objections directed against the model of moral judgement they favour. In the last decades, contemporary Kantians integrated many Aristotelian insights to their theory of moral reasoning. In fact, one of my main suggestions in this book is that contemporary Kantianism in moral philosophy has been deeply transformed by Aristotelian objections, and that such objections incited Kantians to refine and improve their theory of moral judgement. That said, the second reason which explains my choice to focus on contemporary Kantian and neo-Aristotelian accounts of moral judgements is by far the most important to me. In a nutshell, I am convinced that doing so can help us bridge the gap between Continental and Analytic approaches to moral philosophy.

FRANCE, GERMANY AND THE ANGLO-AMERICAN WORLD

In contemporary philosophy, we tend to exaggerate the differences that exist between the Analytic and Continental traditions. While a successful defence of this claim would require more than one monograph, one of my central objectives in this book—perhaps the most important one—will be to show that it holds true when we consider work on moral judgement. Not only have neo-Aristotelian objections been formulated against Kantian theories of moral judgement in the French, German and the Anglo-American philosophical traditions, but such objections are also very similar. Between 1980 and 2010, moral philosophers stemming from these three countries have debated the (im)possibility of grounding universal moral principles as well as the role that principles and virtues can play in moral deliberation. This is the historiographical claim that I will argue in the following chapters. Here is how I will attempt do so.

The first part of this book retraces neo-Aristotelian critiques of Kantian models of moral judgement that developed in contemporary Anglo-American, German and French philosophy. Specifically, I present three distinct objections directed by neo-Aristotelian philosophers against Kantian models of moral judgement. Hopefully, my introductory remarks have already provided readers with clues about the content of these objections. According to the first, Kantians conceive of moral judgements as the application of general principles for which they cannot provide an adequate rational grounding. According to the second, such principles are too general to guide action. Finally, the third objection amounts to the claim that agents who lack virtues will be unable to act rightly even if they are provided with a list of moral principles that they ought to respect. Although each objection is singled out in a specific chapter, we will see that philosophers who formulate one often formulate one of (or both) the others.

Chapter 1 recasts the Rawls-MacIntyre debate as a disagreement on the nature of moral reasoning and judgement rather than a political quarrel. After examining Rawls's interpretation of the categorical imperative and his deontological conception of moral judgement, I present the key objections directed by MacIntyre against Kant and Rawls, as well as his alternative conception of practical rationality and judgement. While doing so, I introduce readers to the neo-Aristotelian claim that moral judgement cannot be appropriately exercised by non-virtuous agent.

Chapter 2 focuses on German neo-Aristotelian philosophers whose work remains unknown by most Anglo-American philosophers, even those working in the Continental tradition. Specifically, the chapter examines how a key theme of German neo-Aristotelianism—the normativity of "Ethos"—developed in the works of three of its central representatives: Joachim Ritter, Hans-Georg Gadamer and Rüdiger Bubner. According to these three philosophers, moral judgements are not rooted in universal moral principles such as those defended by Kantians, but rather in the values of particular "forms of life" (*Lebensformen*) which are themselves embodied in social institutions. I then consider how Habermas's exchange with Bubner helped him to develop his own attempt at rationally grounding moral judgements—discourse ethics—a moral theory to which I devote more attention in chapter 4.

Chapter 3 focuses on the neo-Aristotelian objection that moral judgement should not be conceived of as the application of general moral principles to particular cases. To illustrate this claim, I focus on the works of French neo-Aristotelian Vincent Descombes, who generally argues that deontological principles are not sufficiently precise to guide action. I then discuss Descombes's intentionalist model of moral deliberation as well as his account of practical wisdom, both of which are based on his interpretation of the philosophical thoughts of Elizabeth Anscombe and Peter Geach.

The second part of this book considers three responses to the objection according to which moral philosophers do not have the means to base moral judgements on an account of universal moral principles that all human beings ought to respect. Let us call this the problem of the *rational grounding* of moral judgements. Chapters 4 and 5 are critical assessments of two Kantian attempts to solve this problem in response to the Aristotelian critique. Specifically, chapter 4 focuses on Jürgen Habermas's discourse ethics, and more precisely on his argument that all rational discourse presupposes a commitment to certain universal moral principles. If this is so, then all discussants who engage in rational debate with others will have to admit that their behaviour is constrained by universally binding obligations. As we will see, however, Habermas's philosophy is haunted by a dilemma: either he admits that the conditions that must be met for discussants to successfully ground universal moral principles cannot be met *or* his approach collapses into that of Anglo-American Kantians like Rawls or Christine Korsgaard, a conclusion that he certainly seeks to avoid. Chapter 5 considers a second solution to the problem of rational grounding, one that has recently been defended by Korsgaard. There, I relate some of her key insights to the neo-Aristotelian claim that moral obligations are rooted in the multiple dimensions of our practical identity before assessing her transcendental argument which aims to supports the conclusion that *human beings must value their humanity and that of others if they are to value anything at all.* I also argue that an examination of both Sartre and contemporary French Kantianism can help us conceive of an objection to which Korsgaard's stance remains vulnerable, one that I call the *problem of reflexivity.*

In many ways, chapter 6 is an outlier in this book. Although chapters 4, 5, 7 and all contain critical discussions of Kantian responses to the objections considered in the first part of this book, chapter 6 examines how some contemporary neo-Aristotelians have themselves attempted to solve the problem of rational grounding. By assessing Alasdair MacIntyre's late works, as well as Philippa Foot's ethical naturalism, I show that not all neo-Aristotelians are committed to the claim that a universal moral standpoint from which objective obligations could be grounded is beyond reach. This chapter ends with a discussion of the Foot-McDowell debate which highlights the deep divide between neo-Aristotelians who argue that moral obligations can be grounded in an account of the normativity of nature and those who rather believe that the very idea according to which moral judgements need to be *grounded* is misguided and fundamentally un-Aristotelian in character.

The third and last part of this book examines Kantian responses to the neo-Aristotelian objections that moral principles are too general to guide action and cannot lead non-virtuous agents to act rightly. Chapter 7 focuses on the following claim: even if we admit that moral principles can be rationally grounded, such principles do not truly guide action as they merely allow moral agents to distinguish between permissible and impermissible actions. Let us call this the *problem of indeterminacy* in moral judgement. There, I examine Hannah Arendt's solution to this problem, which builds on Kant's theory of *reflective judgement.* After formulating objections against this solution, I turn to the Kantian account of moral deliberation put forward by Onora O'Neill, Barbara Herman and Nancy Sherman. Specifically, I examine the claim according to which moral rules are imperfect duties which provide agents with some leeway in determining how to act in the case at hand.

Chapter 8 sheds a Kantian light on the relationship between virtue and moral judgement by building on two of Kant's late works—the *Doctrine of Virtue* and the *Pedagogy*—and, once again, on the works of O'Neill, Herman and Sherman. There, I argue that Kantian virtues such as apathy, sympathy and gratitude can bolster moral motivation and assist moral deliberation by helping agents to identify morally salient facts in particular situations. Only the empathetic person, for instance, recognizes her friend's suffering as a reason to offer help. This means that the main difference between the virtuous and vicious person is not purely conative, but also cognitive in character.

Lastly, the book ends with the presentation of a hybrid Aristotelian-Kantian model of moral judgement that Kantian responses to neo-Aristotelian objections help us conceptualize. In the conclusion, I sketch an alternative way to conceive of the universal moral standpoint by drawing on French phenomenology and, more specifically, on Merleau-Ponty's concept of the *lateral universal*. Instead of resorting to philosophical thought experiments, I argue, philosophers should draw from social scientific research and engage deeply with works written in other languages than English to build a conception of moral universalism informed by myriad cultural worldviews.

METHODOLOGICAL REMARKS

This book retraces a debate on moral judgement that opposed contemporary Kantian philosophers to neo-Aristotelians. To my knowledge, it is the first to relate analytic reflections on this topic to philosophical contributions coming from both France and Germany, many of which have not yet been translated. By writing it, I hope to allow readers to familiarize themselves with several French and German philosophical works that have not been extensively discussed—and sometimes not discussed at all—within Anglo-American philosophy. By exploring the different chapters of the book, readers will gain knowledge of the philosophical claims defended by lesser-known philosophers such as Rüdiger Bubner, Vincent Descombes, Alain Renaut and Souleymane Bachir Diagne.[8] Those that are not already familiar with analytic philosophy will also benefit from my critical discussions of the thoughts of Rawls, MacIntyre, Korsgaard, Herman, O'Neill, Sherman, Foot and McDowell. Lastly, readers who are very knowledgeable about contemporary analytic moral philosophy but lack exposure to continental philosophy can turn to chapters which focus on Habermas, Arendt, Sartre and Merleau-Ponty (in the conclusion). In fact, if every reader becomes more familiar with the thought of even *one* of these philosophers, then I will have fulfilled my main objective.

Although this objective is primarily historiographical, the story I intend to tell would not be as interesting as it can be if I did not step into the philosophical arena myself, that is, critically engage with the arguments and objections advanced by these philosophers. Let the reader be warned: my contribution to the history of contemporary moral philosophy will therefore be an opinionated one. When it seems to me that certain objections miss the mark, for instance, I won't refrain from pointing this out. As mentioned, I also sketch an Aristotelian-Kantian hybrid theory of moral judgement in the conclusion of the book to which readers who are not interested in historiographical inquiry can directly turn. According to this Kantian-Aristotelian account, our moral duties are rooted in the multiple dimensions of our social identity. As these duties conflict with each other, moral agents must ultimately rely on their own capacities to determine which action best coheres with their competing obligations, and which obligation should be given priority in a particular situation. That said, my choice to focus on what I call the historiography of contemporary moral philosophy gives a distinctive shape and personality to this book. Unlike many introductions to moral philosophy, it does not contain an exhaustive review of all approaches to ethics (Kantian deontology, Aristotelian virtue ethics, consequentialism, feminist ethics, social contract theory, etc.). In fact, it is much more focused than general introductions to moral philosophy. It focuses on one of its subtopics—moral judgement—and seeks to cover works emerging from more than one philosophical tradition. As a result, it does not cover all recent work on moral judgement produced by analytics philosophers. To do so, I would have had to set aside French and German approaches to moral judgement, and the book would have lost much of its value.

The choice to describe philosophers as contemporary Kantians or neo-Aristotelians whose work I examine in this book is also mine. It is not a riskless one as all of them clearly reject at least *some* important claims made by Aristotle or Kant. Furthermore, some historians of philosophy go as far as arguing that the label "neo-Aristotelian" has become meaningless considering the gap that separates Aristotle's philosophy from its contemporary interpretations. In her remarkable book on *Greek Ethics*, for instance, Monique Canto-Sperber underlines that "contemporary Aristotelians are not Aristotelian in the way they think they are."[9] As she explains, the term "neo-Aristotelian" is sometimes carelessly applied to philosophers who defend incompatible ethical views, but all agree that modern moral philosophy is lacking in some way. How can one avoid such carelessness? In my view, the best way to proceed is to strive to understand contemporary philosophers as they understand themselves. In practice, this means that I do not deny the labels "contemporary Kantian" and "neo-Aristotelian" to philosophers who claim it on the grounds that their thoughts are not sufficiently similar to Aristotle or Kant's own. I find it much more interesting to pay special attention to the reasons for which contemporary philosophers claim such labels. Why does French philosopher Alain Renaut call himself a Kantian although some of his philosophical claims are more reminiscent of Sartre's existentialism than of Kant's own views? For what reasons do Foot and Descombes see themselves as indebted to Aristotle even if they disagree with many claims defended by MacIntyre and German neo-Aristotelians?[10] These are the kind of questions I propose to ask. Interestingly, the philosophers whose work I discuss rarely conceive of themselves as pure historians of philosophy to the extent that they all develop their own conception of moral judgement. That said, they all reject ahistorical philosophical thinking. In fact, one of their common beliefs is that Aristotle or Kant's works contain important insights about the nature of moral reasoning which should not be ignored by contemporary philosophers.

Before I begin, a few final remarks are in order. First, there is a wide array of moral philosophers who describe themselves as contemporary Kantian or neo-Aristotelians, but only some of them are considered in this book. How did I select those that are? In general, philosophers considered in the first part of this book are not neo-Aristotelians *tout court*, but neo-Aristotelians who developed a powerful critique of the Kantian model of moral judgement. In the second and third parts, I focus on contemporary Kantians who actively engaged with neo-Aristotelian objections. Still, I had to leave out some philosophers who meet these criteria and were included in the original version of this manuscript, which is a PhD dissertation I completed at the Université Paris-Sorbonne. Here, I am thinking of David Wiggins and Johnathan Dancy in particular. While writing in French, I aimed to introduce French philosophical audiences to their analytic reflections on moral judgement. In this book, I often seek to do the opposite, which is to introduce English readers to the works of contemporary French and German philosophers.

While my reflection focuses on three intellectual traditions, I also find it important to underline that the conclusions I draw could be enriched by the reflection of philosophers who work outside of France, Germany and the Anglo-American world. In fact, my remarks on translation as a rich intellectual inquiry contained in the conclusion of this book clearly support this claim. Here, I am thinking of current philosophical discussions of Islamic conceptions of the foundations of moral judgement (al-Attar 2017), African moral theory (Metz 2007), the Indian model of moral development (Mulla and Krishnan 2014) and judgement in Confucian ethics (Lai 2009).

Given that I have been educated in Canada, France and Germany, I am much more familiar with the Analytic and Continental philosophical traditions than with such works, which explains the focus of this book. English, French and German are also the only three languages that I am competent to read. Still, I envision this book as a point of departure; once we get a clearer picture of the theories of moral judgement developed in France, Germany and the Anglo-American world, my hope is that it will become easier to compare them with other philosophical models.

The third methodological remark is perhaps the most delicate one. Contemporary European and North American philosophers are only beginning to address the racist history of their discipline. What is more, there is no doubt in my mind that there are racist elements in both Aristotle and Kant's thoughts. For instance, Charles Mills (2017) has convincingly argued that Kant envisioned Black people and Native Americans as natural slaves (*untermenschen*). This echoes Aristotle's infamous claim that some humans are naturally born to govern while others are born to obey, one which served to justify slavery in ancient Athens. In my view, the existence of racist elements in the thoughts of historical Western philosophers should be acknowledged rather than swept under the rug. This does not mean that contemporary Kantians and neo-Aristotelians who occupy the centre stage of my reflection in this book have inherited this racism. In fact, their methodological wager is that it is possible for contemporary philosophers to separate Kant and Aristotle's most valuable insights about the nature of moral judgement from their poorly argued racist views. I too believe that this can be done, or I would not have written this book. For instance, it seems to me that one can endorse the Aristotelian insight according to which moral judgement can only be exercised by virtuous people while rejecting Aristotle's claim that some humans are naturally fit to govern. That said, I find it important to shed light on this methodological choice so that it can more easily be challenged by those who disagree with it. If we are to keep reading Aristotle and Kant—and I believe that we should—then it is likely that we will abandon some of their claims while defending others. Yet doing so does not spare us of the duty to recognize that some of the views held by past philosophers have helped legitimize persisting forms of inequality and injustice, and to unequivocally condemn such views.

A final remark pertains to the many ways in which this book can be read. Readers who are unfamiliar with philosophical work on moral judgement or with both contemporary Kantianism and neo-Aristotelianism will benefit from reading the booking in its entirety. Yet I suspect that many readers who choose to pick up this book will be interested in specific parts of it. For instance, those who are mainly interested in neo-Aristotelianism can focus on the first part of the book (as well as chapter 6), and those who want to read about contemporary Kantianism can move directly to its second and third parts. Other readers may be especially interested in learning more about the German philosophical tradition. These can start by reading chapter 2, which focuses on German neo-Aristotelianism after the Second World War, move on to chapter 4 (on Habermas's discourse ethics) and finally turn to my remarks on Arendt's theory of judgement in chapter 7. The same method can be used by readers interested in French philosophy, who can concentrate on Vincent Descombes's critique of contemporary Kantianism (chapter 3), read my remarks on Sartre and Renaut in chapter 5 and finally reflect upon the Merleau-Pontian conclusion with which I end the book. In other words, this book will easily allow readers to tailor their reading experience to their needs. While the easiest way to read is still to follow the natural order of chapters, I wanted to accommodate rebellious readers, for I am one myself. Throughout the book, I have also deliberately kept endnotes to a minimum.

PART I

The Neo-Aristotelian Critique of Kantian Judgement

Chapter 1

Moral Judgement in an Aristotelian Communitarian Perspective

Why begin a cross-traditional inquiry on moral judgement by discussing the philosophical works of John Rawls and Alasdair MacIntyre? After all, Rawls is primarily known for his reflection on political justice and MacIntyre for his communitarian critique of contemporary liberalism. However, my objective in this chapter is to recast these two thinkers in a somewhat unusual role: that of philosophers of moral judgement. This is because MacIntyre's critique of Kant and Rawls helps us grasp one of three neo-Aristotelian objections which are at the very core of my reflection throughout this book. In a nutshell, this objection amounts to the claim that contemporary Kantians typically fail to discuss the set of virtues which agents must possess in order to make good moral judgements. Within Macintyre's philosophy, however, this objection directly relates to a second one, which pertains to the putatively universal foundations of moral judgement that some Kantians believe they have identified. Although it would be difficult for me to completely avoid discussing this second objection, it is worth noting that I devote significant more attention to it in the next chapter, which focuses on German neo-Aristotelianism.

With regard to Rawls, a critical examination of his philosophy will allow me to introduce some key components of the Kantian conception of moral judgement, which is the central topic of this book, including ruled-based reasoning, universalization tests and the very concept of moral duty. Such an examination is also a useful point of departure to better appreciate some of the claims made by Kantian philosophers to whom I turn in the second part of this book (Jürgen Habermas and Christine Korsgaard, for instance). Beyond his political views, how does Rawls conceive of moral judgement and how is this conception Kantian in character? In MacIntyre's perspective, what are its central shortcomings? As the reader will see, answering such questions is a fruitful way to begin a reflection on the role that principles and virtues play in moral reasoning. It also sheds light on parts of Rawls's philosophy which are less frequently discussed than his conception of political justice, for instance his interpretation and defence of Kant's categorical imperative. Let me therefore begin by considering Rawls's views on duty, desire and the categorical imperative. Then, I'll turn to MacIntyre's attack on contemporary Kantian moral theory.

RAWLS ON DUTY, DESIRE AND THE CATEGORICAL IMPERATIVE

In *A Theory of Justice*, Rawls (1999a, 53) famously defends the two following principles of justice:

> First: each person is to have an equal right to the most extensive scheme of equal basic liberties compatible with a similar scheme of liberties for others.

> Second: social and economic inequalities are to be arranged so that they are both (a) reasonably expected to be to everyone's advantage, and (b) attached to positions and offices open to all.

Although such principles entail institutional arrangements that have been widely debated by contemporary political philosophers, they also give rise to *principles for individuals* which specify how reasonable people ought to behave (Rawls 1999a, 93). "In addition to principles for institutions," Rawls explains, "there must be an agreement on principles for such notions as fairness and fidelity, mutual respect and beneficence as these apply to individuals" within a complete philosophical conception of right.

Principles for individuals define moral requirements that can be divided into two types: *obligations* and *natural duties*. Obligations are duties that people acquire as a result of their voluntary acts. If I freely promise you that I will help you move on Tuesday, for instance, then I acquire the obligation to help you move on Tuesday. In addition to promising, there is a wide range of voluntary acts through which I can acquire obligations. These include accepting a position of authority (judge, mayor, senator, etc.), taking another person as my spouse, or even accepting to play a game. In contrast to obligations, natural duties apply to all people without regard to their voluntary acts. Such duties are deemed *positive* when they require us to do something good to others and *negative* when they require us to refrain from doing something bad to them. By way of example, our natural duty of mutual aid is a positive duty in that it requires us to help those in need. If a child is drowning and you have reasons to believe that you could save her life, then you have a duty not ignore her and walk by as if nothing bad were happening. Conversely, our natural duty not to injure fellow human beings is a negative duty to the extent that it merely forbids us to do something bad to them. In Rawls's view, we cannot acquire the obligation to perform a particular kind of action when we already have a natural duty to do so. For instance, it does not make sense to promise to others that we will not injure them and then consider that we have acquired this obligation through our promise. This is because we have a natural duty not to injure others regardless of what we have promised to them.

One of our fundamental natural duties is the duty of justice, which requires us to comply with the rules made by just institutions when they exist, and to contribute to the creation of such institutions when they have not yet been created. Of course, the amount of time and energy that each person should invest in the fight for social justice depends on their life circumstances. What is more, Rawls is well aware that our natural duties and obligations sometimes conflict with one another. If I spend most of my time caring for a sick family member, for instance, then I am arguably not in a position to contribute to the creation of just political institutions to the same extent of other citizens. In chapter 7, I will consider Rawls's solution to the problem of conflict between rules of duties—which focuses on the concept of *lexical ordering*—in greater detail. For now, let me point out that a basic picture of moral judgement already emerges from the preceding remarks. According to this picture, some moral obligations fall upon us for the very reason that we are rational beings whose actions often have a positive or negative impact on the well-being of others. Furthermore, we acquire a second set of moral obligations through the social roles we accept to play and the voluntary actions we perform. When such obligations conflict, we face the task of deciding which obligation we ought to prioritize (although I have admittedly not yet paid to this problem all the attention that it deserves). As we will see in the second part of this book, this is the basic model of judgement that several contemporary Kantians take as a point of departure for their reflection on how rational beings ought to behave. Before turning to such philosophers, let us consider why Rawls believes that his *Theory of Justice* and the model of moral judgement which it contains is properly *Kantian* in nature.

Note first that Rawls uses Kantian language throughout his *magnum opus* and incites us to envision his theory of justice as being universalist in character. Like Kant's moral law, the principles of justice "are to be universal in application" and "must hold for everyone in virtue of their being moral persons" (Rawls 1999a, 114–16). Borrowing a judicial metaphor from Kant's practical philosophy, Rawls indicates that such principles are the "final court of appeal in practical reasoning" as they "override the demands of law and customs, and of social rules generally." Moreover, such principles should be made public so that they are known by everyone. This publicness condition is "clearly implicit in Kant's doctrine of the categorical imperative insofar as it requires us to act in accordance with principles that one would be willing as a rational being to enact as law for a kingdom of ends." A Kantian universalist interpretation of Rawls's theory of justice is also supported by the claim that evaluating society from the point of view of the original position amounts to seeing it *sub specie aeternitatis*, that is, "not only from all social but also from all temporal points view" (Rawls 1999a, 514).[1] More specifically, this perspective amounts to a "certain form of thought and feeling that rational persons can adopt within the world." In a nutshell, we can say that—like Kant—Rawls believes he has identified normative principles that are universally valid and apply to all rational beings simply because they are rational beings.

Rawls's perspective remains Kantian when he describes his theory of justice as being *deontological* rather than *teleological* in nature. Teleological moral theories begin with a reflection on the nature of the human good. According to this perspective, what moral philosophers must do to define the duties and obligations which fall upon us amounts to painting a picture of a good human life, and then identifying the moral rules that we must respect for all human beings to have a reasonable chance of living such life. By way of contrast, Rawls's theory of justice is not based on a complete theory of the human good. This is because he believes that one can separate the philosophical reflection on the basic rules of coordinated living from more ambitious attempts to describe the good life. Even if people have incompatible conceptions of what counts as a good human life, they can identify some "primary goods" that all people desire to possess and agree on rules which stipulate how such goods should be distributed amongst them. By way of example, people certainly disagree about the role which religious belief ought to play in life, but religious believers and atheists can still agree that everyone should enjoy a political good—freedom—which allows them to choose whether they want to practice a particular religion. This feature of Rawls's philosophy is known as *the priority of the right over the good*, and it is to none other than Kant that Rawls attributes its discovery. In his commentary on the second chapter of Kant's "Analytic of Pure Practical Reason," indeed, he writes that:

> The burden of this chapter is to explain what has been called Kant's Copernican Revolution in moral philosophy. Rather than starting from a conception of the good given independently of the right, we start from a conception of the right—of the moral law—given by pure (as opposed to empirical) practical reason. We then specify in the light of this conception what ends are permissible and what social arrangements are right and just. (Rawls 1999b, 509)[2]

Yet perhaps there is no place where Kant's influence on Rawls's philosophy is more evident than in the section of *A Theory of Justice* titled "The Kantian Interpretation of Justice as Fairness." There, Rawls stresses that his theory is based on a Kantian conception of *autonomy*, which he opposes, like Kant, to the concept of *heteronomy*. In general, autonomy demands that the principles upon which an agent acts "are not adopted because of his social position or natural endowments" or the "specific things that he happens to want" (Rawls 1999a, 222). In Kant's practical philosophy, duties that fall upon us are independent of empirical desires. When an agent bases her action on her empirical desires instead of her rational understanding of the demands of morality, her action becomes heteronomous. By way of contrast, autonomous actions are performed *from duty*, that is, by agents who are motivated to perform them because they understand that morality requires them to do so.

Now, Rawls considers that the thought experiment which grounds the principles of justice—the original position—perfectly embodies Kantian autonomy. Specifically, the original position is a situation in which "free and equal persons who are deprived of all knowledge of their personal characteristics and social and historical circumstances" must choose principles of justice to live by (Freeman 2019). Because they are deprived of such knowledge, Rawls describes them as standing behind a veil of ignorance which makes it impossible for them to choose principles of justice in a heteronomous manner. To see this, imagine that I ask myself the following questions: "If I did not know that I am a married white man who teaches philosophy in California and enjoys hiking and wine club memberships, which principles of justice would I select to regulate social life? Which of my opinions on justice comes from my current particular desires and which are tied to more general features that I share with all other human beings?" In Rawls's view, attempting to answer this question in a sincere manner will prevent me from choosing principles which are catered to my desires and advantageous to my social position—say, all philosophy professors should be excused from paying taxes. This suffices for us to say that I did not select such principles *heteronomously*.

Importantly, once principles of justice have been selected in the original position, people are required to implement them in real life *even when doing so frustrates their subjective desires*. In other words, they ought to act autonomously in the Kantian sense of the term. As we have seen, the duty of justice requires all citizens to obey and contribute to the establishment of just institutions. Of course, this duty applies to them independently of whether such institutions will better or worsen their current social condition. Like Kant's philosophy, Rawls theory of justice rests on the idea that people are capable of subordinating instrumental rationality—the calculations through which they determine which actions would best satisfy their individual desires—to moral reasoning. If they do so successfully, then they will avoid selfish behaviour and act in ways that allow them to fulfill their natural duties and obligations.

In works subsequent to *A Theory of Justice*, Rawls deepened his analysis of the relationship between instrumental rationality and moral reasoning. In his article "Kantian Constructivism in Moral Theory," he argues that such an analysis borrows many elements from Kant's moral psychology. As he explains, his:

> Kantian doctrine joins the content of justice with a certain conception of the person; and this conception regards persons as both free and equal, as capable of acting both reasonably and rationally, and therefore as capable of taking part in social cooperation among persons so conceived. (Rawls 1980, 518)

Here, the key distinction is between *reasonable* and *rational* action. What Rawls calls the "Rational" is a person's ability to freely set goals for herself, and then to reflect upon the most efficient way to pursue such goals.[3] In his perspective, the Rational must always yield to the "Reasonable," which refers to people's capacity to identify and obey moral requirements. In Rawls's own words, "the Reasonable subordinates the Rational because its principles limit, and in a Kantian doctrine limit absolutely, the final ends that can be pursued" (Rawls 1980, 530). Simply put, reasonable citizens can do anything they want *provided* that their actions do not lead them to violate their natural duties and obligations.

Interestingly, Rawls believes that the contrast between the Rational and the Reasonable mirrors Kant's own distinction between *pure practical reason* and *empirical practical reason*. In the works of both Kant and Rawls, the inner life of moral agents is portrayed as a battleground between two kinds of reasoning. While empirical practical reason helps us effectively indulge in our passions (e.g., "If I accept this job, I will become rich and finally be able to buy this apartment in San Francisco"), pure practical reason constrains our tendency give in to our desires (e.g., "but the oil industry is destroying the environment, and I ought to refuse this job not to be morally complicit in this"). What unites Kant and Rawls in terms of moral psychology is their belief that pure practical reason can win the fight against pure practical reason. Admittedly, Rawls is much more confident in the latter's strength than Kant is. While Kant portrays human beings as being continuously tempted by evil, Rawls believes that moral education and socialization will lead ordinary citizens to develop a "sense of justice which will incite them to comply with their natural duties and obligations."[4]

So far, we have seen that Rawls reflects upon moral judgement through a Kantian lens. In both *A Theory of Justice* and later works, he depicts moral reasoning as a matter of identifying courses of action which will allow agents to fulfill their natural duties and obligations. To act rightly, moral agents must find the psychological strength to subordinate their subjective desires to their sense of justice, which incites them to prioritize the moral obligations that fall upon them over the satisfaction of their interests. What is more, Rawls confers a universalist character to his theory by arguing that the original position allows us to see society *sub specie aeternitatis* and identify universal moral requirements. Before turning to MacIntyre's criticism of Kant and Rawls, I want to push this idea further by considering the parallels that Rawls draws between the original position and Kant's categorical imperative.

In *Themes in Kant's Moral Philosophy*, Rawls offers a peculiar interpretation of Kant's first formulation of the categorical imperative—the formula of universal law—which requires all rational beings to "act only according to that maxim by which you can at the same time will that it should become a universal law" (Kant 1996, 73).[5] At the core of such interpretation is a four-step schematic rendering of the categorical imperative that he calls the "CI-Procedure." According to his perspective, the CI-procedure "helps us determine the content of the moral law as it applies to us as reasonable and rational persons endowed with conscience and moral sensibility" (Rawls 1999b, 498). More specifically, it allows us to picture how social life would be transformed if the subjective principle on which a moral agent acts—what Kant calls a "maxim"—was simultaneously adopted by all rational beings. As is well known, the first formulation of the categorical imperative is a universalization test, and Rawls tells us that this test incites us to represent how the world would be transformed if particular maxims were universalized. This is what he calls an *adjusted social world*.

Let us unpack this idea by considering the CI-procedure step by step. At the first step, we begin with an agent's maxim, which has the form of a hypothetical statement. More precisely, maxims depict actions as means to reach particular ends. To see this, imagine that I reason in the following manner: "*If* I want fewer people to live in poverty, *then* I should give 10 percent of my salary to charity." In this case, I believe that I should give money to charity as doing so would allow me to satisfy one of my particular desires (that there be fewer people living in poverty). Rawls (1999b, 499) expresses this idea with the following technical statement:

> I am to do X in circumstances C in order to bring about Y. (Here X is an action and Y a state of affairs.)

The second step of the CI-procedure generalizes a particular action by portraying it as one that all people ought to perform so that:

> Everyone is to do X in circumstances C in order to bring about Y. (Here X is an action and Y a state of affairs.)

With the example of charitable giving, for instance, the second step of the CI-procedure would yield the statement according to which "everyone is to give 10 percent of their salary to charity so that fewer people live in poverty." Then, the third step of the CI-procedure requires us to imagine that generalized statements yielded by the second step—general precepts of the form "Everyone is to do X . . ."—are *things that all people always do*. This is what Rawls calls *laws of nature*, which are of the following kind:

> Everyone always does X in circumstances C in order to bring about Y. (Here X is an action and Y a state of affairs.)

Keeping the same example, we get the statement "Everyone always gives 10 percent of their salary to charity so that fewer people live in abject poverty."

Lastly, we come to the fourth step of the CI-procedure. Here is how Rawls describes it:

> We are to adjoin the law of nature at step (3) to the existing laws of nature and then calculate at best we can what the order of nature would be once the effects of the newly adjoined law of nature have had a chance to work themselves out.

To determine whether we have a moral imperative to perform an action, we thus need to imagine what the world would look like if *everyone* committed it, and then wonder if this world is preferable to the one in which we currently live. Imagine, for instance, that the main difference between a world in which everyone always gives 10 percent of their salary to charity and our current world is, as hoped, that fewer people live in poverty. With other conditions remaining the same, this possible world is preferable to the actual world and hence I can conclude that I ought to give 10 percent of my salary to charity.

To summarize, Rawls portrays Kant's formula of universal law as a heuristic device which allows us to compare and evaluate possible worlds. More surprisingly, he also considers that such a heuristic device needs to be accompanied by limits on information in order to function well. As he explains:

> I believe that Kant may have assumed that the decision at step (4) is subject to at least two kinds of limits on information [. . .] The first limit is that we are to ignore the more particular features of persons, including ourselves, as well as the specific content of their and our final ends and desires [. . .] The second limit is that when we ask ourselves whether we can will the adjusted social world associated with our maxim, we are to reason as if we do not know what place we may have in that world. (Rawls 2000, 175–76)

Here, the similarity between the CI-procedure and Rawls's original position is striking. In his view, the limits on information that such a procedure places on us are precisely the same as those featured in his famous thought experiment. In the original position, hypothetical subjects choose principles of justice without knowing how, precisely, their life will be affected by their implementation. Similarly, the limits on information which accompany the CI-procedure require us to evaluate possible worlds without knowing the place that we may have in them. If these suggestions are plausible, then it seems that Rawls understands the original position as facilitating the very same kind of moral reasoning as Kant's formula of universal law. In other words, the formula of universal law and the original position are two thought experiments that require us to do essentially the same thing, which is to ignore features of our own life—our social position, interests, desires, life goals, etc.—to better identify rules by which everyone ought to live. Considering Rawls's remarks on universalism, pure practical reason and Kant's categorical imperative, it is therefore hardly surprising that one of the most influential neo-Aristotelian philosophers—Alasdair MacIntyre—considered the former to be an epigone of the latter. Let us now see how.

THE CRITIQUE OF KANTIANISM IN MACINTYRE'S COMMUNITARIAN ARISTOTELIANISM

In *Whose Justice? Which Rationality?*, MacIntyre laid out an impressive history of theories of practical rationality developed within the Western philosophical canon. There, he also defended a conception of moral reasoning which is heavily influenced by Aristotle's philosophy and opposed to Kant's own. Even more important for our discussion is the fact that MacIntyre rejects three Kantian ideas that serve as foundations of Rawls's own philosophy: (i) the attempt to reach a universal standpoint from which impartial moral principles could be defined; (ii) a conception of moral reasoning as the application of moral principles to particular case; and (iii) the categorical imperative itself. Once we have grasped the objections he directs against such ideas, we will be in a better position to pinpoint the main features of his alternative theory of moral judgement, one which focuses on the acquisition of moral virtues.

MacIntyre's entire philosophy is based on his negative appreciation of European philosophical Modernity. In his view, an important part of contemporary moral thinking is based on ideas and concepts that have lost their meaning throughout the Enlightenment. When defending this view, MacIntyre is indebted to Elizabeth Anscombe who famously argued that the Modern attempt to secularize religious concepts has led to philosophical confusion. During Modernity, Anscombe argues in her article "Modern Moral Philosophy" (1958), many philosophers ceased to believe in the existence of an almighty God who creates absolute moral duties—ones that are free from limitations, exceptions or qualifications—through his commands. When they did, they simultaneously lost the ability to represent absolute foundations for moral judgement. Who (or what) else beyond an omnipotent God could have the power to impose unconditional obligations on humans? Several philosophers have attempted to answer this question and find new foundations for moral judgement, but, in Anscombe's view, none have succeeded. Still, many of them have kept their habit of writing *as if* we could conceive of absolute moral obligations that are binding for all.

MacIntyre's reflection adds to Anscombe's own. According to him, contemporary moral philosophers have not only rejected the religious framework which once made their moral theories plausible, they have also abandoned the teleological picture of the world which was the backbone of Greek moral wisdom. The starting point of Aristotle's reflection on ethics is that human beings have, like all things, a natural end (or *telos*). Without understanding what this end is, we will not be able to know how we ought to act. Another way of saying this is that moral philosophy's main task is to help us attain "human-nature-as-it-could-be-if-it-realized-its-*telos*" (MacIntyre 2007, 53). This itself requires us to conceptualize three things: (i) a first state of affairs in which a human being has not yet realized her *telos*; (ii) a second state of affairs in which she has and (iii) the process through which she transitions from the first state of affairs to the second. As we will see, this process is one through which agents exercise rationality and acquire moral virtues. This tripartite account of ethics was first attacked by Christian thinkers. First, Protestant and Jansenist thinkers rejected the idea that human beings can realize their telos *by themselves*, that is, through rational reflection and action alone. More specifically, such thinkers emphasized human depravity and the necessity of divine grace for salvation. In order to live good lives, human beings need God's assistance. Second, the development of modern natural sciences put pressure on the very idea that human beings have a *telos*, that is, a natural goal toward which they strive. This was a cornerstone of Aristotle's representation of the world, but it has been abandoned by modern and contemporary scientists (as well as philosophers).

Nevertheless, many Enlightenment thinkers shared an unshakeable faith in the powers of human reason. The principles of human morality are not to be found in religious revelation, they argued, but can be established through philosophical reflection alone. There may not be an almighty God whose commands we ought to obey, but this does not mean that all is lost when it comes to morality. For his part, MacIntyre believes that such an optimism was ill-conceived and that the Enlightenment project of justifying morality through rational reflection alone was ultimately a failure. Having abandoned the pre-Modern teleological conception of the world, Enlightenment philosophers inherited a stockpile of moral principles from ancient Greek and early Christian thinkers, but struggled to make sense of them. This is because they could no longer see that such principles were meant to help humans reach their natural end. In other words, they were means to an end that was no longer thinkable.

Perhaps the most damaging idea that was born out of this confusion is the Modern distinction between facts and values. In MacIntyre's view, Aristotle did not consider statements relating to what humans ought to do (e.g., "Zoe should stay home while she is sick") to be fundamentally different from descriptive statements (e.g., "Zoe lives in San Jose, California"). Again, this is due to Aristotle's belief that all things—including human beings—have a *telos*. If this is the case, then there is a sense in which statements which pertain to actions agents must perform to reach their natural end counts as descriptions of the world. In an Aristotelian perspective, that human beings ought to acquire the virtues is a fact inscribed in the very fabric of reality. By way of contrast, following David Hume, many contemporary moral philosophers clearly distinguish between descriptive and prescriptive statements and argue that the latter cannot be derived from the former. This is the meaning of Hume's famous observation according to which statements containing an "ought" cannot be a deduction from statements merely containing an "is" (Hume 1888, 469–70). Here, the idea is that only descriptive statements reflect state of affairs. Moreover, the truth or falsity of these statements can be established through empirical methods (Ayer 1936). As for prescriptive statements, they are of an entirely different kind. They are the mere expression of people's subjective preferences and cannot be true or false to the extent that they are not empirically verifiable.[6]

Once this distinction had been accepted, MacIntyre argues, the Enlightenment project of justifying morality through reason had to fail. If prescriptive statements merely express subjective preferences, then moral debates resemble wars through which combatants try to impose their views on each other to the best of their ability. When this happens, there is no objective moral criterion that can allow us to claim that one camp is right and the other is wrong. If I am a skillful rhetorician, I may convince you that you should endorse my moral views, but that does not mean that such views are true. In fact, they are neither true nor false, and this conclusion would also hold if *you* had convinced *me* that I should endorse your views. Then, when you are criticized for holding particular moral views, you will be able to point out that the moral criterion others use to criticize you is based on their subjective preferences, and that nothing prevents you from rejecting it on the grounds that you do not share these preferences.

Here, my intention is not to argue that MacIntyre's historical diagnosis is correct. Instead, the important point is that his pessimistic picture of the history of moral philosophy is the driving force behind his critique of both Kant and contemporary Kantians. According to him, Kant is a perfect example of a Modern moral philosopher who unsuccessfully attempted to theorize absolute moral obligations. As for contemporary Kantians like Rawls, they have fallen into the same trap.

As I mentioned above, MacIntyre's critique of Kantianism revolves around a few central ideas. First, he criticizes contemporary Kantians for attempting to reach a neutral philosophical standpoint which would allow them to formulate universal and impartial moral principles. Through abstract philosophical reflection, such philosophers endeavor to free themselves from the social context in which they are embedded and the historical contingencies which influence their judgement. As MacIntyre (1988, 3) writes:

> Rationality requires, so it has been argued by a number of academic philosophers, that we first divest ourselves of allegiance to any one of the contending theories and also abstract ourselves from all those particularities of social relationship in terms of which we have been accustomed to understand our responsibilities and our interests. Only by so doing, it has been suggested, shall we arrive at a genuinely neutral, impartial, and, in this way, universal point of view, freed from the partisanship and the partiality and onesidedness that otherwise affect us.

According to MacIntyre, philosophers who claim to envision social reality from a neutral standpoint are delusional, as there is no such thing as a truly impartial observer of the moral landscape. All moral and political theories are rooted in a specific socio-political context and tend to reflect ideas that were dominant at a specific time and place in history. Perhaps the most masterful Modern attempt to grasp moral truths from a universal standpoint was that of Kant. As MacIntyre (2006, 115) notes, the Kantian conception of the universal has had a lasting impact on moral philosophy since it was first formulated:

> This appeal away from the local and particular to the universal requires just that kind of conception of the universal which it has been the aim of Enlightenment and post-Enlightenment moral philosophers to supply. And we may plausibly suppose that such a philosopher, whether engaged in Kantian discovery or in Rawlsian construction, would recognize in the person responsive to this kind of appeal his or her own intended audience.

In general, MacIntyre portrays Kant and Rawls as having committed the same philosophical mistake, which amounts to devaluing the socially embedded ethical reflection in which ordinary people engage. Such people bear concrete socio-historical identities, but they do not necessarily attempt to abstract away from such identities when thinking about how they ought to act. In contrast, and as we have seen, Rawls describes people's knowledge of their social identity in both his description of the original position and his rendering of the formula of universal law. Furthermore, he strives to place limits on the information available to people who engage in moral reasoning to control for their biases. In MacIntyre's view, however, this is a vain attempt. Sociohistorical situatedness is part of who we are, and no clever thought experiment has the power to neutralize what we have inherited from the social context in which we live. If we lose sight of this point, then we risk importing contingent historical values into allegedly impartial philosophical reflection and masquerading them as universal moral principles. This diagnosis applies to the moral duties theorized by Kant just as well as to the principles of justice defended by Rawls.

MacIntyre's critique of Kant and contemporary Kantianism goes beyond his negative appraisal of moral universalism. His objections also target the idea according to which exercising moral judgement essentially amounts to rule-following. Here, his key criticism is one to which I will devote significant attention in this book: moral principles are usually too broad to allow agents to determine how best to act in particular situations. In fact, following such principles does not guarantee that one will act rightly. One striking example of a supposedly valid moral principle that risks leading us astray is Kant's formula of universal law. In a 1957 article titled "What Morality Is Not," MacIntyre illustrates this claim by commenting on a moral dilemma discussed by Jean-Paul Sartre.[7] In *Existentialism Is a Humanism*, Sartre (2007, 30–34) explains that during the Second World War, a student of his was faced with a difficult moral decision; he could either leave France to join the Free French Forces and fight Nazis or stay with his mother who was dependent upon his help. What is more, the mother had already lost a son during the 1940 German offensive and would have been plunged into despair if she lost a second child.

What should Sartre's student have done? Remember that the formula of universal law requires one to act only according to that maxim by which one can at the same time will that it should become a universal law. *Pace* Kant, MacIntyre argues that it would have been morally acceptable for Sartre's student to act according to a maxim without willing that such a maxim should become a universal law. The student "might choose either to stay or to go without attempting to legislate for anyone else in a similar position" and "without being willing to allow that anyone else who chose differently was blameworthy" (MacIntyre 1957, 329).[8] In other words, there is simply no right answer in this case. If Sartre's pupil had decided to leave his dependent mother, he would have violated his obligation to help those in need. Arguably, he would also have been a bad son. If he had chosen to stay, he would have violated his obligation towards his country and, more importantly, towards French citizens whose lives were about to get much worse because of the Nazi invasion.

More radically, MacIntyre (2007, 45–46) contends that several *immoral* maxims would pass Kant's universalization test:

> It is not just that Kant's own arguments involve large mistakes. It is very easy to see that many immoral and trivial non-moral maxims are vindicated by Kant's test quite as convincingly—in some cases more convincingly—than the moral maxims which Kant aspires to uphold. So "Keep all your promises throughout your entire life except one," "Persecute all those who hold false religious beliefs" and "Always eat mussels on Mondays in March" will all pass Kant's test, for all can be consistently universalized.

This passage contains an influential critique of Kant's moral philosophy, which amounts to the claim that selfish individuals will often be able to tailor maxims so that immoral actions they desire to perform become compatible with the formula of universal law. For instance, Kant famously argued that rational beings have an absolute duty not to make false promises on the grounds that "I will make false promises when it achieves something I want" is not a universalizable maxim. His reasoning is the following: if this maxim became a law of nature, then the social practice of *promising* would collapse as no one would trust others when they are giving their words. If this were the case, then people would simply stop making promises as doing so would have become meaningless. In response, MacIntyre points out that liars can easily justify their lies by claiming that the maxim they use is "I will keep all my promises throughout my entire life except one (or two, or three, or four, etc.)." Arguably, a maxim of this type could pass Kant's universalization test. If people know that others only lie in rare circumstances, indeed, then it seems that the social practice of promising will not collapse, and that Kant's argument against making false promises fails.

Note, however, that Macintyre's objection applies to universalization tests—which are often used to justify moral principles—not to the use of moral principles itself. Even if universalization tests are not an appropriate method of verifying if moral principles are valid, this does not mean that they cannot be justified through other methods and that they do not have any role to play in practical reasoning. MacIntyre concedes this point, but he also underlines that moral principles are often too indeterminate to guide action and frequently admit exceptions. Although people look down on liars, most of them would still argue that there are situations in which lying is not only permissible, but *compulsory*. For instance, we usually consider civilians who lied to Nazis and protected Jews by allowing them to hide in their home are moral heroes, not scoundrels. If this is so, then it seems that acting rightly sometimes requires more than blindly following a set of moral rules of the kind "*You shall (not) x!*" According to MacIntyre, this might be the most important lesson we can learn from ancient Greek ethics. As Aristotle writes in his *Nicomachean Ethics* (1984, 1795), "All law is universal but about some things it is not possible to make a universal statement which will be correct." Morality counts as one of those things, for there are situations in which we would not do justice to the circumstances of the case at hand if we simply followed moral principles. When this is so, we must rely on something else than rules to identify the best possible course of action. In MacIntyre's perspective, this is the most significant difference between Aristotle's and Kant's conceptions of moral judgement. As he explains (2007, 150), "Perhaps the most obvious and astonishing absence from Aristotle's thought for any modern reader" is that "there is relatively little mention of rules anywhere in the *Ethics*." This is because the Stagirite did not believe that the exercise of moral judgement is a "routinizable application of rules." By way of contrast, in Kant's moral writings, "We have reached a point at which the notion that morality is anything other than obedience to rules has almost, if not quite, disappeared from sight" (MacIntyre 2007, 236).

PHRONESIS AND THE PRACTICAL SYLLOGISM

If exercising judgement does not amount to blindly following rules, what does it amount to, precisely? What should moral agents rely on when general moral principles fail them? MacIntyre's answer is that they should rely on virtues. Of course, this raises new philosophical questions. First, what are virtues? Second, how are they acquired? In Rawls's perspective, virtues are "sentiments, that is, related families of dispositions and propensities regulated by a higher-order desire, in this case a desire to act from the corresponding moral principles" (1999a, 167). Considering his critique of rule-based reasoning, however, the reader can probably guess that MacIntyre conceives of them in a radically different fashion than contemporary Kantians like Rawls do.

Central to MacIntyre's reflection on moral judgement is the virtue of practical wisdom (*phronesis*) and Aristotle's practical syllogism. In general, a syllogism is a deductive reasoning in which a conclusion is drawn from two premises, each of which (i) shares a term with the conclusion and (ii) contains a term which is not present in the conclusion. According to Aristotle, syllogisms are theoretical when their conclusion is a statement. Here is an often-used example:

P1. All humans will die.
P2. Socrates is a human.
C. Therefore, Socrates will die.

In contrast, syllogisms are practical when their conclusion is an *action*. Those are the kind of reasoning in which moral agents engage right before they act. The first premise of a practical syllogism is a general statement which pertains to what is good for an agent. For instance, let us imagine a soldier who believes that it is generally good for her to defend her village against invaders. The second premise of a practical syllogism describes the circumstances in which the agent finds herself. To illustrate this point, let us say that our soldier now realizes that her village is currently under attack by invaders. Knowing that (P1) it is generally good for her to defend her village against foreign invasions and (P2) her country is currently subject to a foreign invasion, the soldier then (C) picks up her battle equipment and begins fighting off the attack. She reasoned, then acted, and we can say that her practical syllogism is now complete.[9]

Of course, not all actions which are the outcome of a practical syllogism will be good ones, morally speaking. This is because the soundness of a practical syllogism not only depends on the logical relationship between its premises and its conclusion, but also on the validity of its premises.

In many cases, however, moral agents will formulate a first premise which does not correctly identify something that is truly good for them. Other times, they will formulate second premises which do not capture all the morally salient facts of the situation in which they find themselves.[10] Such remarks bring us to MacIntyre's conception of practical wisdom. In an Aristotelian perspective, an ethical virtue is a settled disposition to act in the right manner. For instance, moderation is the settled disposition to indulge in things without excess. Like all virtues, it has both an intellectual and an emotional component. The moderate person knows what the moderate way to behave in various situations is, but she is also emotionally disposed to behave in such way. As a result, she reliably performs moderate actions.

Now, Aristotle also contends that "ethical virtue is fully developed only when it is combined with practical wisdom" (Kraut, 2018). In a nutshell, practical wisdom is a virtue of the mind which allows its possessors to adequately describe the circumstances of the case at hand. Indeed, "one of the marks of *phronesis* is that someone is able to identify just which circumstances are relevant and therefore which premises must be utilized in the deliberative construction" (MacIntyre 1988, 132). In other words, *phronesis* enables moral agents to build good practical syllogisms by making its possessors sensitive to morally relevant facts (that is, ordinary facts which matter from a moral point of view).

Let us imagine, for instance, that my toddler begs me to go for a swim while we are walking by the Pacific Ocean at sunset. When deliberating, one thing that comes to mind is that this could be a bonding experience and that good parenting requires me to be attentive my child's needs and desires. Considering that the waves are not too strong, why would I deny my daughter a swim? If I notice a shark fin piercing the water, however, then swimming will no longer be an option. This is a very simple example, and most parents would probably engage in a similar kind of reasoning before granting permission to their child to go for a swim. Sometimes, however, moral life is more complex. To tactfully break bad news to a friend, for instance, moral agents must find the right moment, the right phrasing, and the right tone. They must also pay attention to small details in their friends' behaviour and decide whether now is the right time to break this news. Here, the key point is that moral life requires us to pay attention to a vast amount of (often subtle) facts, and that our capacity to notice such facts will have a decisive impact on the moral value of our actions. From MacIntyre's neo-Aristotelian perspective, agents who are skilled at noticing such facts are said to possess practical wisdom. But how does one develop this virtue?

In Aristotle's view, one cannot acquire practical wisdom without acquiring all other virtues. This is the Aristotelian claim known as the unity of virtue. More specifically, Aristotle classifies virtues into two distinct types (1984, 1742). First, there are virtues "which pertain to the part of the soul that engages in reasoning" (Kraut, 2018). Those are said to be intellectual virtues (or virtues of the mind) and are themselves divided into those which pertain to theoretical reasoning and those which—like practical wisdom—pertain to practical reasoning. Second, there are virtues which "pertain to the part of the soul that cannot itself reason but is nonetheless capable of following reason." These are ethical virtues (or virtues of character) and include courage, moderation, justice and many more. Those are acquired through imitation and habit: by attempting to act like courageous people, for instance, we gradually become courageous ourselves. If we progressively train ourselves to acquire each individual ethical virtue, then we will eventually develop practical wisdom. In other words, people cannot reasonably hope to be able to build good practical syllogisms without first molding their character, and the best way to mold one's character is to follow the example of great people. Importantly, MacIntyre underlines that acquiring and exercising practical wisdom is not primarily a matter of following moral principles. As he explains:

> That Aristotle did not consider phronetic activity itself to be rule-governed [. . .] is clear. For in exercising phronesis we understand why this particular situation makes the exercise of some particular moral virtue or the application of some particular rule of justice in acting in some particular way the right thing to do.

And there are no rules for generating this kind of practically effective understanding of particulars. (MacIntyre 1988, 116)

At this stage of my reflection, however, an important question about MacIntyre's theory of moral judgement remains unanswered. As we have seen, formulating good second premises of practical syllogisms requires agents to pay attention to morally relevant facts, and this itself is made possible by the acquisition of practical wisdom. As for the first premise, it must point to something that is good for human beings. At first sight, this seems to imply that *there are some things that are universally good for human beings*. If this is so, however, how can MacIntyre reconcile his defence of Aristotle's practical syllogism with his forceful critique of universalism in contemporary moral theory? The Scottish philosopher's wager is that one can reflect upon the human good without envisioning the moral landscape from a neutral point of view as Kant and contemporary Kantians claim that they have done.

Any contemporary reading of ancient philosophical works raises several questions that ancient philosophers themselves were not in a position to conceptualize. Perhaps the best example of this is MacIntyre's reflection on the problem of historical relativism. During the nineteenth and twentieth centuries, German historians became interested in the fact that members of different societies held contrasting and incompatible moral views throughout human history. This problem has been at the centre stage of philosophical reflection on the foundations of moral judgement ever since. In fact, the problem of historical relativism undergirds much of MacIntyre's criticism of universalism. As mentioned, when Kantian philosophers claim to have grasped universal moral rules through *a priori* philosophical thinking, their arguments mostly reflect the views that came to be dominant in the time and place where they live. Yet the realization that moral and political ideas are historically contingent need not plunge us into despair, for this fact does not entail that all moral judgements are the mere expression of subjective or arbitrary preferences.

To see this, MacIntyre asks us to pay attention to the goods which are internal to the practices in which we engage daily. When I try to learn to play the piano, for instance, I am driven by a representation of what playing the piano *well* amounts to. In fact, my objective is precisely to get progressively closer to a state in which I play the piano well myself. Such a conclusion holds for several human practices; not only do piano players try to become *good* pianists, but parents typically attempt to be good parents, teachers to be good teachers, and so forth. Furthermore, MacIntyre argues that most human practices come with *internal standards of excellence*, and the first step in answering the central question of moral philosophy—"How should I live my life?"—amounts to paying attention to such standards. To live good lives, we should begin by reflecting upon the practices in which we already engage as well as what it means to engage in such practices well.

In some cases, the internal standards of excellence which belong to a human practice are quite easy to pin down. For instance, I do not need to think that long to understand what it means to be a good cook. After all, I have tasted good dishes before, and I know that the goal of cooking is to produce well-balanced dishes.[11] Other practices have internal standards of excellence which are considerably harder to define. For instance, what does it mean to be a good parent? Are good parents mostly permissive or strict? And what does it mean to be a good professor? Do good philosophy professors mostly teach students facts about the history of philosophy? Should they instead help students acquire critical thinking skills? Does good teaching essentially depend on content or is it rather a way of being with students, one that allows them to understand that you are there to help them become the person they desire to be? After many years of teaching, those are not questions to which I have found a definitive answer.

Now, one problem with MacIntyre's discourse on practices and internal standards of excellence is that reflecting upon such standards does not itself allow us to decide in which practices we ought to engage in the first place. We know that there are good soldiers and good painters, but should I be a soldier or a painter? According to MacIntyre, each person must ultimately make this decision for herself. Yet doing so requires one to forge a *narrative conception of herself*, that is, represent her life as a story with a beginning and an end between which she will pursue specific internal standards of excellence by engaging in a set of practices. Hopefully, she will succeed in giving some coherence and unity to all her activities. "As a nurse, parent and friend," we can imagine an elderly person thinking, "I have strived to remove hardships from the lives others." In the absence of such narratives, it becomes harder for us to provide our lives with meaning, that is, to understand *why*, ultimately, we have decided to engage in a specific set of human practices. Interestingly, narratives also help us interpret the behaviour of others. Borrowing an example from MacIntyre, let us picture a situation in which we observe an old man gardening. At first sight, it might seem that this man gardens because he enjoys doing so. This is a reasonable assumption for most. If we spoke to the man, however, we would realize that he hates gardening, but that he deeply loves his wife who likes it when the backyard is tidy. For this man, gardening is part of a larger practice which amounts to being a good partner which sometimes requires him to do things that he dislikes, as this will make his companion happy. Here, the key point is that practices become *meaningful* in the context of narratives in which they are embedded, and that one cannot identify their meaning without understanding such narratives. As MacIntyre notes, "Until we know this, we shall not know how to characterize correctly what the agent is doing" (2007, p. 207).

Is MacIntyre an existentialist philosopher? At the end of the inquiry on moral reasoning, is there nothing more than a radically free choice to forge a narrative for oneself, and then decide what practices will be the centre of one's life? This is not so. When forging a particular life narrative, MacIntyre contends, we should conceive this narrative as being part of a particular historical *tradition* which opens human possibilities and closes others. More specifically, every historical tradition emphasizes the value of certain human goods and practices which allow agents to pursue such goods. Within the liberal philosophical tradition, for instance, the pursuit of individual freedom is portrayed as being especially worthwhile. According to this framework, having the power to freely pursue one's preferences without being impeded from doing so by others is intrinsically valuable. In a nutshell, this is part of a good human life. By way of contrast, other traditions emphasize the well-being of communities over that of individuals or, more precisely, argue that individuals can only thrive *as members* of a community. In his article on "Person and Community in African Traditional Thought," for instance, Ifeanyi Menkiti (1984, 171) contends that "as far as Africans are concerned, the reality of the communal world takes precedence over the reality of individual life." Lastly, within the neo-Aristotelian tradition defended by MacIntyre, individual freedom is not intrinsically good, but has value to the extent that it allows people to become virtuous agents.

To sum up, great historical intellectual traditions can serve as moral beacons when we reflect upon the way in which we should live our life. Instead of creating our life narrative *ex nihilo*, we should see ourselves as belonging to something that is greater than us, that is, a community of individuals dedicated to the pursuit of human goods valued by a particular tradition. In fact, we can envision historical traditions as philosophical interlocutors. In MacIntyre's own words, a tradition is an "argument extended through time" to which we can turn when we are unsure about how we ought to behave or desire to test the narrative which we have forged for ourselves. Returning to practical wisdom, MacIntyre goes as far as describing a moral agent's capacity to embed practices into narratives and then link narratives to traditions as a virtue which allows her to make good judgements in particular situations. This "sense of tradition" (2007, 223) can indeed help moral agents build good practical syllogisms. To see this, remember that the first premises of practical syllogisms must identify something that is good for humans to pursue (health, friendship, knowledge, love, freedom, pleasure, equality, etc.). If this is so, then formulating such premises amounts to choosing a human good I ought to pursue amongst a set of possible ones. Historical traditions can help us do this to the extent that they are collective discourses on the value of human goods which often contain considerations on which goods should be prioritized over others. In MacIntyre's view, they are the ultimate repository of moral reasoning.

Yet I wish to conclude this chapter by suggesting that, at this stage, MacIntyre's discussion of tradition does not contain a fully satisfying answer to the problem of historical relativism. Why this is so is not especially hard to see. Simply put, there exist myriad historical traditions which each value and rank human goods differently, but no universal standpoint which allows us to determine which traditional ranking of goods is the best one. Indeed, MacIntyre cannot reasonably criticize Kantian philosophers for attempting to reach a universal standpoint and then use such standpoint to arbitrate between the conflicting claims of historical traditions. If this is so, how can a moral agent rationally defend her choice to embed her life narrative within a particular tradition? In chapter 6, we will answer this important question. For now, I want to consider a second philosophical context in which such question was raised. As I noted earlier, reflections on historical relativism and moral universalism have been central to the German philosophical tradition since the nineteenth century. It is therefore hardly surprising that, in this country, the neo-Aristotelian critique of Kantian judgement focused on such themes.

Chapter 2

German Neo-Aristotelianism and the Normativity of *Ethos*

In an article on the contemporary revival of Aristotelianism in Germany, Belgian-Québécois philosopher Richard Bodéüs (1989) discusses the work of philosophers whom he describes as "North American Continentals." When using this expression, Bodéüs does not refer to native Canadian, American or Mexican philosophers working in the continental philosophical tradition, but rather to German Jewish philosophers who fled Germany to escape Nazism and settled down in the United States. Strauss, Jonas, Horkheimer, Arendt, Adorno: the list of eminent German twentieth-century philosophers who found refuge in North America is an impressive one. In this chapter, however, my ambition will not be to critically examine the work of German philosophers in exile. Instead, I wish to answer a question that Bodéüs's choice to speak of "North American Continentals" naturally raises: if there were German philosophers in exile, who were the "mainlander Continentals," that is, German philosophers who stayed in Germany during the Second World War and occupied university positions in its immediate aftermath.

As the reader can imagine, this is a delicate historiographical project as postwar philosophy in Germany was built in the shadow of Nazism. During the 1950s, the Nazi regime had fallen, but Germany's national conversation on how it came to be and how a relapse into authoritarianism could be avoided was only beginning. What is more, several intellectuals who were engaged in this collective reflection had participated in the Nazi regime during the war. Arguably, many did so against their will. This is the case of teenage conscripts who—like Jürgen Habermas—were coerced into participating in the German war effort (often as auxiliary staff rather than proper soldiers). Yet an older generation of professors had compromised with Nazism more substantially, for instance by signing the *Vow of allegiance of the Professors of the Germany University and High Schools to Adolf Hitler and the National Socialist State* in 1933. Two influential German neo-Aristotelians—Joachim

Ritter and Hans-Georg Gadamer—signed this pledge, but their acceptance of Nazism was deemed sufficiently passive for them to maintain their university position in the newly born German Democratic Republic.[1]

Why mention such philosophers at all in a book devoted to moral judgement? First, I find it important to emphasize that influential thinkers can easily betray philosophical ideals like truth and justice when their privileges are at stake. This is a humble reminder that those who theorize about moral judgement are not necessarily able to exercise it themselves. Second, reflecting upon Nazism can help us identify an important risk tied to the critique of Kantian universalism which amounts to uncritically celebrating the value of dominant social norms. As the reader will see, this is a central theme of this chapter. Lastly, my discussion of German neo-Aristotelianism and its Kantian detractors would remain incomplete if I did not mention that both groups of philosophers feared a relapse into authoritarianism.

For instance, the conservative neo-Aristotelianism defended by Ritter and his pupils after the Second World War is based on the idea that the deadliest ideologies of the twentieth century—fascism and authoritarian communism—arise when human reason becomes overconfident in its capacity to transform society for the better. Once a universal standpoint of justice has supposedly been reached in *a priori* philosophical reflection, then the society we live in unmistakably falls short of philosophical ideals. For this reason, it becomes tempting to rebel against current social and political institutions and build new ones from the ground up. According to this conservative mindset, philosophical universalism and reckless revolutionary impulses go hand in hand. In response, Kantian thinkers like Habermas argue that moral universalism *safeguards* society *against* authoritarianism. In his view, abandoning the quest for universal moral standards deprives philosophers of the means to criticize current injustices. This in turn makes it all too easy for intellectuals to accept rotten compromises like Ritter and Gadamer did when they signed the *Vow*.

In what follows, I will not try to hide that my sympathy is with those who hold the latter point of view, not the former. Yet I still want to reconstruct the conservative point of view for historiographical reasons. As mentioned, understanding Habermas requires one to engage with his reaction to German neo-Aristotelians. Focusing on Ritter and Gadamer's thought will also allow me to introduce the concept of *ethos*, which is a key piece of the neo-Aristotelian critique of the Kantian conception of moral judgement that developed in postwar Germany. Then, I will show how neo-Aristotelian ideas put forward by Ritter and Gadamer served as the backbone of a debate on moral judgement which opposed Rüdiger Bubner to Habermas.[2] As we will see, ultimately at stake in this debate are the very foundations of moral judgement. Are dominant social norms the benchmark of moral reasoning or does moral judgement rests on universal moral principles the validity of which is entirely independent of these norms and practices? All philosophers discussed in this chapter attempted to answer this question in one way or another.

THE CONCEPT OF *ETHOS* IN JOACHIM RITTER'S PHILOSOPHY

Joachim Ritter's philosophy is not well known outside of Germany as most of his works have not been translated into English. From a historiographical point of view, this remains surprising given that "Ritter's circle was probably the liveliest in Germany" during the 1950s and 1960s (Tugendhat 1992, 9).[3] Many students who were active members of this circle—the *Collegium philosophicum* in Münster—later became figureheads of neoconservatism in postwar Germany. These include Robert Spaemann, Odo Marquard and Herman Lübbe, all of whom heavily criticized left-wing student movements which, in their view, threatened the political stability of newly founded democratic institutions in West Germany. As Werner-Müller (2013, 116–32) points out, what united members of the so-called Ritter school is a "melancholy modernism" according to which Germans had to protect their recently recovered individual freedom without expecting too much from liberal democracy in the aftermath of Nazism. The new liberal regime might not meet the expectations of the left with regard to social justice, but it was nonetheless preferable to the one that preceded it as well as the relapse into authoritarianism that might follow if Germans were not careful. After fascism, stability was more important than progress. To avoid the worst, Germans had to settle for less.

Members of the *Ritterschule* also believed that modern individuals have had to pay a heavy price for their hardly won freedom. Certainly, they no longer must live in a hierarchical and restrictive social order in which their individual liberty is violated by those who rule. Yet they have also lost the moral beacons which once regulated social life, namely religion and tradition. Most importantly for the subject matter of this book, Ritter and his pupils were deeply skeptical of human reason's capacity to justify its moral and political choices. In their writings, liberal democracy is not portrayed as the only political regime compatible with universal moral rights, but as an imperfect regime that can be reasonably preferred to others even in the absence of sophisticated philosophical arguments in its favour. In the 1950s, Germans had been through the hell of Nazism and they did not need such arguments to be convinced that democracy was preferable to authoritarianism. Politically speaking, Ritterians' skepticism about the power of human reason "translated into a presumption in favour of the tried and the tested" (Werner-Müller 2003, 122). The status quo needed no philosophical justification. Instead, "those advocating change had to carry the burden of proof." Furthermore, promises of a better future did not count as proof. The new liberal order left much to be desired, but it was nonetheless preferable to the naïve hopes of the left which had led people astray in the past and could do so once more.[4]

Beyond his political influence, Ritter remains known (in Germany) for his defence of Aristotle's practical philosophy, which was heavily influenced by his reading of Hegel's political thought. In general, he argues that contemporary moral philosophers have a misguided tendency to separate reflection on moral judgement and reasoning from political philosophy. By way of contrast, Aristotle's conception of judgement hinges on his political theory of the ancient Greek city-state (*polis*). While the *Nicomachean Ethics* is often read as a standalone philosophical work, Ritter reminds us that such work ends with Aristotle inviting the reader to critically assess the value of various political constitutions, an inquiry which he undertakes in the *Politics*. As for Ritter's own neo-Aristotelian theory of moral judgement, it focuses on the concept of *ethos* which refers to the mores, traditions and customs that undergird collective life in a given community. Rules that regulate family life, religious conventions that govern worship, ways in which one is expected to behave in public; all of these create an *ethical substance* which should serve as the basis of people's moral reasoning when they wonder how they ought to act. As Klaus Günther rightly underlines (1993, 181–182), the main task that Ritter attributes to moral agents amounts to understanding the various norms contained in this ethical substance, and to ensure that their individual judgements adequately reflect it. In other words, it is by following ethical standards which are embodied in social institutions of their community such as families, churches, local associations, and educational organizations that moral agents can come to act rightly.

As for state constitutions, they determine the nature and extent of the power that institutional leaders will be allowed to yield over members of the community. In fact, listening to the counsel and obeying the directives of institutional leaders is likely to help us live an ethical life. The ethical substance of a community is not solely composed of individual thoughts and actions, but also of social relations between its members. This is because people who stand in positions of authority relative to us can give us moral advice. When they do, they help us exercise moral judgement.

This is what Ritter means when he writes (2003, 110) that "practical philosophy is, as an ethic, (also) politics." Admittedly, Ritter's point of view is not purely Aristotelian, but also Hegelian in nature. Indeed, the concept of *ethos* is strongly reminiscent of Hegel's notion of *Sittlichkeit* (or "ethical life") which he famously opposed to Kantian *Moralität*. While *Sittlichkeit* encompasses the ethical substance formed by the customs, mores and traditions of a particular community as they are embodied in its social institutions,

Moralität refers to an abstract set of moral principles which need not be embedded in social institutions to be valid. In fact, from a Kantian standpoint, such principles can be used to *criticize* customs, mores and traditions.

Within Ritter's own philosophy, both Aristotle and Hegel are portrayed as philosophers who paid special attention to the authority of shared communal norms. Such norms can teach us what goods we ought to pursue and thus help us construct the major premises of our practical syllogisms.[5] As he writes (2003, 297), "Hegel builds on the Aristotelian political tradition through his admission of the standpoint of ethical life (*Sittlichkeit*)."[6] Conversely, Kant is depicted as having neglected the ethical substance conveyed by social institutions. In his philosophy, such institutions only have moral authority if the kind of living they promote incite agents to fulfill moral obligations derived from the moral law. What is more, these duties can be identified through *a priori* philosophical reflection, that is, without observing how human beings live with one another in communal settings. In a nutshell, Ritter accuses Kant of having wrongly believed that moral agents can find ethical standards of living within their inner consciousness without paying any attention to those that concretely regulate social life.

Now, is it not dangerous to argue that individual moral consciousness should always defer to traditions, mores and customs? Can the values embodied in social institutions not lead us astray when we strive to determine how to act rightly? Whether Ritter truly considers that we *always* ought to give priority to mores and traditions over individual moral reflection remains hard to tell. On the one hand, his interpretation of modern natural law theories suggests that this is the case. By "natural law," modern philosophers refer to a set of supra-historical universal norms which can be used to criticize *positive law* (i.e., the set of laws which have been enacted in various societies). According to natural law theorists, concrete legal orders must respect the fundamental precepts of natural law to be valid. When they do not, then we can safely conclude that they are unjust. According to Ritter, however, the contrast between unchanging universal norms and concrete legal orders does not exist within Aristotle's practical philosophy. For Aristotle, "What is just is given by the customs and the institutions of civic life" (Ritter 2003, 160). In fact, Ritter go as far as writing that "for Aristotle, there is no separation between what is and what ought to be, between morality and legality" (163). According to this Hegelian interpretation of the *Nicomachean Ethics*, concrete legal orders cannot be deemed unjust according to external moral standards. Instead, they are the very benchmark in comparison to which things can be said to be just or unjust

One obvious concern with Ritter's traditionalist-institutionalist theory of *ethos* is that it leaves no room for a critical perspective which would allow moral agents to criticize authoritarian institutions. In the aftermath of Nazism, it also seems to me that Germans needed this critical perspective more than ever. Without a doubt, Ritter and his followers were staunch defenders of the liberal order. This does not mean, however, that they had the philosophical means to justify this order against authoritarian alternatives. If we conceive of positive laws and institutions as grounding justice—not the other way round—then we deprive ourselves of the means to criticize such institutions. As we will see, this very thought undergirds Habermas's entire philosophical project in the 1980s. Before I turn to Habermas's philosophy, however, let me note that there are reasons to believe that Ritter's thought is not so radically conservative that it eliminates all possible grounds for a philosophical critique of socio-political institutions. A first indication of this is that his deep-rooted Hegelianism commits him to the claim that a central achievement of modernity is the philosophical discourse on subjective freedom. Although modern subjects can choose to conceive of themselves as the heirs of a particular tradition or the members of a given community, this remains a free personal commitment that no one can force upon them. Certainly, they can be coerced into *obeying* social norms, but they always remain free to reject such norms in their inner consciousness, that is, to consider that they *ought not* follow them even if they are coerced into doing so. This implies that subjects can rely on an inner conception of justice and resist the claim that the political institutions under which they live are necessarily just. A second reason to believe that Ritter does not in fact argue in favour of blind obedience to all socio-political institutions pertains to the distinction between laws and social norms. According to his perspective, there are cases in which the laws of a particular society poorly reflect the traditions, mores and customs by which its members live. For example, we can imagine a society in which political authorities try to enact laws which are incompatible with the unwritten norms which have regulated social life for many centuries. When this happens, there might be reasons to reject such laws. Indeed, Ritter (2003, 162) argues that Aristotle himself "does not hesitate to give priority to customs over positive laws." This brings us to conceive of a second point of view from which political institutions and laws can be critically assessed. In a nutshell, moral agents can evaluate whether laws reflect their community's unwritten *ethos*, and refuse to obey them when they do not.

Nevertheless, Ritter's discourse on *ethos* will be but poor consolation for philosophers who worry that both a society's unwritten customs and its current laws can be unjust; in fact, my intention here is not to offer a defence of Ritter's Hegelian-influenced Aristotelianism, quite the contrary. In the end, it seems to me that his conservative philosophy involves a very risky wager which amounts to the belief that people will live ethical lives if they primarily conceive of moral judgement as a matter of complying with traditional norms and abandon the project of defining universally valid moral principles. In what follows, we will see that this wager is not only Ritter's, but also that of two other German neo-Aristotelians who, like MacIntyre, reject the quest for a neutral philosophical standpoint. Those two neo-Aristotelians are Hans-Georg Gadamer and Rüdiger Bubner.

GADAMER ON JUDGEMENT AND PRACTICAL WISDOM

Born in 1900, Hans-Georg Gadamer is recognized as one of the most important German interpreters of ancient philosophy of the second half of the twentieth century. What is more, the chapter of *Truth and Method* dedicated to the hermeneutic relevance of Aristotle is often described as a key moment in the development of practical philosophy in postwar Germany. Yet Gadamer's primary philosophical intention was never to develop a political philosophy or an ethic. His interpretation of Aristotle's *Nicomachean Ethics* is part of a broader reflection on the interpretation of historical texts and the nature of human understanding.[7] In the eyes of many, what makes Gadamer a practical philosopher is his description of hermeneutic understanding as a form of Aristotelian practical wisdom. Without summarizing Gadamer's entire philosophical hermeneutics, I wish to discuss two aspects of his thought which are directly relevant to the subject matter of this book: his criticism of Kant's conception of the faculty of judgement and his neo-Aristotelian remarks on the sensorial dimension of moral decision-making. Then, we will see that Gadamer is, like Ritter, deeply interested in Aristotle's concept of *ethos*.

In the previous chapter, we have seen that neo-Aristotelian philosophers typically argue that following a set of general moral principles often does not allow moral agents to determine how best to act in concrete situations. First, there are cases in which such principles conflict with one another and moral agents ought to decide which principle takes precedence over all others that apply to the case at hand. Second, moral principles leave many possible courses of action open, and agents are always faced with the task of determining which specific action is the best one to perform. Third, moral principles sometimes admit of exceptions and agents must be able to identify situations in which an exception is warranted. I have also argued that such considerations lead neo-Aristotelians to contend that moral agents must acquire a set of virtues (including practical wisdom) in order to reliably make good ethical decisions. For his part, Gadamer is interested in a Kantian concept that contemporary philosophers often envision as an analogue to Aristotelian *phronesis*: the faculty of judgement (*Urteilskraft*). In his *Critique of the Power Judgement*, indeed, Kant (2000, 66) characterizes *Urteilskraft* as "the faculty for thinking of the particular as contained under the universal." In the *Critique of Pure Reason*, he similarly defines it as "the faculty of subsuming under rules, i.e., of determining whether something stands under a given rule" (Kant 1998, 268). Although Kant's remarks remain hard to interpret, he seems to be describing a skill or aptitude that would enable moral agents to perform cognitive tasks which are essential in moral judgement. Let us say that I find myself in a situation in which lying would allow me to save a life. To act rightly, I must decide whether this is a situation which falls under the general rule according to which "I ought not to lie" or, as many would argue, that an exception to this rule is warranted in this case.[8] This is precisely the kind of mental operation that Kant seems to have in mind when he discusses the faculty of judgement.

In chapter 7, I will offer a much more detailed analysis of Kant's *Urteilskraft* when considering Hannah Arendt's theory of moral judgement, which heavily builds on this notion. For now, let me point out that Gadamer is struck by the fact that, contrary to what I have suggested, Kant does not describe the faculty of judgement as a properly *moral* aptitude. In fact, he primarily discusses *Urteilskraft* in the context of a more general reflection on *aesthetic* judgements, that is, judgements which pertain to the *beautiful* as opposed to the *good*. In other words, the concept of *Urteilskraft* is notoriously absent from Kant's central works of moral theory such as the *Critique of Practical Reason* and the *Metaphysics of Morals*. In fact, it seems that Kant never truly made room for the idea that good moral judgements depend on skill.[9] In Gadamer's view, this is a missed opportunity. As the lying example suggests, good decision-making requires moral agents to depart from general principles when they feel that following them would not lead to the best outcome. As Gadamer (2004, 35) explains, good decision-making is more specifically a matter of *taste*:

> Judging the case involves not merely applying the universal principle according to which it is judged, but co-determining, supplementing, and correcting that principle. From this it ultimately follows that all moral decisions require taste—which does not mean that this most individual balancing of decision is the only thing that governs them, but it is an indispensable element. It is truly an achievement of undemonstrable tact to hit the target and to discipline the application of the universal, the moral law (Kant), in a way that reason itself cannot. Thus taste is not the ground but the supreme consummation of moral judgment.

Here, the reader might be puzzled by the affirmation that taste allows us to make correct moral judgements "in a way that reason itself cannot." Yet the idea that wise judgement has a non-rational quasi-sensorial dimension runs deep in contemporary Aristotelianism. In the passage quoted above,

Gadamer relates this non-rational quasi-sensorial dimension to the sense of taste, but many neo-Aristotelians compare it to visual perception. In fact, Gadamer himself does so in other parts of *Truth and Method*. "The task of making a moral decision," he writes, "is that of doing the right thing in a particular situation—i.e., *seeing* what is right within the situation and grasping it" (Gadamer 2004, 314). Anglo-American neo-Aristotelians tend to do the same. For instance, John McDowell (1979, 335) depicts virtue as "consisting in a sensitivity, a perceptual capacity." For his part, David Wiggins (1976, 43) claims that knowing how to act in the case at hand requires a "situational appreciation, or, as Aristotle would say, perception (*aisthesis*)." Here, the common idea is that the acquisition of practical wisdom and other virtues lead moral agents to develop a sensory aptitude to see beyond moral principles or—to put it less metaphorically—understand when particular situations warrant exceptions to such principles. Indeed, a core feature of the neo-Aristotelian mindset amounts to the claim that virtuous agents not only reason well, but also perceive the world in a fundamentally different way than those who have yet to acquire the virtues.

An example will be useful to illustrate this point. Until now, we have seen that Gadamer stresses that moral judgement involves a special ability to "see" what one is required to do in a particular situation. Now, in his view, such ability also plays a central role in legal hermeneutics (that is, the interpretation of legal texts). For instance, good adjudication requires judges to pay special attention to the particular context in which laws are made. Consider the following example, which was originally discussed by H. L. A. Hart and Lon Fuller.[10] Let us picture a law which forbids people to take a vehicle into a public park. Imagine now that members of the local government responsible for the maintenance of the park wish to set an old military truck on a pedestal to honour veterans of the Second World War. In this case, should we consider that the government's plan runs contrary to the law which prohibits people from taking a vehicle into the park? Here, it seems that a judge cannot answer this question in a satisfactory manner by merely focusing on the phrasing of the law. Certainly, military trucks count as vehicles, but there is also an important difference between driving one's car in the vicinity of a public park and setting a historical military truck on a pedestal. Arguably, doing the latter does not run contrary to the law if we admit that the *purpose* of such law is to protect park users from motorists, not to prevent them from looking at memorials. To make a sagacious judgement in this case, a judge must "see" that the case at hand is compatible with the spirit of the law. Such an example perfectly illustrates Gadamer's (2004, 216) claim that "administering justice is a special task that requires both knowledge and skill," one which sometimes lead wise judges to "refrain from applying the full rigor of the law" given that "to do otherwise would not be right." In certain cases, making an exception to a moral principle or a law simply makes sense, or so Gadamer argues. By way of contrast, mechanically applying general statements to particular cases would lead us to make bad moral or legal decisions.

We can now relate Gadamer's remarks on judgement to the conservative neo-Aristotelianism discussed in the first part of this chapter. Like Ritter, Gadamer believes that an agent's ability to "see" what she ought to do in particular cases will be enhanced by her understanding of a community's *ethos*. To make the right decision in the military truck example, for instance, a judge needs to understand what the community who formulated the law which prohibits people from taking vehicles into the public park was trying to accomplish. To do so, she must come to see that the ethical result which members of the community were trying to generate is a situation in which the physical safety of park users is better protected than it currently is. Like virtuous agents, wise judges can identify which human goods the norms in force in a particular community aim at and take decisions accordingly. Ultimately, there is an ethical substance which gives laws their purpose, and good interpretation of such laws required judges to forge links between legislation and *ethos*.

To be sure, Gadamer reaches such conclusion by following a different philosophical path than Ritter. A main source of inspiration for his philosopher is Heidegger's conception of *Geworfenheit*, or throwness.[11] Regardless of the socio-historical context in which a human being is born, it is always the case that she is thrown into a family, community, country and historical context which she did not choose. This is the condition of *Dasein* or, more simply put, the human condition. Now, the fact that we are thrown into a particular historical situation matters immensely for our practical lives. Indeed, the context in which an agent is born comes with norms and expectations to which she *must* respond. Certainly, she has the freedom to meet or reject such expectations, but the very fact that she must do one or the other demonstrates that she cannot escape them. It is also likely that communal norms and expectations shape this agent's understanding of the nature of the good life. In Gadamerian terms, we can say that moral agents are *prejudiced*, that is, their individual judgement is never free of social-historical influences. In other words, we always envision what we ought to do in a particular situation through lens that have been "given" to us. Within Gadamer's philosophy, "prejudice" (*Vorurteil*) is not a pejorative term. Its meaning is closer to "pre-judgement" than to "bias." In fact, Gadamer describes prejudices as enabling understanding rather than preventing it. When we face difficult moral decisions, we might feel overwhelmed by the many courses of action that are open to us. In such situations, communal norms and values can serve as moral beacons. The decision to perform *such* or *such* action need not come purely from within; the moral baggage that has been transmitted to us through education and that we now carry can be of assistance. We see the world through a particular community's lens, ones that help us see what it means to act rightly.

The link between practical wisdom, prejudice and *ethos* is one that Gadamer explicitly attributes to Aristotle. As he writes in "On the Possibility of a Philosophical Ethics":

> Aristotle's view is focused more intensely on the conditionedness of our moral being, on the dependence of the individual decision on the practical and social determinants of the time [. . .] His analysis of *phronesis* recognizes that moral knowledge is a way of moral being itself, which therefore cannot be prescinded from the whole concretion of what he calls *ethos*. Moral knowledge discerns what needs to be done, what a situation requires; and it discerns what is doable on the basis of a conviction that the concrete situation is related to what is considered right and proper in general. (Gadamer 2007, 284)

Ultimately, there is no hope and no need for moral agents to free themselves from the social determinants of the time. The criterion of the right action depends on a collective traditional understanding of "what is considered right and proper in general." Put differently, an action is said to be right to the extent that it is compatible with a historically contingent conception of the good life embodied in the institutions and social practices of a particular community. The problem, of course, is that what is considered right and proper in general in a particular society sometimes strikes us a morally repulsive by contemporary standards. Is there a way to overcome this problem? Can we reach a point of view which would allow us to see how we ought to behave in light of communal norms *and also* critically assess such norms? This very question is at the core of the philosophical debate between Rüdiger Bubner and Jürgen Habermas.

RÜDIGER BUBNER'S CRITIQUE OF HABERMAS

When Habermas laid out the foundations of discourse ethics in the early 1980s, neo-Aristotelianism had established itself as a major movement in contemporary German practical philosophy. Yet the influence of German neo-Aristotelianism never matched that of critical theory in the Frankfurt school tradition. Considering its strong emphasis on social transformation and emancipation, critical theory was always naturally suited to serve as the intellectual backbone of progressive political movements of the 1960s and 1970s. Today, Habermas remains an iconic representative of the Frankfurt School and—more than any other public intellectual in Germany—a fierce opponent of conservative neo-Aristotelianism. As we have seen, such conservatism is traditionalist without being reactionary as a central objective of Ritter and his pupils was always to defend liberal democracy and individual freedom. Without a doubt, this defence was a melancholic one. Ritterians envisioned twentieth-century Germany as a heavily individualistic and technocratic society in which traditional modes of collective life were on the verge of disappearance. For this reason, they encouraged contemporary Germans to freely embrace the powers of tradition—*ethos*, religion and artistic practice—which could serve as the basis of ethical reflection.

To a large extent, Habermas's philosophy is a response to this conservative discourse. One of his main criticisms amounts to the claim that German neo-Aristotelians celebrate socially dominant norms without having the philosophical means to assess whether those norms are rationally justified. As mentioned above, such criticism is one that I share. As Habermas recurrently points out, the norms and values that influence people's behaviour at a particular point and time in history are not necessarily the right ones. Indeed, human history contains countless examples of societies which promoted (or still promote) injustice, inequality and oppression. This is what Habermas means when he writes that "there may be good reasons to consider the validity claim raised in a socially accepted norm to be unjustified" (Habermas 1990, 61). Before we start honouring traditions, we should therefore ensure that their moral content is universally valid. Yet conservative neo-Aristotelians fail to provide us with a rational criterion that would enable us to do so. As a result, they run the risk of defending radically unjust norms:

> If we wish to remain faithful to the Aristotelian conviction that moral judgment is bound to the ethos of a particular place, we must be prepared to renounce the emancipatory potential of moral universalism and deny so much as the possibility of subjecting the structural violence inherent in social conditions characterized by latent exploitation and repression to an unstinting moral critique. (Habermas 1993, 125)

Contrary to Ritter and Gadamer, Habermas spent a large part of his philosophical career arguing that moral agents can reach a "posttraditional level of moral judgment" that "liberates us from the structural constraints of familiar discourses and established practices" (Habermas 1993, 125). To do so, they must resort to a universal procedure the validity of which is independent from socially dominant norms and that can be used to evaluate them. In a nutshell, defining such procedure is the main objective of Habermas's Kantian-inspired discourse ethics.[12] More specifically, what Habermas names "discourse ethics" is based on his analysis of human communicative practices. Its core idea is the following: when interlocutors *sincerely* debate the validity of a particular moral norm—that is, argue in favour or against this norm in the hope that they will come to an agreement with others—they implicitly recognize that several *rules of argumentation* must be respected for their rational discussion to succeed. If such rules are not respected by participants of a discussion, then collective rational inquiry will fail. Indeed, whichever answer to the question, "Is this truly a moral norm that we should all live by?" comes out of the discussion will not be valid. Imagine for instance that I argue in favour of a particular moral principle while successfully preventing others from criticizing my arguments by denying them the right to speak. It seems obvious that the activity in which my censored opponents and I have engaged is not true critical inquiry. This is because letting people who disagree with me share their views is a necessary condition of such inquiry.

Such considerations already allow us to understand that Habermas's point of departure for discourse ethics is a reflection on the conditions of possibility—sometimes called "transcendental conditions"—of joint critical inquiry. What conditions must be met, Habermas asks himself, for a conversation to count as an *ideal* rational discussion?[13]

The most important of these conditions is that all participants in a conversation about a particular moral norm the observance of which would affect them must be free to endorse or reject it once they have considered the consequences that its universal adoption would entail. Habermas names this requirement the *principle of universalization*—or (U)—which he defines as the following:

> (U) *All* affected can accept the consequences and the side effects [the norm's] *general* observance can be anticipated to have for the satisfaction of *everyone's* interests (and these consequences are preferred to those of known alternative possibilities for regulation). (Habermas 1990, 65)

Habermas portrays this principle as a reinterpretation of Kant's Formula of Universal Law. As is the case with Rawls's original position, (U) requires that we compare and evaluate hypothetical social worlds in which people live by different moral rules, and to choose the world we want to live in amongst a set of possible ones. Contrary to Rawls, however, Habermas does not believe that this issue can be settled by a thought experiment carried out by a lone philosopher sitting in his office. According to his perspective, *only real discussions* allow us to understand which moral norms are *actually* (not hypothetically) endorsed by all people who are affected by them. Only such norms can be said to be valid. This claim leads Habermas to argue that the best way to ensure that a moral norm is compatible with (U) is to follow a second principle, which he names the *principle of discourse ethics*—or (D). Such principle stipulates that "only those norms can claim to be valid that meet (or could meet) with the approval of all affected in their capacity as participants in a practical discourse" (Habermas 1990, 66). This point is worth stressing. In Habermas's view, Kantian philosophers can certainly aspire to identify the conditions that must be met for moral norms to be universally valid, but they cannot themselves know *which particular norms meet* such conditions. To find out, they need to participate in real discussions in which all people affected by the possible adoption of a norm debate its value. By way of contrast, both Kant and Rawls attempt to define substantial moral principles that people ought to follow through *a priori* philosophical reflection. For Habermas, this is a mistake. *A priori* philosophical reflection simply cannot lead us to identify the ethical standards by which people ought to live.

In the second part of this book, I will have the occasion to explain why this last claim by Habermas forces him into a philosophical dilemma. For now, I want to underline that his criticism of Kant and Rawls looks like an amicable discussion compared with the belligerent debate which opposes him to neo-Aristotelians. What the latter typically forget is that a certain set of moral rules can be invalid even if a majority of people obey them. The very fact that a moral norm is socially dominant in a particular community is never a sufficient reason to consider that it is valid. This is because some agents affected by this norm might still reject it if they were given the opportunity to do so in the context of an ideal rational discussion. Again, a brief look at history reveals that norms are frequently imposed on people and power relations often prevent the oppressed from expressing their discontent. In Habermas's view, that members of the Ritter School who—like him—had witnessed the rise of Nazism could not see this was sadly ironic. In fact, the philosophical framework endorsed by Ritterians would deprive a moral agent living under Nazi rule of the means to criticize the national-socialist *ethos*. How could such agent do so without reflecting upon this *ethos* from the standpoint of free conversational inquiry and engaging in real discussions?

As mentioned, this is the question that Rüdiger Bubner attempted to answer when he crossed swords with Habermas. Like MacIntyre, Bubner's attack on Kantians builds on the claim that the philosophical standpoint they aim to reach is nothing but a chimera. That said, the specific arguments he puts forward in defence of this claim are worth considering. A prolific student of Gadamer, Bubner (1976) argues that philosophers who defend universal moral principles are unconsciously guided by the historical context in which they have formulated them. For instance, Rousseau's contractualist political philosophy stemmed from the need to rethink political legitimacy when European absolute monarchies came under attack. As for the political philosophy developed by Kant in his *Doctrine of Right*, it amounts to an attempt to justify private property against its detractors.

At a more fundamental level, Bubner argues that Kant's insensitivity to historical relativity threatens his practical philosophy. Unsurprisingly, one of his key arguments focuses on Kant's most famous philosophical principle: the formula of universal law. Even if we consider that such a principle is a universally valid moral principle, Bubner contends, the results that it will yield will necessarily vary depending on historical context. As we have seen, the categorical imperative allows moral agents to evaluate maxims (e.g., "I will lie whenever I need to," "I will always refrain from stealing," etc.). Yet the people philosophers describe as "moral agents" are always real individuals who live in a particular society at a specific time and place and history, that is, what Bubner describes as a "form of life" (*Lebensform*). Such forms of life are likely to influence which precise maxims historical agents choose to evaluate with recourse to Kant's formula of universal law. In other words, even if people use the same universalization test to assess their maxims, the content of these maxims will change throughout history. In each historical context, some maxims are more likely to be tested than others. By way of example, the maxim "I will attempt to liberate all prisoners of war" is more likely to have been evaluated by military veterans of a war-torn country than by people who live in a country which never experienced war over the course of their lifetime. If moral agents living at various points in human history use Kant's universalization test to evaluate different maxims, they risk behaving in dissimilar ways. Indeed, two moral agents might end up abiding by different sets of moral rules because the maxims they have evaluated with recourse to the formula of universal law diverge. As Bubner (1973, 232) explains, "the Categorical Imperative is nothing more than a logical meta-rule for testing the reasonableness of rules guiding action," one that yields different results depending on the content which is fed to it. Even if we accept that the formula of universal law is binding for all rational beings, the outcomes it will generate will still vary from one form of life to another, and the agents who belong to such forms of life might live very different moral lives.

Not all Kantians will be moved by this critique. First, one could argue that the maxims that agents will submit to the universalization test throughout human history will not be fundamentally dissimilar to one another. This is because human beings often face similar moral dilemmas regardless of the contingent historical context in which they live. In the seventeenth century, people were probably just as tempted to lie as they are now. Second, if the results yielded by Kant's formula of universal law differ without contradicting each other—a conclusion which is compatible with Bubner's argument—this might not be a problem at all. Certainly, some moral agents will never consider acting on the maxim according to which "I will attempt to liberate all prisoners of war" over the course of their lifetime, but this does not compromise Kantian ethics. What would do so is the demonstration that the universalization test sometimes yields contradictory results, that is, the same action can be judged to be permissible *and* impermissible depending on the content of maxims.[14]

Should we discard Bubner's critique for this reason? Interestingly, Habermas's own interpretation of the Kantian universalization test might be more vulnerable to it than the formula of universal law itself. To see this, let us picture a discussion amongst the members of community x at time t^1 in human history. Let us also assume that such discussion satisfies Habermas's principle (D), that is, that a set of norms s^1 has received the approval of all people affected by it in their capacity as participants in a practical discourse. Now, imagine that at t^2 in human history, members of community x hold a new discussion which satisfies (D) and end up endorsing a new set of norms s^2. Is there anything which prevents s^1 and s^2 from conflicting with each other? This does not seem to be the case. Here, an example will be useful to illustrate this argument. British sexual mores evolved drastically between 1800 and the present day. In 1800, we can imagine that the British people might have endorsed a norm according to which "sexual activities between members of the same sex are morally impermissible" in the context of a discussion which satisfies principle (D). More than two hundred years later, it is more likely that they would endorse the opposite norm (i.e., "sexual activities between members of the same sex are morally permissible"). If it is so, then Habermas will have to admit that principle (D) can yield contradictory results at different points in human history, and this seems to support the conclusion that discourse ethics does not generate moral principles that are universally valid in any meaningful sense of the term. That said, one line of response available to Habermas and his followers is that, in nineteenth-century England, discussions which portrayed homosexuality as immoral probably did not meet principle (D). Indeed, it is very likely that at least *some* people who were attracted to members of the same sex would have rejected the principle according to which it is. Without a doubt, these people were also affected by the sexual norms of the society in which they lived. If this is so, then a discourse ethicist would consider that any social norm prohibiting sexual activities between members of the same sex enforced in nineteenth-century Britain was in fact invalid.

A more promising line of objection directed by Bubner against discourse ethics amounts to the claim that discussions which Habermas has in mind never actually take place. More specifically, it is never the case that participants of an ideal discussion suspend judgement on the validity of *all* norms, and then examine such norms one by one to determine whether they should be endorsed or rejected. In a given community, all forms of collective action—including the decision to engage in discussion with others—presuppose that people already agree on some norms the validity of which cannot be questioned. Certainly, members of a particular community typically disagree on important moral issues. Yet the very representation of these people as being *members of the same community* implies that they share some ethical standards which are not up for debate. In the absence of this ethical agreement, no collective rational discussion would happen in the first place. This is what Bubner means when he writes that "what makes collective action possible cannot also emerge from collective action" (1984, 208). In other words, the validity of social norms which make joint rational inquiry possible is not itself established through joint rational inquiry. Any discussion through which these norms are subject to a critical assessment already rests on the assumption that at least some of them are valid. If this is so, then it is always the case that some social norms are accepted without having been critically assessed by all affected parties in the context of an ideal rational discussion.

Bubner's critique of discourse ethics does not only focus on Habermas's view of how moral principles can be rationally grounded through principle (D). In a typically neo-Aristotelian fashion, he also discusses the role that moral principles can play in moral reasoning. For such principles to be useful, he argues, there must be a social agreement on which actions count as correct applications of them.[15] Consider the lying example once more. To respect the Kantian principle according to which "one should never lie," I must understand what, precisely, counts as lying. Yet there is room for disagreement on this question, and it remains possible that people belonging to different communities will accept different definitions of lying. Let us say that I utter a claim that I know to be false without intending to deceive my audience. Am I really lying? Borrowing an example from Thomas Carson (2006 290), we can imagine a student who tells a college dean that he did not cheat on an exam. The student knows this to be false, and he also knows the dean knows this to be false. Yet there is a university policy in place which prevents dean from punishing liars who did not admit to cheating. In this situation, the student is not trying to deceive the dean, but merely using the university policy in his favour. While some would argue that the student's utterance count as a lie, others would deny that this is the case.

The point is that moral principles usually come with what Bubner (1974, 180) calls a margin of tolerance (*Toleranzmarge*). This margin encompasses actions that *come close* to being infringements of such principles, but do not unambiguously count as such. Furthermore, the extent of a moral rule's margin of tolerance is never fixed by the rule itself, but depends on the views of members of communities who live by it. While some communities will count the student's utterance as a lie, others will not. In Bubner's view, this suggests that any theory of moral judgement should make room for the Aristotelian concept of practical wisdom. Indeed, what allows moral agents to understand whether a particular action counts as a correct application of principle is not itself a principle, but an *aptitude* that they have acquired through moral education. In general, human beings develop a holistic understanding of the norms that regulate social life within their community which includes an ability to tell what actions fall within their scope.

For his part, Habermas believes that the neo-Aristotelian discourse on *phronesis* makes moral discussions more confusing. When considering the cheating student scenario, what we want to know is whether the student's answer *should* count as a lie and, if it does, whether the student should be punished in the same way as liars usually are (even if he did not attempt to deceive anyone). By way of contrast, arguing that different communities will have distinct views on this subject—and that wise people from these communities will understand what these views are—is not especially interesting. What is more, it does not help readers understand whether it is morally acceptable for them to behave as the student did *regardless of the communal ethical standards under which they live*. Before concluding this chapter, this is the philosophical point to which I wish to draw attention. In practical matters, giving the last word to communal ethical standards risks leading us to social conservatism. And as we have seen, the costs of social conservatism sometimes include complicity in injustice.

At this stage of my reflection, however, two important remarks are in order. First, neo-Aristotelians like MacIntyre and Bubner do have more sophisticated views on the problem of historical relativism that the ones I have considered so far. In second part of this book, I will therefore need to assess such views.[16] Second, the very idea that moral agents can tell how they ought to act *regardless of the communal ethical standards under which they live* implies that philosophers can define a supra-traditional criterion of moral judgement, which is precisely what neo-Aristotelians usually deny. As mentioned, MacIntyre and Gadamer consider that contingent historical circumstances always end up influencing our ethical views, and such influence prevents any attempt to reach philosophical neutrality to succeed. Again, whether contemporary Kantian philosophers can overcome this criticism is an issue that I reserve for the second part of this book. For now, I wish to continue retracing the neo-Aristotelian of Kantian judgement as it developed in continental Europe over the last two decades of the twentieth century. Doing so will incite me to consider an argument according to which grounding moral judgement in an account of universally valid moral principles is not only *impossible*, but also *unnecessary*. This is Vincent Descombes's view, a contemporary French philosopher to whom I now turn.

Chapter 3

A French Aristotelian Perspective on Deliberation

Writing about contemporary French philosophy in English is always challenging. This is not only because translating philosophy is always a delicate endeavour, but also because philosophers who have been trained in the Anglo-American world have a very particular conception of what contemporary French philosophy is. When graduate students enroll in seminars on "contemporary French philosophy," they typically expect to read works from post-structuralist thinkers (Deleuze, Derrida, Foucault, etc.) and reflect upon issues such as the critique of the subject.[1] According to this critique, great philosophers of the Western tradition have naïvely assumed that human behaviour is guided by rational reflection. However, in reality, humans are moved by irrational impulses and desires of which they remain unaware.

As interesting as it might be, this is not the philosophical discussion to which I wish to draw attention in this book. Instead, I want to assess the work of a French Aristotelian philosopher who deliberately rejected the influence of post-structuralist *maîtres à penser* and focused an important part of his reflection on moral judgement and practical rationality: Vincent Descombes. Born in 1943, Descombes first wrote his doctoral dissertation on Plato in 1970, and then published a history of French philosophy between 1933 and 1978 in which he discussed the works Kojève, Merleau-Ponty, Foucault, Althusser, Derrida and Deleuze.[2] In the 1980s, however, he discovered analytical philosophy of action, a subdiscipline that heavily influenced the theory of moral and political reasoning that he developed in the 1990s. In what follows, I will devote most of my attention to some of Descombes's untranslated essays in which he strongly criticizes what he names the Kantian "foundationist" conception of moral judgement. In such essays, Descombes also draws from the works of Aristotle, Peter Geach and Elizabeth Anscombe to build an alternative "intentionalist" theory of moral judgement to which I devote the second section of this chapter. Before I move on to the second part of this book, I also wanted to include a short summary of the neo-Aristotelian objections discussed in its first part. Readers will find it at the end of this chapter.

VINCENT DESCOMBES'S CRITIQUE OF KANTIAN "FOUNDATIONISM"

In many ways, Descombes is an odd Aristotelian thinker. Contrary to MacIntyre, whose philosophical reflection owes much to Aquinas, he defends a theory of moral judgement which he believes is fundamentally at odds with the scholastic tradition. In his view, medieval scholastic thinkers typically conceived of moral judgement as the application of general principles to particular cases.[3] In this way, their practical philosophy shares a fundamental feature with that of contemporary Kantians. Interestingly, Descombes is also quite critical of German neo-Aristotelianism for reasons that I have examined in the previous chapter. Simply put, this philosophical movement quickly turned into a conservative political discourse which he rejects. Lastly, a third reason to believe that Descombes's Aristotelianism is unconventional is that he is uninterested in building a virtue ethics. According to his perspective, virtue ethicists often put forward a critique of principled-based accounts of moral judgement, but they paradoxically end up defending a moral principle according to which agents should "act like the virtuous would in the same circumstances." When this is the case, then the same objections that virtue ethicists direct against contemporary Kantians can be directed against their own preferred moral theory.

Yet there is no doubt that—like many philosophers he criticizes—Descombes is strongly indebted to Aristotle. As he explains, the basis of his philosophical reflection is a "claimed alliance between Aristotle and Wittgenstein," a twentieth-century Austrian philosopher who famously argued that most philosophical problems are based on conceptual confusions (Descombes 2007a, 384). In fact, an important part of Descombes's argument against Kantian conceptions of moral judgement amounts to the claim that Kantians are conceptually confused to the extent that they mistake theoretical reflection for practical reasoning. In other words, Kantians are typically unable to see that practical reasoning is a "different form of reasoning, which has its own rules of validity" (Descombes 2007b, 21).[4] To see this, consider how moral philosophers typically envision the way moral agents ought to justify their moral and political decisions. According to Descombes (1994, 11–18), there are two fundamental views about this question. While these views seem antithetical at first glance, they share a central feature with one another. The first view is that of Kantian philosophers whom Descombes calls "foundationists." It contains two central steps. At the first step, moral and political actors demonstrate that their individual decisions are compatible with general principles (e.g., "You ought not to lie"). At the second step, agents must now explain why the general principles they have chosen to respect should be followed by all moral agents. However, one problem with this foundationist conception is that moral agents (and philosophers) tend to disagree about the principles that everyone ought to follow. When I attempt to justify my actions by pointing out that they conform to a given principle, indeed, we can easily imagine that someone would respond the following: "While it is true that your actions are in conformity with principle p, I disagree that I ought to follow principle p." When this happens, Kantians often try to demonstrate that principle p derives from a meta-principle which all rational agents must follow—the formula of universal law or the principle of discourse ethics, for instance—but the disagreement about which meta-principle grounds all other moral principles is just as profound as that which focuses on moral principles themselves.

The second philosophical view about the justification of moral and political decisions is that of philosophers whom Descombes names "decisionists." Such philosophers conceive of justification in the very same way as Kantian foundationists, but they also argue that it is doomed to fail. This is because it remains rationally impossible for Kantians to demonstrate that there are moral principles that all rational agents ought to respect. In the end, whether a particular agent should respect a moral principle depends on her subjective desires. For the affirmation "I ought not to lie" to be true, it needs to be the case that I desire not to lie. Yet subjective desires undoubtedly vary from one person to another, and there is not a single principle that all human beings always desire to respect. A common feature between the foundationist and decisionist views is the claim that moral and political decisions must be grounded in universally valid moral principles. For his part, Descombes argues that moral and political actors can perfectly justify their particular decisions *without grounding them*. To do so, he develops a neo-Aristotelian discourse according to which the multiple layers of our social identity are the ultimate source of reasons for action.

In Book II of his *Nicomachean Ethics*, Aristotle unambiguously ties the aim of our actions to what we can call our practical identities (for instance, my identity as a son, brother, husband, father, philosophy professor, friend, member of this community organization, and so on). Using the example of a medical doctor, he underlines that the bearers of a specific practical identity need not deliberate about the ends they ought to pursue. This is because ends are internal to practical identities, and all bearers of particular identities should pursue ends that are internal to them:

> We deliberate not about ends but about what contributes to ends. For a doctor does not deliberate whether he shall heal, nor an orator whether he shall convince, nor a statesman whether he shall produce law and order, nor does anyone else deliberate about his end. (Aristotle 1984, 1756)

The important point here is that it would be absurd for a doctor to wonder if, in general, he really ought to attempt to heal his patients. Indeed, the very point of having doctors in the first place is to ensure that their patients will be healed. In Aristotle's perspective, the end "to heal" *teleologically* belongs to the practical identity "doctor." The very function of doctors is to promote health, and this fact allows us to conclude that all doctors have reasons to heal their patients. What doctors may deliberate about is not *whether* they ought to pursue the end that belongs to their practical identity—and this independently of their subjective desires—but *how* they should pursue this end when treating *such* or *such* patient.

Note that one can accept this teleological conception of practical identities without endorsing Aristotle's philosophy of the natural (as opposed to social) world. For instance, I can accept the claim that a doctor's function is to heal his patients without believing they have this function *by nature*. The fact that doctors must heal patients is not "written in the reality of things"; it simply derives from the fact that human beings who live in society attribute this task to them. Furthermore, that doctors possess this function does not entail the claim that human beings possess a function *qua* human beings. Pace *Aristotle*, there might not be a central activity in which all human beings should engage by nature.[5] In fact, in many contemporary Aristotelian accounts of the normativity of practical identities, Aristotle's natural teleology plays little to no role. For example, MacIntyre (1999, x) underlines that his most influential work—*After Virtue*—does not rely on what he defines as Aristotle's "metaphysical biology." Instead, its philosophical basis is a teleological understanding of identities and practices which is rooted in the forms of social life.

Similarly, Descombes develops a non-naturalistic teleological account of the normativity of practical identities. In his view, such teleological account can be used to answer one of the most famous challenges pertaining to the foundations of moral judgement: Elizabeth Anscombe's thought experiment involving a "rational Nazi." In this thought experiment, a Nazi soldier is caught in a trap where he is sure to be killed during the Second World War. He nonetheless can exterminate Jewish people before he dies. In fact, he is firmly committed to doing so under the pretext that it is his function to do so *qua* Nazi soldier. According to his perspective, "It befits a Nazi, if he must die, to spend his last hour exterminating Jews" (Anscombe 1957, 72). Here, Anscombe uses the example of one of the worst crimes in human history to show that teleological accounts of the normativity of practical identities are lacking. What is disturbing in this hypothetical scenario is that the imagined Nazi uses a teleological understanding of his own practical identity *qua* Nazi to justify the pursuit of a morally reprehensible end. What is more, such an end is internal to his identity: it befits a Nazi to pursue it like it befits a doctor to heal patients. This raises the worry that teleological accounts of practical identities are a poor guide to morality. It may be true that exterminating Jewish people is an end internal to the practical identity "Nazi," but this evidently does not constitute a moral reason to pursue this end.

In Descombes's view, however, we can resist the conclusion that neo-Aristotelian discourses on practical identities legitimize the pursuit of bad ends. To show this, he once again compares his own response to Anscombe's thought experiment with that of Kantians. When considering the "rational Nazi" scenario, Kantians are likely to argue that the Nazi acts irrationally by violating moral principles that all rational agents ought to respect. As discussed above, however, this philosophical strategy might not bear fruit. By way of contrast, Descombes argues there is no need to resort to universally valid moral principles to demonstrate that Nazis act irrationally when they engage in genocidal violence. According to his perspective, a less philosophically demanding solution is available. To defeat the Nazi in thought—that is, to demonstrate that he is not acting rationally when he pursues an immoral end—we should turn the normativity of practical identities thesis against him. To do so, Descombes begins by arguing that our social identities are complex. For instance, people typically have a profession, but they are often also part of a family, have friends, and may be part of associations such as political parties or religious groups. Moreover, many difficult moral decisions they face come from the fact that the ends which are internal to their practical identities cannot always be pursued simultaneously. It may be my role *qua* friend to help my colleague move and my duty *qua* father to attend my daughter's martial arts exam, but I might not have time to do both. When this happens, I am forced to choose between the two.

In Descombes's view, the same goes for Nazis. In the real world, Nazis are not like the one in Anscombe's thought experiment, that is, people about whom we know nothing else other than the morally reprehensible end that they are firmly committed to pursuing. They also bear complex identities from which conflicting obligations can spring. To borrow Descombes's own example, imagine a Nazi who bears the following two practical identities: he is a member of the NSDAP, but he is also the rector of a renowned German university. Now, like Anscombe's hypothetical Nazi, this person judges that it befits him to do anything he can to support the NSDAP. In his view, he has only one objective *qua* Nazi and *qua* rector: to help the party's leader achieve his political objectives. According to Descombes, the Nazi rector is right to think that it befits him to act in such manner *qua* Nazi, but he is mistaken in believing that it also befits him to act in such a way *qua* rector. The end internally tied to the practical identity "rector" is to promote higher education and research, not to support a political party by agreeing with everything its "enlightened" leader desires to accomplish, even when this hinders the pursuit of knowledge. Returning to Aristotle's remarks on deliberation, it is also true that rectors should not deliberate about whether to promote the pursuit of knowledge. Deliberation is of means, not of ends, and promoting the pursuit of knowledge is quite simply what rectors are for. When our rector prioritizes the leader's ends over the pursuit of knowledge, he may be an "excellent" Nazi, but he is being a terrible rector.

Descombes's rector example is intended to show that agents can make rational mistakes by misidentifying the ends and standards of correctness that internally belong to their practical identities. The Nazi rector's mistake is not to believe that his identity *qua* Nazi is to promote the political objectives of the NSDAP, but to consider that promoting these objectives is also his duty *qua* rector. Indeed, the idea that a good rector is one who subordinates knowledge and truth-seeking to ideological ends is just as absurd as claiming that the central end an Olympic runner ought to pursue is to bake good cakes. Once again, the underlying Aristotelian idea that unites these two cases is that agents cannot choose to assign external ends and standards of correctness to the practices in which they engage. Instead, practical identities and their associated practices have internal ends and standards of correctness that agents ought to pursue and respect:

> Will our ideologist say that athletes in his country are the best, even if they only win by fraudulent means? Will he say that his soldiers are the best according to his own "table of values" even if they do not win battles, or if they only do so at the cost of the total ruin of their country [. . .] If we claim that any notion of success and failure is arbitrary and depends on our opinions, we do away with the *practical sense*: we abolish the difference between doing one thing and not doing it. (Descombes 1994, 37–38)

In the end, Descombes believes that Nazis will be rationally defeated when we demonstrate that their ideological way of thinking rests on their philosophical inability to identify the ends that internally belong to the practices in which they engage. It is true that the end pursued by the Nazi rector is internal to his identity *qua* Nazi, but when he attributes this end to all dimensions of his identity, he replaces the end internal to such dimensions with an external one. It is in this very manner, argues Descombes, that monomaniacal reasoners who pursue one single objective are irrational: by concentrating on one sole end, they assign such an end to practices to which it does not teleologically belong, and fail to recognize that their practical identities may create conflicting duties. Defending the ideology of the NSDAP at all costs is incompatible with promoting the pursuit of knowledge, but the Nazi rector remains oblivious to this fact.

In summary, Descombes's philosophical gamble is that one can demonstrate that the Nazi is acting irrationally without requiring him to endorse the *standpoint of rational agency as such*. As we will see in chapter 5, contemporary Kantians such as Christine Korsgaard defend the claim that a Nazi must shed the multiple layers of his social identity to correctly identify the moral obligations that he must truly fulfill. Doing so would allow him to understand that he must ultimately act *qua rational human being*, not *qua* Nazi. For his part, Descombes solution to Anscombe's challenge is based on the claim that moral agents cannot rationally assign *one single end* to all their practical identities. For my part, I am not convinced by this solution. In fact, in the second part of this book, I will argue that Descombes's neo-Aristotelian teleological understanding of practical identities faces an important problem, and that a great deal of contemporary Kantian philosophy should be understood as an attempt to avoid the pitfalls of the neo-Aristotelian discourse on the normativity of practical identifies. For now, I want to stress that—like that of MacIntyre and German neo-Aristotelians—Descombes's critique of contemporary Kantianism is not limited to his attack on foundationist conceptions of moral judgement. It also includes an important objection against what he calls "normativist" accounts of moral reasoning.

AN INTENTIONALIST ACCOUNT OF PRACTICAL REASONING

Consider the following syllogistic account of moral reasoning (Descombes 2007b, 119):

> First premise (which introduces generality into the agent's reasoning): a principle (that is, a "great principle" or a standard of conduct) is stated in the imperative tense or by means of a deontic operator such as "it is compulsory for one to," "one ought to," etc.
>
> Second premise: the agent's situation is described as a particular case which falls under this general rule.
>
> Conclusion: the subsumption of the case under the rule is sufficient to determine what the agent should do. The syllogism allowed the agent to understand what her duty is. (Descombes 2007b, 111)

Is there anything wrong with this picture? In Descombes's view, there is. The central problem with this "normativist" account of practical reasoning is that it is not action-guiding. Indeed, it does not identify a particular action that a moral agent ought to perform. This remains difficult to see if we stay at a high level of philosophical abstraction, but a simple example will help us grasp this point. In one of the most famous debates in which he engaged during his life, Kant discussed a case which is now known as the "murderer at the door" with French-Swiss political theorist Benjamin Constant. In this hypothetical scenario, a murderer at my door asks me if I know where to find an innocent person that she is looking for, and which happens to be hiding in my home. When reflecting upon this case, Kant famously argued that you should not lie to the murderer. As he argued in "On a supposed right to lie from philanthropy" (1996, 613), "To be *truthful* (honest) in all declarations is therefore a sacred command of reason prescribing unconditionally, one not to be restricted by any conveniences." According to the traditional interpretation of Kant's argument, this is because lying is not a universalizable maxim. If we lived in a world in which people always lied, then the basis of mutual trust would be absent, and there would no such things such as promises and contracts. Indeed, what would be the point of signing a contract with someone who you know will not respect it?

Now, Descombes's point is not that Kant's argument in favour of the absolute prohibition of lying is a good (or bad) one. Instead, his claim is the following: even if we accept such prohibition, it will barely help us determine how to act in the case of the murderer at the door (or in other real or hypothetical situations in which lying appears to be a reasonable course of action). Certainly, if I agree with Kant that my general duty not to lie is an *absolute* one, then I will know that I should not tell the murderer that the innocent person is *not* hiding in my home. Yet there is still a wide range of actions that I can commit *hic et nunc* without disobeying my duty not to lie. For instance, a first option amounts to simply telling the murder that the innocent person is in fact hiding in my home. If I do this, however, I will arguably be complicit in the murderer's killing, and this is bad. A second option would be to tell the murderer something that does not count as a lie, but might still incite her to leave my house. Imagine, for instance, that I tell her the following: "I know for a fact that the person you are looking for has the habit of hiding in this neighbourhood." Hopefully, the murdered will think that the meaning of my statement is something along the following lines: "The person you wish to kill is probably in this neighbourhood, but not in this house." A third option— my preferred one—is to refuse to answer the murderer's question, swiftly close the door, lock it and then swiftly alert the person whom I am hiding in my house that her prospective murderer is here.

Those are only three options, but it is quite easy to imagine a dozen more. In short, I can do many very different things without lying to the murderer. Negative duties—that is, mere prohibitions, tell us what actions we *ought not* to commit, but they do not tell us which particular action we *ought* to commit. In Descombes's view, however, moral reasoning must be such that it allows us to choose between the many courses of actions that are available to us in particular situations, which is why Kantian accounts of it are flawed. As he (2007b, 113) explains:

> Deontological reasoning, the conclusion of which is that a given obligation falls upon a subject, is, in reality, a theoretical reasoning that relates to practical matters. Such a reasoning reminds or teaches the practical subject what one of his duties amounts to. It does not tell him what to do [. . .] in the sense of *leading to an action*. It is therefore not a practical reasoning for all it says is: whatever you do, do not lie.

As for positive duties, they are not of the form, "Whatever you do, do not ϕ," but rather of the form, "You ought to ϕ!" At first sight, it therefore seems that such duties are action-guiding. Upon closer examination, however, we can see that positive duties are not any less general than negative duties; quite the contrary. Consider for instance Kant's claim that we have a moral duty to develop our natural talents. There is an incredibly wide range of ways in which moral agents can do this. Depending on what they are naturally good at, they can choose to become artisans, pursue a PhD, learn to play a musical instrument, study therapy and counselling, become expert chess players, and so on. While negative duties are of the form "Whatever you do, do not ϕ," positive duties are of the form, "Whatever you do, make sure that some things that you do count as ϕ-ing." Yet neither tells us how, precisely, we ought to act.

According to Descombes, Kant also neglected the fact the deontic statements sometimes conflict with each other. In his *Doctrine of Virtue* (1996, 379), for instance, he writes: "If it is a duty to act in accordance with one rule, to act in accordance with the opposite rule is not a duty but even contrary to duty; so *a collision of duties* and obligations is inconceivable." Yet such statement directly contradicts our ordinary moral experience, which is replete with situations in which we feel that it is quite simply impossible for us to fulfill all our duties at the same. Again, an example will be useful to illustrate this idea. Let us admit that, as moral agents, we have both a negative moral duty not to lie and a positive moral duty to protect the life of others to the best of our ability. If such a statement is true, then any moral agent who finds herself in a situation in which lying is the most effective way to protect the life of another person will face a conflict of duties. Fortunately, this conflict is not impossible to solve unless both these duties turn out to be absolute. If they are not, then our moral agent can eliminate the conflict she faces by giving priority to one of her duties over the other. For instance, she might conclude that people's right to be protected from injury and death takes precedence over their right not to be lied to, and then decide to lie for this reason. The same method of moral reasoning can be applied to less dramatic familiar and perhaps more familiar examples. Let us say that I promise my friend to help her move into her new apartment. On the day of the move, however, I learn that my brother is suffering from severe anxiety, and that he could really benefit from my advice. Arguably, it will be reasonable for me to break my promise to help my friend move even though I have a general moral duty not to break my promises. This is because breaking *this* specific promise is a way for me to fulfill a second duty which falls upon me, that of being a good brother. If my brother's anxiety is severe and debilitating, being by his side appears to be the best thing to do, morally speaking.

Here, note that the type of reflection in which I must engage to solve these hard moral cases is of a different nature than the "normativist" reasoning summarized by Descombes at the beginning of this section. When I give priority to my anxious brother over my friend, I recognize that there is a variety of ends that humans can legitimately pursue, but that those ends cannot all be simultaneously pursued at the same time. Caring for others is a wonderful thing to do, but it sometimes prevents me from being a good friend or, at least, the friend that I wish I were on moving day. In Descombes's view, this suggests that truly practical reasoning is an intellectual process through which agents identify the best possible course of action in particular situations by subordinating certain ends to others. This is what he calls *deliberation*. To clarify this concept, Descombes (2007b, 24) uses the example of policy-making, but we can easily apply his reasoning to the examples I have just discussed:

> To know what to do, it does not suffice to rationally demonstrate that it is good to adopt policy A [. . .] Indeed, it may well happen that another reasoning leads me to conclude that it would not be good to adopt policy A in the end (because this would mean that I have to refrain from enacting policy B, which is more urgent).

Interestingly, the very fact that legitimate human ends can conflict with each other and that our moral life is plagued by dilemmas suggests that practical reasoning has a different *logical* structure than that of theoretical reasoning (i.e., the kind of reasoning that allows us to form true beliefs about *how things are* as opposed to *what I ought to do*). To argue this point, Descombes builds on the philosophy of English logician Peter Geach. In his book *Logic Matters*,

Geach (1972, 386) distinguishes between theoretical and practical reasoning through the demonstration that "practical inference is *defeasible* in a way that theoretical inference is not." Specifically, he argues that an instance of deductive theoretical reasoning can be unsound for two different reasons. First, it can be *invalid*, which means that its conclusion does not derive from its premises. For example, the following inference is invalid:

P1: All men will die.
P2: x will die.
C: x is a man.

As the reader can easily see, there is a wide range of beings that can die but do not qualify as men (e.g., women, non-human animals, and plants). Second, an instance of deductive theoretical reasoning can be unsound even if the conclusion of such reasoning derives from its premises. This happens when at least one of its premises is false. By way of example, consider the following reasoning, which is deductively valid, but only contains one true premise:

P1: All whales are mortal.
P2: Socrates is a whale.
C: Socrates is mortal.

Now, instances of practical reasoning can also be unsound in these two ways. Yet Geach underlines that there is a third distinct way in which *only* practical reasoning can be unsound. To see this, consider the following story, which Geach once read in a political weekly:

> I do not dispute Col. Bogey's premises, nor the logic of his inference. But even if a conclusion is validly drawn from acceptable premises, we are not obliged to accept it if those premises are *incomplete*; and unfortunately there is a vital premise missing from the Colonel's argument—the existence of Communist China. (Geach 1972, 77)

When discussing this case, Geach explains that he cannot remember the details of this specific political dispute. This need not matter here for our interest relates to logic rather than politics. What the above-cited quote suggests is that a practical reasoning can be defeated through the demonstration that its premises are true, but *incomplete*. In other words, an instance of practical reasoning which appears to be sound (because it is valid and only contains true premises) can still be undermined by the introduction of a new premise, even if this new premise is also true. While Geach's political weekly example is interesting, Descombes's preferred one illustrates this point even more clearly. In seventeenth-century France, fabulist Jean de La Fontaine wrote a short story titled "The Bear and the Gardener" (*L'Ours et l'Amateur Des Jardins*). In this fable, a bear ponders how to kill a fly which risks awakening his elderly friend from a peaceful slumber. The bear then concludes that the very best way to kill the fly amounts to squashing it by throwing a brick at it. This would not be a bad reasoning, Descombes argues, if it were not for the fact that there is a crucial piece of information missing from the bear's reasoning. In Lafontaine's fable, the fly is resting on the sleeping man's nose, who ends up being killed by the brick. While "one can kill a fly by throwing a brick at it" is a good premise to consider, in this case, the bear's thought that he should do so is defeated by a second premise, namely, "bricks can also hurt people." The moral of the story, La Fontaine concludes, is that nothing is as dangerous as a foolish friend.

Descombes draws two conclusions from this fable. The first is that instances of practical reasoning—including moral reasoning—can be defeated if reasoners do not pay attention to all relevant features of the case at hand. The second conclusion relates to practical wisdom. According to Descombes, *phronesis* is an intellectual virtue which enables wise moral agents to pay attention to such relevant features. Unlike the bear, wise agents do not fail to integrate important premises into their moral thinking. When we make moral judgements, some features of the situation in which we find ourselves can reasonably be ignored, but others should not. Because of this, good judgement is a matter of *discernment*, that is, of correctly distinguishing between the morally relevant and irrelevant features of singular cases. In other words, *phronesis* is:

> A sense that allows one to distinguish between what is relevant and what is not. It does not relate to what *exists*, but to what *matters*. It relates to an order of value or priority: there are important things—those that one cannot afford to neglect—and there are secondary things, which one can consider to be insignificant or indifferent to the thing which concerns us. (Descombes 2007b, 304)

It is also worth noting that, in La Fontaine's fable, the bear's failure to notice a morally relevant fact prevents him from fulfilling a goal that he freely set for itself. In fact, Descombes chose this example to illustrate that deliberation is a form of *first-person reasoning*, one in which agents engage to effectively pursue ends that they endorse. For deliberation to lead to an action, it must be undertaken by agents who are reflecting upon reasons for action that they see as their own. This entails that any person who reflects upon how *others* ought to act does not, strictly speaking, engage in practical reasoning. Practical reasoning ends with an action, and no agent can *make others act* for others have a will of their own. At best, second-person or third-person reasoning will end with a suggestion or a command—with a "you should" or a "she ought to—" but never with an "I act." As Descombes (2007b, 134) puts it, "the role of the will in deliberation is to provide the motive without which reasoning will not lead to anything more than an opinion without a practical follow-up."

To sum up, Descombes portrays deliberation as a practical reasoning through which (i) an agent reflects upon the best way to reach an end that she endorses, (ii) requires her to grasp all the morally relevant features of the case at hand and (iii) ends with an action as opposed to a deontological statement about how she ought to act. Unlike the one described at the very beginning of this section, such an account of practical reasoning is not *normativist* but *intentionalist*, for it always begins with an intention and ends up with an action. In Descombes's perspective, the two central steps of intentionalist reasoning can be described as follows:

1. First premise: it states what the desired outcome is; what is to be achieved, obtained or maintained in one way or another. For example, the aim of *this* doctor facing *this* patient is to restore her health.
2. Second premise: it indicates what initiative the agent can take immediately to reach the end set in the first premise. In the example given by Aristotle: the starting point of the doctor's reasoning is that the patient must regain physical equilibrium. To do so, one will have to warm her up [. . .] and this is something that can be done right now. The final term of the reasoning is the beginning of an action: if it is indeed the doctor *as such* who has deliberated, she will now take action. (Descombes 2007b, 116)

Ultimately, Descombes argues that contemporary Kantians are so preoccupied with the philosophical grounding of universal moral principles that they forget to analyze how moral agents deliberate once they have understood how they generally ought to behave and formed the desire to do so. As we have seen, the thought that "I ought to comply with duty x" is not the last step of practical reasoning, and this for three reasons. First, it remains possible that such a duty will conflict with other moral duties which fall upon me, in which case I will have to decide which of my duties should be given priority. Second, I must see this duty as *mine* and form the desire to perform an action that will allow me to respect it. Third, I must decide which particular action amongst all possible ones best allows me to fulfill it. When I do so, there is a risk that I will fail to notice a morally relevant feature of the situation in which I find myself and end up performing a bad action. In summary, the most challenging steps of moral judgement come *after* I have come to understand what my general duties are, not before.

THE NEO-ARISTOTELIAN CRITIQUE OF KANTIAN JUDGEMENT: A SUMMARY

With discussions of MacIntyre's communitarianism, German neo-Aristotelianism and Descombes's theory of deliberation behind us, we are now in a position to summarize the critique of Kantian judgement discussed in the first part of this book. Before I do so, one methodological remark is in order. When assessing the claims made by MacIntyre and Bubner and Descombes, I have deliberately stopped myself from developing a full-blown critique of their own philosophies. Before criticizing the arguments that such thinkers have put forward, I wanted to reconstruct such arguments to the best of my ability. In the second part of this book, however, my perspective on neo-Aristotelianism will be much more critical. To an extent, this is because I believe that the neo-Aristotelian picture of moral judgement is flawed. Yet I also have historiographical reasons to critically assess neo-Aristotelianism. In short, I firmly believe that fully understanding contemporary Kantian moral theory requires one to grasp the ways in which Kantians have responded to the three neo-Aristotelian objections I have discussed so far as well as the criticisms of neo-Aristotelianism they have formulated in return. To a large extent, contemporary Kantianism is an attempt to *overcome neo-Aristotelianism*.

Before I turn to contemporary Kantianism, however, let me summarize the neo-Aristotelian objections I have discussed so far and sketch the main line of response I will assess in the second part of the book.

1. A first neo-Aristotelian objection against the Kantian model of moral judgement relates to the grounding of moral principles that agents must respect to perform good actions. Here, the claim is that Kantians attempt but fail to reach an impartial standpoint which would allow them to formulate universally valid moral rules. Upon closer examination, this putatively neutral viewpoint always turns out to be the historically contingent one of a particular community. What is more, the values it embodies often conflict with that of other communities which existed at a different point in time or space—or both—in history. As we have seen, this objection is salient in both MacIntyre's and Bubner's work.

To rebut this objection, contemporary Kantians typically use one of three strategies. First, there are Kantians who simply acknowledge that the normative principles they defend are not *a priori* and universal. From the middle of the 1980s until his death, for instance, Rawls (1993) described his theory of justice as fairness as one that reflects the fundamental moral intuitions of contemporary liberal democracies. Second, some Kantians argue that only philosophers who heavily rely on armchair thought experiments are vulnerable to the neo-Aristotelian objection which pertains to the foundations of moral judgement. By way contrast, a philosophical reflection on the conditions of possibility of argumentative discourse, which lets real discussants ground moral principles themselves, avoids it. This is Habermas's strategy, which I critically assess in the next chapter. The third Kantian line of response is even more ambitious. It amounts to offering a transcendental argument the conclusion of which is that all rational agents must endorse specific moral principles if they are to value anything at all. The most influential version of that argument has been offered by Christine Korsgaard, whose work I consider in chapter 5.

2. A second neo-Aristotelian objection amounts to the claim that Kantians offer an impoverished account of moral reasoning. Certainly, such philosophers extensively debate the validity of deontic statements of the form "you ought to φ" or "you ought not to φ," but such statements are too general to be action-guiding. Simply put, they do not allow moral agents to identify the best action they can perform in the case at hand. Doing so requires agents to identify all morally relevant facts in myriad situations they find themselves, and this itself implies that they have acquired the virtue of practical wisdom (*phronesis*).

Once again, there are several Kantian lines of response to this objection. For instance, some Kantians readily admit that principle-based moral reasoning has limits, but argue that Kant's philosophy can easily accommodate the idea that some agents are wise while others lack judgement. In Hannah Arendt's view, Kant's remarks on reflective judgement in the *Critique of the Power of Judgement* lay the foundations of a model of moral and political judgement which is fundamentally dissimilar from the one neo-Aristotelians have in mind when they criticize Kantians. By way of contrast, some Anglo-American Kantians reject the idea that a coherent model of moral judgement can be extracted from Kant's third *Critique*, but nevertheless attempt to accommodate the neo-Aristotelian claim that good judgement requires practical wisdom. I turn to such issues in chapter 7.

3. The third neo-Aristotelian objection I have discussed relates to the second one. Simply put, it amounts to the claim that Kantians neglect the virtues. As discussed in chapter 1, MacIntyre defends the Aristotelian view that *phronesis* can only function jointly with moral virtues such courage, justice and moderation. If this is so, then good moral judgements can only be achieved by fully virtuous moral agents, and a theory of moral judgement should always be accompanied by a philosophical account of the virtues (what they are, how they can be acquired, what precise role they play in moral reasoning, etc.).

In chapter 8, we will see that several contemporary Kantians have developed a Kantian account of moral education and the virtue in direct response to this objection. Drawing from Kant's later works—especially the *Metaphysics of Morals*—philosophers such as Onora O'Neill and Nancy Sherman have argued that good moral reasoning must rely on Kantian virtues such as apathy, sympathy, gratitude, solicitude, solidarity and tolerance.

PART II

Three Perspectives on the Foundations of Moral Judgement

Chapter 4

Habermassian Discourse Ethics and the Grounds of Moral Judgement

How did Kantians respond to the neo-Aristotelian objection according to which formulating universal moral principles—which could then serve as the basis of moral judgements—is an impossible task? This is what I have called the problem of *rational grounding*, and the next two chapters of this book are critical assessments of Kantian attempts to solve it. While carrying out my critical assessment of these attempts, one of my suggestions will be that neo-Aristotelianism is at the forefront of contemporary Kantians' philosophical reflection. To understand Kantians like Onora O'Neill, Christine Korsgaard and Jürgen Habermas, I contend, we need to envision their philosophical projects as attempts to *overcome neo-Aristotelianism*. Indeed, Kantians feel compelled to refute objections directed by neo-Aristotelians against their theory of moral judgement. In addition, they believe that alternative conceptions of moral judgement put forward by neo-Aristotelians is deeply flawed and typically criticize it in return.

In the first part of this chapter, I summarize MacIntyre and Bubner's proposed solutions to the problem of historical relativism discussed in the first part of this book. I then turn to contemporary Kantianism and consider Onora O'Neill's and Jürgen Habermas's criticisms of these solutions. As we will see, the main point of contention between these two pairs of thinkers amounts to knowing whether members of a historical philosophical tradition can critically assess their beliefs without envisioning the moral landscape from a universal standpoint. In the second part of the chapter, I introduce two paths borrowed by Kantians in their attempt to reach this universal standpoint: the dialogical path and the monological path. To do so, I retrace a methodological debate between two contemporary French Kantians whose work has yet to be appreciated by Anglo-American philosophers: Jean-Marc Ferry and Alain

Renaut. Lastly, in the third part of the chapter, I explore one of these two paths by examining Habermas's dialogical theory of moral judgement, which he names discourse ethics. Ultimately, I argue that discourse ethics faces an insurmountable dilemma. As a philosophical theory of moral judgement, discourse is either incapable of grounding universally valid moral principles *or* collapses into a monological theory of moral judgement such as the one defended by Christine Korsgaard, whose work I consider in chapter 5.

OVERCOMING NEO-ARISTOTELIANISM

The first part of this book left us with unfinished neo-Aristotelian business. There, I suggested that MacIntyre's philosophy leads us to contemplate the problem of historical relativism. In the Scottish philosopher's view, a moral agent can determine how she ought to act by reflecting upon goods which are internal to practices in which she engages. If I am a teacher, for instance, then I can understand how I *ought* to act *qua* teacher by thinking about what it means to *teach well*. This aligns with Descombes's Aristotelian remarks according to which, once I have become a teacher, it would be unwise for me to wonder *whether* I should attempt to teach well. Teaching well is simply what good teachers do. However, there exists a wide range of human practices in which moral agents can choose to engage, and teaching is but one of them. For this reason, moral agents not only face the task of determining *how* they can reach goals and standards of excellence which are internal to practices, but they must also decide in which practices they should engage in the first place. According to MacIntyre, a moral agent can do this by forging a *narrative conception* of herself. More precisely, she must conceive of her life as a story the main character of which is dedicated to the pursuit of human goods such as knowledge, friendship, love, health, play, and so on. By way of example, it will make sense for someone who is interested in the pursuit of knowledge and concerned by social inequalities to accept a job as a teacher at a school who serves underprivileged students.

Of course, forging a narrative conception of oneself is rarely a simple task. After all, there are many human goods that I can reasonably pursue throughout my life, but life is too short for me to pursue them all (to the same extent, at least). This raises the question of knowing which human good(s) I should prioritize over others. Here, MacIntyre's claim is that I can answer this question by envisioning my life story as part of a historical tradition which depicts certain human goods as being more valuable than others. Simply put, what practices I should engage in depends on the narrative conception I have forged for myself, but this narrative conception should itself be influenced by the *ranking of human goods* provided by the historical tradition of which

I am a member. Ultimately, each moral agent must realize that she is part of something greater than herself—a tradition which has the power to give structure and meaning to her individual existence—and how she ought to act is determined by the content of this tradition.

The philosophical problem that these considerations entail is not especially hard to see. Just as there are many practices in which I can engage and many narrative conceptions that I can forge for myself, there are many historical traditions of which I can become the member. What is more, each tradition contains a different ranking of human goods that will itself yield a different answer to the question of knowing which ones I should spend the most time, energy and effort pursuing. In other words, historical traditions compete which each other as each of them claim to contain the best understanding of what it means to live a good human life. Should I become a loving househusband and father, a devoted professor or a religious hermit? Should I devote my life to the pursuit of knowledge or to the pursuit of pleasure? This depends on the tradition to which I choose to belong, and distinct historical traditions contain incompatible answers to these questions. A fifth-century (BCE) Athenian citizen might have a very different view about this than a twenty-first-century Indian feminist, and we have yet to find a way which would allow us to arbitrate between their views should they come to conflict with one another. If there are only rival traditions but no universal standpoint to arbitrate between their competing claims, then it seems that the right answer to the question of knowing how we ought to live our life is *relative* to a particular tradition. In a nutshell, this is the problem of historical relativism.

MacIntyre indeed argues that there is no such thing as a universal moral standpoint which would allow us to determine which traditional ranking of human goods is best. Each tradition ranks human good in a different manner, but moral agents do not have access to a universal ranking of traditions. As he explains (1988, 166):

> When two rival large-scale intellectual traditions confront one another, a central feature of the problem of deciding between their claims is characteristically that there is no neutral way of characterizing either the subject matter about which they give rival accounts or the standards by which their claims are to be evaluated. Each standpoint has its own account of truth and knowledge, its own mode of characterizing the relevant subject matter. And the attempt to discover a neutral, independent set of standards or mode of characterizing data which is both such as must be acceptable to all rational persons and is sufficient to determine the truth on the matters about which the two traditions are at variance has, generally, and perhaps universally, proved to be a search for a chimera.

In the absence of a neutral way to critically assess competing claims, can conflicts of traditions be overcome? MacIntyre believes that they can. Throughout history, representatives of a historical tradition have often come to the realization that a rival tradition is superior to their own. This happens when scholars of a tradition begin raising questions that they are unable to answer without borrowing ideas from *another* tradition, which itself suggests that the traditional conception of human experience to which they previously adhered is incomplete. When a tradition is supplemented with ideas stemming from another, it enters a state of crisis which can be resolved in either of the two following manners. In some cases, the finding that a rival tradition is better equipped to answer philosophical questions leads scholars to embrace it and abandon their own tradition. Other times, representatives of a tradition which is currently undergoing a crisis successfully integrate ideas from a rival tradition without contradicting the fundamental tenets of their own. When this happens, they produce a *synthesis*.

According to MacIntyre, European intellectual history contains several syntheses of traditions. By way of example, Thomas of Aquinas produced a synthesis of Aristotelian philosophy and Christian theology which remains influential today. Like Aristotle, Aquinas believed that humans are rational beings who possess a natural end (*telos*), and this informed his ethical views about how they ought to behave. The Dominican friar also endorsed Aristotle's view on the unity of virtue according to which a moral agent cannot fully possess one virtue without possessing them all. Yet Aquinas's philosophy is not a mere restatement of Aristotle's own for the former also integrated the latter's ideas into a Christian framework. As a Christian, he portrayed the human will as fundamentally flawed and argued that no human being can become truly virtuous without the help of God. To illustrate this claim, MacIntyre (1988, 205) turns to the virtue of charity (*caritas*), which Aquinas depicts as a divine gift:

> Charity is the form of all virtue; without charity the virtues would lack the specific kind of directedness which they require. And charity is not to be acquired by moral education; it is a gift of grace, flowing from the work of Christ through the office of the Holy Spirit.

While Aristotle laid the foundations of the intellectual edifice erected by Aquinas, the latter still judged that the former had paid insufficient attention to grace, that is, to the idea that human beings must receive the help of a higher Being if they are to live exemplary moral lives.

By portraying Aquinas's philosophy as a successful synthesis between Aristotelian philosophy and Christian theology, MacIntyre aims to demonstrate that representatives of rival traditions are not doomed to talk past one another. While the search for the standpoint of universal morality amounts to a chimera, it remains possible for members of a tradition to evaluate their moral views by comparing them to those held by representatives of another tradition. If this is so, then philosophical reflection on the foundations of moral judgement need not lead to historical relativism. This is at least the case if, by using the expression "historical relativism," one refers to a philosophical position according to which (i) moral claims are only true relative to a particular historico-traditional standpoint and (ii) representatives of rival historical traditions are deprived of the means to rationally evaluate the content of these traditions in light of each other's views. All things considered, people are not prisoners of the historical context which gave rise to the tradition to which they adhere. If they show intellectual generosity and willingly engage in a rational dialogue with other traditions, then they might come to the realization that some of their moral views are false.

Do MacIntyre's considerations on dialogue between traditions truly represent a way out of the problem of historical relativism? I doubt that it does. First, nothing guarantees that the representatives of rival traditions will indeed engage in a productive dialogue with one another and willingly accept to examine their own moral beliefs by considering their adversaries' views. In certain cases, members of a tradition might simply not feel the need to search for new moral ideas which could enrich their worldview. As we will see below, however, that members of a tradition are confident in the ideas it contains does not entail that these ideas are true. Furthermore, even if members of a tradition do engage in a search for new moral ideas, they might be unable to produce a successful synthesis of a rival tradition and their own. As MacIntyre himself recognizes, the Aristotelian conception of moral judgement he defends cannot be reconciled with all of its rivals, and particularly not with the Humean view according to which practical rationality amounts to nothing more than instrumental reasoning. More specifically, Aristotelians typically argue that humans can use their rational capacities to determine which human ends contribute to happiness and ought to be pursued by all moral agents. By way of contrast, Humeans believe that reason is a slave to the passions and only allows us to determine what the most effective means to satisfy our subjective desires are. For this reason, MacIntyre (1988, 329) contends that "anyone who is an Aristotelian is thereby committed to denying Hume's central claims and vice versa." If an Aristotelian engages in dialogue with a Humean, both are likely to reject the fundamental premises on which their rivals base their arguments, and there will not be any rational way to decide which premises are the right ones. In other words, the problem of relativism will resurface.

A second reason to believe that MacIntyre's philosophy is still haunted by the spectre of historical relativism is that it ultimately requires us to have faith that, when they are successful, syntheses of traditions bring us closer to moral truth. Yet it remains unclear that such syntheses always lead to moral progress. Indeed, why not believe that some of them can lead us astray? For instance, what warrants the claim that Aquinas's philosophy is preferable to both Aristotelianism without Christianism and Christianism without Aristotelianism? Alternatively, might it not be possible that moral truths lie in a different historical tradition, one that has nothing to do with either Aristotelianism or Christianism? Certainly, Thomists will disagree, but this is not itself a sufficient reason to believe that their moral views are correct. After all, history contains many examples of traditions which were once embraced and defended by ardent believers, but that we now envision as morally deficient. By the standards of contemporary liberal democratic thinking, all traditions according to which human beings of different gender, race and sexual orientation are not entitled to the same political rights count as such. And while I see no reason at all not grant that all human beings deserve the same basic rights without exception, what makes us so sure that our views about the nature of a good human life will not be seen as deeply flawed by future generations? Looking back at the rise and fall of traditions throughout history, it seems that we have few reasons to believe that the moral views we now cherish will not eventually perish. This might not be a problem if we knew that the moral views which will eventually supersede our own are superior to ours, but this might not be the case. Nothing guarantees that the future will be one in which humanity progresses towards morality and justice. More fundamentally, however, it seems that MacIntyre's philosophy deprives us of the viewpoint we need to determine *what counts* as progress towards morality and justice. Certainly, we can hope that the clash of traditions throughout history will yield true moral views, but we do not have access to a criterion which would allow us to know which moral views are true. All we can do is judge historical traditions in light of contemporary moral standards in the very same way as the members of traditions we are now judging have judged those that came before them.

This might seem like a pessimistic view of the foundations of moral judgement. Yet in the contemporary philosophical landscape, this view is a point of departure, not an endpoint. In fact, I wish to suggest that the conceptualization of the problem of historical relativism led several Kantians to reject neo-Aristotelianism and attempt to overcome it. In other words, contemporary Kantianism should be envisioned as a philosophical project which aims to ground universal moral principles that would allow us to rationally arbitrate disputes between people who hold incompatible moral views. Consider for instance some claims made by Onora O'Neill, a leading contemporary Anglo-American Kantian philosopher. In her view, neo-Aristotelian philosophers fall into two broad families. First, there are Aristotelian *universalists*.

Like Kantians, these philosophers believe that we can rationally arbitrate moral disputes with recourse to objective moral standards. In chapter 6, I will discuss the views of Aristotelian universalists in greater detail.[1] For now, let me point out that these views significantly differ from that of neo-Aristotelians I have considered so far, who are O'Neill's true philosophical adversaries. As she explains, neo-Aristotelians like MacIntyre belong to the family of "Aristotelian *particularists*" who "hope to orient ethical reasoning without appeal to universal principles of inclusive scope" (O'Neill 1996, 13). More specifically, these philosophers "seek to anchor ethical claims by appeal to the actual practices or traditions or patterns of judgement of particular communities." Put differently, Aristotelian particularists consider that historically contingent agreements on the truth of a set of ethical standards amongst the members of a particular tradition or moral community are the true basis of moral judgement.

For her part, O'Neill argues that Aristotelian particularists do not have the conceptual means to rationally criticize moral communities who successfully perpetuate themselves through time, but whose collective life is nonetheless based on unjust norms. In her view, a community of agents whose moral life is regulated by traditional norms might indeed engage in atrocious activities and commit evil actions. After all, fascists too can appeal to the value of their tradition. In general, that a community successfully regulates its collective life by appealing to traditional ethical standards is not a sufficient reason to believe that its representatives behave morally. In O'Neill's view, these standards amount to nothing more than *unjustified assumptions* until we rationally demonstrate that they are compatible with universal moral principles. She writes:

> The most fundamental objection that contemporary theorists of justice make against contemporary accounts of the virtues mirrors the most fundamental criticism made against them. It is that, even if appeal to particular, established standards, practices and commitments or sensibilities could resolve (an adequate range of) ethical questions and conflicts, still no good reasons would have been given for thinking that the resolutions proposed are ethically authoritative, important or even adequate. (O'Neill 1996, 20–21)

As the reader can guess, this quote is an implicit but direct response to MacIntyre's arguments. As we have seen, it is he who suggests that a tradition can be envisioned as morally superior to another if the former allows its members to resolve a wider range of ethical questions and conflicts than the latter. According to O'Neill, however, this line of argumentation compares to what Kant (1996, 18) called a "private use of reason." In a Kantian perspective, using one's reason in a private way is tantamount to reasoning on the basis of ethical standards that are those of closed associations or private clubs instead of resorting to principles that the entire public can follow and no one can rationally reject. As Kant argues, those who make a private use of their own reason do not have the courage to rely on their own understanding, but allow tradition to eternally remain their self-appointed guardian. They engage in ethical reflection just like meticulous employees of dubious organizations carry out their work: others provide them with norms they are expected to blindly follow, and the thought that questioning these norms is part of their duty as moral agents never crosses their mind.[2]

This Kantian reaction to neo-Aristotelian defences of traditional moral thinking can also be found in contemporary German moral theory. To see this, consider Bubner's own discussion of the way members of a historical community can critically assess their ethical standards without appealing to universal moral principles. In his view, we can conceive of a two-step procedure which allows members of a given community to determine whether they live by good ethical standards. When this is the case, Bubner contends that this community amounts to a rational "form of life" (*Lebensform*). The first step of the procedure leads agents to wonder whether their community socializes its members effectively so that they develop a tendency to spontaneously obey social norms. Borrowing Bubner's own terminology, we can say that a community who successfully achieves this objective possesses social institutions which stabilize actions in need of regulation (Bubner 1984, 210). As we have seen, a foreseeable objection against this claim is that a community can effectively socialize its members and stabilize action, but still be regulated by fundamentally unjust norms. If this is so, then the criterion of effective socialization alone cannot serve as the basis of a properly moral assessment of collective life in this community. By way of example, one could argue that extremely repressive societies in which people obey dominant social norms out of fear stabilize action (to some extent, at least). Bubner foresees this objection, and this itself motivates him to add a second step to his proposed evaluative procedure of the rationality of forms of life. To count as a rational form of life, a community must (i) stabilize actions in need of regulation *and* (ii) ensure that its members do not envision social norms they are expected to follow as ones that frustrate their individual needs and aspirations. Instead, they must see these norms as ones that allow members of the community to flourish.

For his part, Habermas rejects the conclusion that all communities who meet Bubner's two criteria count as properly moral communities. At the very least, it seems that Bubner's procedure leaves many important questions unanswered. When he argues that the members of rational forms of life envision social norms as compatible with their needs and aspirations, for instance, does he mean that *all* people believe that such norms enable *everyone* (including themselves) to fulfill their desires? If this is so, then Bubner's criteria appear to be underinclusive. In all well-functioning human societies, there are at least *some* members who will consider that dominant social norms frustrate their desires. Expecting that all members will be perfectly reconciled with social norms seems unrealistic. Yet if we relax Bubner's criteria and argue that rational forms of life are those in which *most* people have a positive appreciation of dominant social norms, then these criteria will be overinclusive. For example, imagine a community in which a majority of people support the ethical standards on which collective life is based, but in which religious minorities are systematically oppressed. Surely, this society flouts the requirements of human morality, but Bubner's two-step procedure seems to entail that it does not or, at least, does not clearly support the conclusion that it does. In a nutshell, this is the philosophical objection that Habermas directs against Bubner's discourse on the rationality of forms of life. Interestingly, this objection is fundamentally similar to the one that O'Neill directs against MacIntyre. Ultimately, both O'Neill and MacIntyre incite us to consider the same philosophical problem: historically speaking, many human communities have treated a majority of their members quite well while tolerating injustice against religious, racial or sexual minorities. That most members of a community see it as based on adequate ethical standards does not warrant the claim that all of its members are treated with the respect they deserve. To critically assess communal life, we cannot simply rely on ethical standards that are authoritative *from the perspective of community members*. Instead, we need to resort on universally moral principles that members of a community *might* or *might not* actually endorse.

This philosophical objection incites Habermas (1984, 227) to argue that Bubner fails to escape the kind of ethical conservatism espoused by Ritter and other German neo-Aristotelians:

> Bubner [. . .] does not want to allow concrete morality to be affected by moral considerations that exceeds the horizon of a given lifeworld (*Lebenswelt*), nor does he want to sacrifice the claim to reason of a hermeneutically renewed traditionalism. This ambiguity disturbs his attempt to specify standards of rationality by which the *ethos* of forms of life can be judged: sometimes he characterizes the immanent rationality (of these forms of life) in a functionalist manner; other times he does so in a normative manner. Bubner develops a neo-Aristotelian conception of morality. This conception is neo-Aristotelian insofar as it only retains the suggestion [. . .] that what has happened in history is also what has been tried and tested.[3]

Here, Habermas's prose is complex and in need of commentary. Simply put, what the German social theorist argues is that, like MacIntyre, Bubner denies that there exists a neutral philosophical point of view from which universal moral principles could be defined, and then used to evaluate the lived ethical practices of particular communities (i.e., what he calls the "horizon of a given lifeword"). At the same time, Bubner attempts to avoid Ritter's philosophical conservatism. In other words, he hesitates between two philosophical positions. On the one hand, he is tempted to argue that there is a way to morally assess traditional norms which regulate collective life in particular communities. This is the task that Bubner's two-step procedure is meant to accomplish. On the other hand, he maintains that any community which stabilizes action and convinces its members that its internal ethical standards are correct count as rational. This forces him to accept that traditional standards can be morally valid *independently of their content*. As long as members of a community *see them as valid*, then this community will remain stable through time, and this itself suggests that its internal ethical standards are true.

If neo-Aristotelianism does not safeguard against the possibility of injustice, can we truly formulate universal moral principles that would? Certainly, Habermas believes that this is the case, but I have yet to examine Kantian attempts to conceptualize the neutral standpoint the existence of which neo-Aristotelians are so committed to deny. This is precisely what I will do in the remainder of this chapter as well as in the next one. As we will see, contemporary Kantians disagree amongst themselves with regard to the philosophical methodology they must use to conceive of universal moral norms. While some believe that we should ground moral judgement in a theory of communicative practice, others argue that we can derive these norms from *a priori* thought experiments.

MONOLOGICAL AND DIALOGICAL APPROACHES TO THE FOUNDATIONS OF MORAL JUDGEMENT

Let us agree with O'Neill and Habermas that neo-Aristotelians like MacIntyre and Bubner deprive themselves of the means to criticize the norms of historical communities from a properly moral point of view. Let us also grant that the best way to do so would be to formulate universal moral principles that could be used to evaluate these norms. For instance, if we can demonstrate that "all humans should be granted the same political rights," this will allow us to establish that all communities who do not grant humans equal rights are morally deficient. Without a doubt, the challenge for Kantians is to explain *how*, precisely, this philosophical task can be achieved.

When thinking about morality, a good way to begin is to reflect upon our individual desires and consider how the pursuit of these desires will affect the well-being of others. For example, it is quite uncontroversial to claim that most human beings long for safety, and it is also obvious that people will need to refrain from acting in ways that pose a serious risk to the safety of others if we are to create a society in which all people are safe. Certainly, some risky actions will be prohibited by the government and backed up with the threat of punishment, but we also expect people to abide by moral rules that are not enforced by the state. At the time of writing, the state of California does not require me to wear a protective mask at the store to minimize the likelihood that I will infect others with COVID-19. Judging by the reactions of fellow shoppers in San Francisco's Sunset District (where I live), most people believe that I should still do so. After all, covering my face with a mask is a very uncomplicated thing to do, and if doing so can save even just one human life, I believe I have the moral obligation to do so. Of course, some people disagree with me on this issue. In their view, pressuring others into wearing a mask is liberticidal, and one moral rule they think we should live by is "let people live without masks and, if you do not like it, stay home." When these people are confronted with the negative reaction of masked shoppers—a frown or a snarky comment, perhaps—they defiantly ignore them (or worse). In this debate, I strongly believe that the masked are right and the unmasked are wrong, but my intention here is not to explain why this is so. Instead, I want to raise the following question: when we face moral disagreements, how can we establish that some are right and others are wrong? Given that people disagree about the moral rules that everyone ought to follow, what method allows us to define our moral obligations towards others?

Contemporary Kantian philosophers are divided on this issue. Proponents of a monological approach to moral theory believe that philosophers can identify universal moral principles through solitary reflection. They might not be *likely* to do so, but this remains a possibility. For instance, John Rawls (1999a) has famously argued that a thought experiment which he named the original position enables us to formulate two principles of justice which should regulate communal life. As we will see in the next chapter, Christine Korsgaard also contends that *a priori* moral reflection allows us to conceive of moral obligations that all rational beings ought to fulfill. Arguably, this is the philosophical methodology that most resembles that used by Kant himself. Rawls's and Korsgaard's reflections are based on the key methodological belief that the *content* of at least some universal moral principles can be defined through individual philosophical reflection.

Often, this philosophical reflection involves imagined subjects. Remember for instance that Rawls's original position features hypothetical reasoners who select principles of justice while being deprived of knowledge which relates to their personal characteristics and socio-historical circumstances. Yet there is an important difference between reflecting upon what hypothetical subjects would say and discussing with real people. In Habermas's view, this difference is one that matters. In fact, Habermas belongs to a second group of Kantians who are deeply sceptical that universal moral principles can be defined through philosophical reflection alone. According to proponents of a dialogical approach to moral theory, indeed, only real discussions allow us to pinpoint moral principles that are binding for all.[4] This is because moral principles are never binding unless all people affected by them are provided with the opportunity to object to them in the context of a discussion through which their authority is established. As the reader can imagine, these discussions rarely happen in philosophers' offices.

Consider Habermas's criticism of the original position. As James Gordon Finlayson (2019, 148) rightly points out, Habermas argues that hypothetical individuals placed behind a "veil of ignorance" will never be able to grasp the interests "of the actual citizens whom they model, and on whose behalf they choose." This problem is not tied to Rawls's specific thought experiment. Instead, Habermas's point is that *no philosophical thought experiment* can allow us to identify the interests of real people. To know what these interests are, one must engage in dialogue with them, and philosophers who refrain from doing so simply cannot know what these interests are. If this is so, then there is also no guarantee that the moral principles selected by hypothetical subjects in thought experiments are compatible with real people's interests, and these principles therefore have no moral authority. This would not be the case if the moral principles in question had been debated by all people affected by their implementation in the public sphere. When moral principles are endorsed by all affected people in the context of a real discussion, then they truly are valid. Until this discussion takes place, however, the only conclusion that philosophical reflection can hope to establish is that one or many philosophers *believe* they are valid, not that they actually are.

As we will see in the next section, Habermas contends that one central role for philosophers is to determine what conditions real discussions must meet if they are to allow participants to ground moral principles. Before I turn to this issue, let me point out that Habermas's criticism of monological approaches to the foundations of moral judgement was fiercely debated amongst contemporary French Kantians. For example, Alain Renaut objects to Habermas's dialogical approach to moral theory by arguing that Rawls's original position and real discussions are two different means to fulfill the very same end. To see this, consider what moral agents can reasonably expect will happen when they engage in real discussion with others to establish rules that will regulate communal life. Surely, no reasonable discussant can expect that *only rules which personally benefit them* will be adopted by their interlocutors. To be a fair discussant, one must understand that people have different interests which sometimes conflict with one another, and the rules on which all can agree will necessarily be the object of a compromise. Differently put, discussants must be ready to agree on a set of rules which benefits all people even if a different set of rules would personally benefit them more. In Renaut's view, this is precisely what happens in Rawls's original position. As Rawlsian subjects are behind the veil of ignorance, they cannot do otherwise than identify principles which promote the common good. If they choose principles which only advantage a subset of people, then they risk discovering that they do not belong to this subset once the veil of ignorance is lifted. Because of this structural similarity between the reasoning of real discussants and that of Rawlsian subjects, Renaut (1993a, 134) contends that:

> Correctly understood, the veil of ignorance is nothing but a symbolic representation of what argumentative discussion allows, namely the elevation of each person from differentiated individuality to the universality of the practical subject.

In other words, both the original position and Habermassian real discussions allow us to trade the standpoint of personal interest for the standpoint of universality. To see this, consider the following example. In real life, the financially well-to-do do not have a strong incentive to advocate for redistributive principles that would help people with a low income gain access to basic goods and services such as healthcare and education. Of course, some of them will do so on altruistic grounds, but others will oppose a massive redistribution of wealth which does not personally benefit them. Yet, behind the veil of ignorance, the rich do not know that they are rich. As a result, they have a strong incentive to identify redistributive principles that would leave everyone in a decent financial situation. In fact, doing so guarantees that, once the veil of ignorance is lifted, they will be able to meet their basic needs regardless of their income level. Now, what Renaut suggests is that real public discussions between people with unequal income who *must* agree on redistributive principles would lead them to the same conclusion. Certainly, people with a low income are likely to advocate for more redistribution than the rich, but everyone will have to consider the interests of the opposite group if they truly hope to reach an agreement. In Renaut's view (1993a, 134), Rawls and Habermas incentivize moral agents to reflect upon the common good in two different but equivalent ways: while the second requires them to engage in real discussion with others, the first uses a thought experiment which involves the "methodical abstraction of what differentiates us from others" (Renaut 1993a, 134).

In response to Renaut, Jean-Marc Ferry—a French disciple of Habermas—argues that the conclusion according to which real discussants would reach the same conclusion as Rawlsian hypothetical subjects remains highly speculative. Indeed, Ferry reminds us that philosophers overstep the boundaries of reasonable reflection when they pretend to know what real discussants would actually agree on. Without observing public discussions, there is simply no way for them to know this. Certainly, the original position incites us to ask ourselves, "What kind of redistributive principle would I want implemented if I were in a financially dire situation?" Yet Ferry argues that such hypothetical reflection is in no way equivalent to listening to the real testimony of people who struggle to make ends meet. In the original position, people only need to "produce an account of what they would experience if they found themselves in conditions which they imagine could be theirs" (Ferry 1994b, 70–71). Yet this imagined experience might not correspond to the lived experience of people who are in these conditions. In Ferry's own words (1994b, 70), each person "needs the account of others in order to know how they experience a condition which is merely imagined [. . .] in the original position." Ultimately, gaps between imagined and lived experiences open the possibility that philosophers who engage in hypothetical reflection will formulate moral principles that people with a low income actually reject. If this is so, then Renaut is wrong to claim that thought experiments and real discussions are two different ways of achieving the same results.

I find it hard not to side with Ferry in this debate. If one wants to know what moral principles people who find themselves in *such* or *such* conditions endorse, then the most straightforward way to do so is quite simply to ask them, not to try to put oneself in their shoes with recourse to an abstract thought experiment. Here, it seems to me that Habermassians have a point, and this might be bad news for Rawlsians. To sum up, proponents of a monological approach to moral theory use thought experiments to formulate universally valid moral principles that we could use to evaluate social norms which are currently in force. Yet Habermassians contend that they ultimately fail to do so. In the end, the conclusion that a person x placed in a situation y would endorse principle(s) z amounts to a conjecture.[5] At first sight, this objection brings grist to the mill of neo-Aristotelians who contend that there is no such thing as an impartial standpoint from which universally valid moral rules could be grounded. However, we have already seen that Habermas is also extremely critical of neo-Aristotelianism. This raises the two following questions. First, if Habermas believes that philosophers cannot identify universally valid moral rules through abstract reflection, in what sense does his philosophical project count as a universalist attempt to ground moral judgement? Second, in what sense can discourse ethics be envisioned as an attempt to overcome neo-Aristotelianism? Let us now address these two questions.

THE EMANCIPATORY POTENTIAL OF DISCOURSE ETHICS: A CRITICAL ASSESSMENT

We have seen that Habermas assign strict limits to philosophical reflection. According to his perspective, no philosopher has the required knowledge to formulate moral principles which adequately reflect the true interests of all people who would be affected by the consequences of their general observance. Yet a core claim of discourse ethics is that all affected parties must freely accept these consequences in the context of a real discussion for these principles to be universally valid. This is why the foundational principle of discourse ethics is the principle of universalization—or principle (U)—which stipulates that "*all* affected can accept the consequences and the side effects its *general* observance can be anticipated to have for the satisfaction of *everyone's* interests (and these consequences are preferred to those of known alternative possibilities for regulation)" (Habermas 1990, 65). Here, note that (U) is not itself a *moral* principle in the sense that it does not tell moral agents how they ought to behave. In other words, (U) is not a principle which contains *recommendations for action* ("do not lie," "act as the courageous person would act," etc.). In fact, (U) merely indicates how moral agents must proceed if they want to ground moral principles which themselves contain recommendations for action. Yet it does not say anything about what the content of these principles should be. For this reason, we can envision (U) is a *meta-principle* which defines the conditions that must be met if moral agents are to ground valid moral principles.

As we have seen, Habermas also contends that no one can tell if people who would be affected by the consequences of the general observance of a moral principle of action would actually endorse it *without these people being provided with the opportunity to share their views in a real discussion*. As a result, principle (U) naturally leads us to the principle of discourse ethics—or principle (D)—according to which "only those norms can claim to be valid that meet (or could meet) with the approval of all affected in their capacity as participants in a practical discourse" (Habermas 1990, 66). Like (U), (D) is also a meta-principle which does not say anything about the content of moral principles that ought to be followed by all. According to discourse ethicists, moral agents must decide this amongst themselves. Instead, the function of (D) is to define the *procedure* which moral agents must follow to ground valid moral principles. In a nutshell, this procedure amounts to a public debate.

Now, if Habermas argues that moral agents must decide for themselves what moral principles should regulate communal life in the context of a real discussion, how can he be so sure that (U) and (D) are valid meta-principles? Must it not be the case that discussants also endorse such meta-principles for them to count as valid? In short, Habermas's answer to this last question is the following: yes, but we already know that they do. More precisely, we can determine whether participants in public debates endorse (U) and (D) by observing their communicative practices. Imagine that in a small town, a board of supervisors organize a public forum to decide whether the driving speed limit in residential neighbourhoods should be lowered to 15 mph. All town residents are invited to attend the forum and share their views about this proposed measure. Of course, both residents and organizers of the forum will be expected to follow some rules of discussion to ensure that the forum runs smoothly. In fact, if some of these rules are flouted, then the outcome of the forum will not count as an agreement. By way of example, if members of the local Association of Motorcyclists against Speed Limits get to speak their minds but concerned parents of young children are systematically denied the right to do so, it will not make any sense to claim that residents have collectively agreed not to lower the speed limit in residential neighbourhoods. When a group of people who would be affected by the consequences of the implementation of a new town rule are denied the right to speak, then they have not truly endorsed these consequences in their capacity as participants in a practical discourse. If that is the case, then the new town rule is not valid.

This example is meant to illustrate that, in Habermas's view, principle (U) and (D) are *presuppositions* of argumentative discussions which aim at agreement. More precisely, Habermas believes that all sincere and fair participants in a practical discussion implicitly recognize these presuppositions as valid. This is because respecting (U) and (D) is part of the very meaning we give to "agreeing." When I get to share my views but you do not, there is no possible sense in which we can say that we have agreed on something. Importantly, Habermas considers that his main philosophical role as discourse ethicist amounts to analyzing communicative practices and reconstructing its normative presuppositions, that is, identifying rules of discussion that all reasonable discussants already *know* they must follow if the outcome of a discussion is to count as an agreement. Reconstructing these presuppositions and formalizing them into meta-principles help us understand what people must and must not do in discussions which aim at grounding moral rules. In a nutshell, what they must do is recognize that all participants in a discussion are capable of exchanging reasons with one another and, most importantly, deserve to be provided with an equal opportunity to do so. When people are denied an equal opportunity to argue, then no agreement is possible, and the outcome of the discussion must be rejected as invalid.

These considerations also allow us to understand how Habermas's approach to morality differs from that of neo-Aristotelians. While the latter value social customs and traditions, Habermas more radically argues that customs and traditions do not count as valid moral rules unless we can show that all people who are affected by their general observance have endorsed them in the context of a public discussion. If they have not, then Habermas agrees with O'Neill (1996, 20–21) that "still no good reasons would have been given for thinking that the resolutions proposed are ethically authoritative." In other words, people do not have the moral obligation to respect them. In fact, they should use (U) and (D) to critically assess the moral value of traditional norms, which is precisely what discourse ethicists ultimately believe neo-Aristotelians are unable to do. Even more importantly, by analyzing communicative practices and reconstructing its normative presuppositions, Habermas takes himself to have reached the universal point of view the existence of which neo-Aristotelians typically deny. According to him, (U) and (D) truly are universal principles to the extent that people cannot agree with one another without respecting them. Whenever people attempt to agree on moral rules, they will have to comply with these principles.

In my view, a central strength of Habermassian discourse ethics amounts to its emancipatory potential. If we look back at history, then we will see that many unjust norms became socially dominant in contexts where those who were negatively affected by them were not asked whether they endorsed them. In fact, power relations were such that people who benefited from unjust norms could effectively prevent them from having any say about whether they should be implemented. If people of colour had been part of public discussions about slavery in the United States, this exploitative regime would arguably have ended much sooner than on December 18, 1865. Similarly, if British women had been asked to share their views on universal suffrage, they would probably not have had to wait until 1928 to be granted this right. In other words, Habermas's philosophy helps us see that the justification of unjust social norms and practices typically functions through the exclusion of those who are most concerned by them. It also provides us with a powerful antidote against justifications which do not involve agreement between all affected parties.

Today, discourse ethics can also serve as a blueprint for the radical democratization of social institutions. Let us take higher education as an example. In recent years, universities have begun paying attention to the fact that traditional educational practices have put people of colour and women at a disadvantage compared with white male students. For instance, psychologists have recently found that professors respond to emails from students with white- and male-sounding names at a higher rate than to emails from students with female-, Black-, Hispanic-, Indian- or Chinese-sounding names (Milkman, Akinola and Chugh 2015). As most university professors have traditionally been men, it is now widely known that female students have often been exposed to forms of sexual misconduct that were (and still are) tolerated or excused. One popular response to the problems of implicit bias and sexual misconduct has been to appoint women and people of colour in positions of leadership. This certainly makes sense from a Habermassian point of view: by appointing people who belong to groups of people who are most affected by unjust rules and practices, universities are empowering them to participate in discussions that might yield better ones. To minimize bias, for example, universities could ask all professors to grade students' assignments anonymously. To prevent sexual misconduct, they can also forbid professors to be romantically involved with their students. Regardless of the value of these specific measures, the point here is that all people who would be affected by their general observance should be part of discussions about their possible implementation. The expression "all people" also reminds us that social institutions must do more than appoint women and people of colour to leadership positions to ground valid rules. In order for a rule to be valid, it must also be approved by affected parties who currently hold little power within a particular institution. In educational contexts, this means that students too should be provided with the opportunity to participate in decision-making processes regarding pedagogical practices that affect them. Whether all grading should be blind or professors allowed to be romantically involved with their students are not decisions that solely belong the professors and administrators, but to students too.

While discourse ethics can contribute to the social emancipation of oppressed groups, it also has philosophical shortcomings. A first objection against it amounts to the claim that principles (U) of (D) are not truly universal rules of discussions that all participants in public debates *must* recognize as valid. As Jean-Marc Ferry (1994a, 55) points out, Habermas's philosophical approach is reconstructive and phenomenological. As mentioned, the German philosopher takes himself to have analyzed concrete discursive practices and identified implicit rules of discussion that all discussants cannot avoid following if the outcome of their exchange is to count as an agreement. Like all of us, however, Habermas is a moral agent born at a particular time and place in history. As result, he does not have the capacity to observe all discursive practices that have existed in the past and will exist in the future. This itself suggests that he cannot know whether all discussants have always understood and will always understand discussions which aim at agreement in the same way. Throughout history, the communicative practice which amounts to agreeing with others might have looked very different than in contemporary Western liberal democracies and discussants might have followed different rules of discussion. If this is so, then why consider that (U) and (D) are universal and timeless presuppositions of argumentation? There does not seem to be a way to know this with certainty.

A second objection worth considering is that Habermas's philosophy provides us with little resources against people who act immorally and are not interested in attempting to justify their behaviour through argumentation and discourse. To see this, consider the following hypothetical scenario. Deja, a gifted undergraduate student, believes that moral norms of her community are not *valid* in any meaningful sense of the term as they are historically relative. During a meeting of her introductory course on ethics, Deja engages in a debate about the foundations of moral judgement with her professor Mathis, who is a convinced discourse ethicist. As Deja points out, moral norms which were once socially dominant now contradict those by which we live nowadays, and it is also likely that future moral norms will be incompatible with those of the present. What is more, there is no rational way to determine which moral principles amongst a set of incompatible ones are valid. To contradict Deja, Mathis responds the following:

> Deja, the very fact that you are engaged in a discussion which aims at agreement with me implies that you recognize the validity of certain rules. These are *rules of discussion* that you *must* respect if we are to recognize the outcome of our discussion as authoritative. For instance, if I did not allow you to present arguments against the claims I make, then these claims would not be tested through the force of the better argument, and this would itself give us reason to doubt that they are valid. The same goes for moral rules. Their truth value must be tested through the force of the better argument. We might not agree about their content, but at least we know that this content can be shown to be valid or invalid if certain rules of discussion are followed. These rules of discussion are universal insofar as all discussants must follow them if they hope to show that what they are saying is true.

What can Deja say in response to Mathis? First, even if we grant that all discussants are bound by universal rules of discussion, it seems that people who reject the value of argumentation have no reason to follow them. Notice indeed that Mathis's argument takes the form a hypothetical claim: *if* Deja sincerely engages in discussion with him, *then* she must recognize certain rules of discussion as binding. What is more, if she accepts these rules of discussion, she must also endorse the outcomes of discussions in which participants respected them. Yet if Deja chooses not to engage in discussion, discourse ethicists will not be able to demonstrate that *any* rule is binding for her. Neither rules of discussion nor moral rules that are the outcomes of well-regulated discussions will apply to her. Put differently, the discourse ethicist's main argumentative strategy only works with people who choose to argue in the first place. The claim, "If you engage in practice x, you must recognize the validity of rule y!" is of no use against people who choose not to engage in practice x.[6]

The third and last objection against discourse ethics I wish to consider is a simple one. In my view, it is also the most important. For the sake of our reflection, let us grant Habermas that, as soon as moral agents engage in a discussion which aims at agreement, they must recognize the validity of rules of discussions. Let us also concede that, as Habermas contends, (U) and (D) are adequate reconstructions of these rules of discussion and that these principles bind all discussants *qua* discussants. Now, (D) stipulates that the only way to verify whether a moral principle is valid is to allow all people who would be affected by the consequences of its general observance to share their views in the context of a real discussion. Yet it seems that no real discussion will ever fulfill this requirement. Practically speaking, it does not seem possible to hold a discussion which would include all parties that are affected by the observance of a set of moral rules. This is because *all* humans risk being affected by the moral rules followed by others *in some way*. As a result, it seems that only a real discussion in which all moral agents agree on the same rules would allow us to conclude that these rules are universally valid. Of course, no such discussion has ever taken place and we can hardly imagine a future in which it will. Even if such a discussion did take place, it is also highly unlikely that all parties would unanimously agree that a given set of moral rules should be accepted or rejected. As we know, humans tend to disagree about moral matters.[7]

Note that the objection I have just sketched is epistemic in nature. Without a doubt, Habermas's philosophical project can incite institutional leaders to create inclusive spaces of discussion in which people affected by particular rules and practices are given the opportunity to assess them. This is what the example of higher education included above is meant to illustrate. Yet discourse ethics does not tell us much about the general moral rules by which moral agents should abide in their daily lives. This is because the content of these rules can only be established through a practical discussion involving all affected parties, but such a discussion is unlikely to ever take place. As a result, we cannot *know* what the content of valid moral rules is. "How should I act?" you ask. "I can't tell you," the discourse ethicist responds, for their role is simply to indicate what kind of discussion would allow you to find the answer to your question. In a sense, this counts as a solution to the problem of rational grounding: if discourse ethicists are correct, we might not know the content of moral rules we ought to follow, but we do know how to proceed in order to find out what it is. At the same time, this solution is disappointing. As moral agents, what we primarily want to know is how we ought to behave as opposed to how we could possibly (but are not likely to) find out.

That said, there is a way for Habermas to avoid my objection according to which discourse ethics is philosophically disappointing as it does not allow us to understand what the content of universally valid moral principles is. Remember that principle (D) stipulates that those norms can claim to be valid that meet *or could meet* with the approval of all affected in their capacity as participants in a practical discourse. If we emphasize "*could* meet," then perhaps we can interpret (D) as meaning that a real discussion including all affected parties is *not* required to assess the validity of moral rules. Instead, philosophers could use sophisticated arguments to demonstrate that a particular moral principle *could meet* with the approval of all affected parties if such a discussion ever took place. For instance, one could argue that all human beings deeply care about bodily integrity and that we have few reasons to believe that some would reject the view according to which the right to bodily integrity is a basic moral right. However, if discourse ethicists engage in this kind of hypothetical philosophical reasoning, their philosophical methodology is essentially the same as that of so-called monological Kantians like Rawls who resort to thought experiments to ground moral principles. Indeed, Rawls's project in *A Theory of Justice* is precisely to argue that, under certain conditions, all people *could agree* on principles of justice. Of course, discourse ethicists will probably be reluctant to reason in this monological manner as they would then be vulnerable to their own objection according to which we cannot know for sure that moral principles chosen by imagined subjects would be endorsed by real discussants.

In other words, discourse ethicists ultimately face the following dilemma. They can either claim that only real discussions between all affected parties have the power to ground universally moral principles *or* they can argue that, in the absence of such discussions, philosophers can use philosophical reflection to demonstrate that some moral principles *could meet* the approval of all affected parties. If they accept the first claim, then they will have to admit that moral agents cannot know what principles they must follow as discussions involving all affected parties never happen in the real world. If they accept the second claim, however, then their critique of monological Kantianism will fall apart. As a result, we will not have any reason to prefer discourse ethics to "constructivist" Kantian theories according to which the validity of moral principles can be demonstrated *via* thought experiments. In fact, there is one influential constructivist attempt to solve the problem of rational grounding that I have yet to examine: that put forward by American Kantian philosopher Christine Korsgaard.

Chapter 5

Kantian Constructivism and the Normativity of Practical Identities

In the last chapter, we have seen that Habermas criticizes Kantians for engaging in what he calls monological (as opposed to dialogical) moral theory, that is, for attempting to ground moral principles through armchair philosophical reflection. Considering discourse ethics' own shortcomings, the central aim of the present chapter is to critically assess one of the most influential monological reflections on the foundations of moral judgement in contemporary moral theory: that put forward by American philosopher Christine Korsgaard. Although discourse ethics has had a lasting impact on contemporary German thought, indeed, many Anglo-American Kantians who call themselves "constructivists" remain convinced—*pace* Habemas—that universally valid moral principles can be constructed through philosophical reflection alone.

More precisely, my objective in this chapter will be twofold. First, I want to evaluate the prospects of Korsgaard's defence of Kant's categorical imperative. Second, I wish to demonstrate that, like that of Habermas, her philosophical project can be understood as an attempt to overcome neo-Aristotelianism. In the first part of this book, I have suggested that neo-Aristotelians often conceive of our social identities as a source of reasons for action which create binding obligations. In their view, our identities are *practical*. Not only do they define who we are, but they also determine what we ought to do. As father, professor, nurse, union member or best friend, I have moral reasons to perform certain actions and avoid performing others. I also have duties from which individuals who do not bear these identities are exempt. Call this the "normativity of practical identities" thesis.[1]

Now, I will argue that Kantian constructivists like Korsgaard share this neo-Aristotelian insight, but develop it further by arguing that our practical identities are not normative on their own. If such identities have the power to create reasons for action and binding obligations, Kantian constructivists argue, they must be morally valuable, but such value can only be derived from the value of a more fundamental identity, which is the ultimate source of moral obligation: our identity as rational human agents. In their view, the value of practical identities derives from the value of rational human agency: it is only *qua* rational human agents that we can confer value and normative power to our more specific practical identities.

If such an interpretation is plausible, Kantian constructivists face the task of explaining why our practical identities cannot be valuable and normative on their own, that is, why they must acquire their value and normative power to create binding obligations from elsewhere. They must also account for the fact that rational human agency is itself valuable and normative. In contemporary philosophy, one influential way to do so has been to argue that valuing rational human agency is a precondition of valuing anything else, including our specific practical identities. When I try to assess the value of my practical identities, it would simply be *impossible* for me to avoid relying on my identity *qua* rational human agent. Let us say I am trying to determine if my professional duties as a soldier are morally binding. To decide this, I must first determine if my identity *qua* soldier is morally valuable. The Kantian constructivist will then argue that I can only assess the moral value if my identity *qua* soldier from the standpoint of humanity: I know that I am a soldier, but do I have any reasons to be a soldier *qua* rational human agent? If I believe that this is the case, then I will be able to take my duties as a soldier seriously: I have reasons to be a soldier, and this allows me to take the reasons and obligations that spring from this identity seriously. Interestingly, the fact that I rely on my identity *qua* rational human agent to assess the nature of my duties as a soldier seems to entail that I attribute at least some moral value to my humanity. After all, why would I rely on my rational human agency to assess the value of being a soldier if I did not consider the fact that I am a rational human agent to have any kind of moral significance?

This argument need not be entirely convincing at this point. In what follows, I will argue that it ultimately fails, but I must reconstruct it step by step before drawing such a conclusion. For the moment, we must only note that such an argument lies at the basis of the most important philosophical claim defended by Korsgaard in *The Sources of Normativity* and her more recent works: "If you value anything at all, or, if you acknowledge the existence of any practical reasons, then you must value your humanity as an end in itself." The argument that supports this claim is a transcendental argument: it starts from the assertion that "I value some things" and establishes the necessary conditions of this assertion being true. If it is true that I value some things, Korsgaard argues, then I *must* value my humanity as an end in itself.

My reflection proceeds as follows. In the first section, I briefly reiterate the normativity of practical identities thesis by referring to Descombes's thought. By reconstructing Korsgaard's central argument pertaining to the foundations of moral judgement, I then demonstrate that this thesis is at the heart of contemporary Kantian constructivism (in the second and third sections). In the fourth section, I formulate objections against Korsgaard's argument and argue that, even if we accept it, this argument does not confer on human agency the moral importance she believes it does. Lastly, in the fifth section, my criticism of Korsgaard's constructivism leads me to a novel discussion of contemporary French philosophy. There, I compare Korsgaard's view on the foundations of moral judgement to the one defended by Alain Renaut, whose own Kantianism was deeply influenced by existentialist philosopher Jean-Paul Sartre.

A PROBLEM FOR THE TELEOLOGICAL ACCOUNT OF THE NORMATIVITY OF PRACTICAL IDENTITIES

In chapter 3, I offered a detailed discussion of Vincent Descombes's response to a famous thought experiment designed by Elizabeth Anscombe in which she defies us to prove that a "rational Nazi" behaves in an irrational manner.[2] In Descombes's view, this can be done through the demonstration that the Nazi is not *solely* a Nazi. Like most human beings, his identity is multifold. For instance, we can suppose that Anscombe's Nazi is enmeshed in social relationships. Not only is he a member of the NSDAP, but he might also be a romantic partner, a friend to others, a brother, etc. As we have seen, Descombes also imagines that this Nazi is the rector of a university. Now, a key point in Descombes's argumentation amounts to the claim that the many dimensions of the Nazi's identity entail conflicting obligations. While it might be true that it *befits* a Nazi to seek the glory of the NSDAP, it also befits a rector to promote truth-seeking through academic research, a romantic partner to be kind and loving, a friend to be empathetic and loyal, and so on. Using neo-Aristotelian terminology, we can say that certain ends teleologically belong to our practical identities. A rector does not have to *decide* that he will promote truth-seeking through academic research; this is simply what rectors ought to do *qua* rectors. If Anscombe's Nazi disregards all his obligations *except* his obligations as Nazi, however, he will unavoidably come to neglect the ends that belong to other dimensions of his identity. Even worse, he might come to believe that seeking the victory of the NSDAP is the end which teleologically belongs to *all* dimensions of his practical identity. In Descombes's view, this would be a mistake. If the Nazi reasons in this way, he will have become a monomaniacal reasoner who unduly assigns one single end to all his practical identities, but this amounts to a form of practical irrationality. This will allow us to say that the Nazi acts irrationally, and Anscombe's challenge will have been met.

Is Descombes's response to Anscombe convincing? My suggestion is that his neo-Aristotelian teleological understanding of practical identities faces an important problem. One implicit premise in Descombes's reasoning is that the Nazi rector is irrational because he is *unaware* that his duty *qua* rector is not to promote the political objectives of the NSDAP, but to encourage the pursuit of knowledge. Yet we can easily imagine a Nazi who understands very well that he is failing at being a good rector by pursuing purely ideological ends, but does not care much about this failure. This Nazi rector would make the *conscious* decision to give priority to his practical identity *qua* Nazi over his practical identity *qua* rector. "Good Nazis are bad rectors," he thinks, "but being a good rector is not as important as being a good Nazi." Could we demonstrate that such a reasoning is also irrational? Ultimately, Descombes does not provide us with reasons to believe that we can. Even if we admit that (i) practical identities are a source of reasons for action and (ii) it is irrational to assign one end to all our practical identities, this itself does not entail that we cannot rationally prioritize one dimension of our identity over all others. However, to believe that we can, we need to understand what reasons we have to value some of our practical identities over others as well as where these reasons come from.

In the following two sections, I will argue that Kantian constructivism should be understood as a philosophical attempt to provide a satisfying answer to these questions. If practical identities are a source of reasons for action and create binding obligations, we must understand how they acquired this normative power as well as which identities it is morally appropriate for individuals to bear. As I suggested earlier, Korsgaard argues that the normativity of practical identities ultimately derives from the value of humanity. Let us then examine the argument that supports this conclusion, beginning with the Kantian theory of action on which it rests.

ACTING ACCORDING TO ONE'S OWN LAW

The first step of Korsgaard's argument regarding the value of humanity is a defence of the Kantian claim that free actions can only be performed by an agent who acts according to her own law. In her view, an individual lacking the power to act according to a law she gave to herself would necessarily lack free will. To see this, imagine an individual who is solely moved by her strongest current desires. Such an individual is also deeply unreflective: she consistently follows the beckoning of desire without ever noticing that she does. Korsgaard argues that this individual would not count as an agent capable of free will. She would rather resemble an *automaton* who can respond to *stimuli*, but who lacks the cognitive apparatus and decisional power required to be free. Note, however, that this conclusion would not be true if our individual *reflectively* chose to only act on her strongest current desires, as she would then act according to a law she gave to herself. In this case, this law would be the following: "Act only to fulfill your strongest current desires."[3] Korsgaard's claims relate to Kant's considerations on free will in the *Critique of Pure Reason*, where he explains that the human will is an *arbitrium liberum*, not *brutum*, "because sensibility does not render its action necessary" (Kant 1998, 533). In the human being, "there is a faculty of determining oneself from oneself, independently of necessitation by sensible impulses," and the presence of this faculty in ourselves makes us free agents. More specifically, Korsgaard is committed to the Kantian view that free will necessarily presupposes reflectivity. To be free, agents *must* be able to stand back from their desires and choose whether they represent appropriate motives on which to act:

> When you deliberate, when you determine your own causality, it is as if there is something over and above all of your incentives, something which is you, and which chooses which incentive to act on. This means that when you determine yourself to be the cause of the movements which constitute your action, you must identify yourself with the principle of choice on which you act. (Korsgaard 2009, 72)

In Kantian terms, the principle of choice on which you act is the law you give to yourself. At this stage of the argument, however, it remains unclear why such law must be one *that you give to yourself.* After all, why could you not act freely according to a law that someone else gave you? In which sense, exactly, is this claim contradictory (if it is at all)?

Korsgaard's answer is that acting according to one's own law—that is, acting *autonomously*—is part of the structure of free agency itself. When I act according to a law you gave me, I am the one who decides to do so, and this law thus becomes the principle of choice I give to myself. In other words, unless you constrain me to comply with a law of your choosing, what I do when I act on it is to make your law my own. As an agent, "nothing is a law to you except what you make a law for yourself" (Korsgaard 2008, 109).

Now, if acting freely amounts to acting according to one's own law, are there any constraints on the content of this law? Korsgaard does not believe that there are; the principle that one must act according to one's own law leaves the substance of this law undetermined. For Kant, the problem of free will is that such a will must give itself its own law, but nothing determines what this law must be: "all that it has to be is a law" (Korsgaard 1996, 98). On Korsgaard's reading, the categorical imperative, and more specifically its first formula (i.e., the formula of universal law), is the philosophical principle that expresses this very idea:

> The Categorical Imperative merely tells us to choose a law. Its only constraint on our choice is that it has the form of a law. And nothing determines what the law must be. *All that it has to be is a law.* Therefore the categorical imperative is the law of a free will. (Korsgaard 1996, 98)

In Korsgaard's Kantian perspective, asserting that one must act according to one's own law simply is alleging that one must comply with the Categorical Imperative. Note that, by defending such a view, Korsgaard remains faithful to the methodology of the third section of the *Groundwork for the Metaphysics of Morals*, where Kant attempts to demonstrate that freedom itself entails the Categorical Imperative or, in his own words, that once "freedom of the will is presupposed, morality together with its principle follows from it by mere analysis of the concept." Nevertheless, Korsgaard's version of Kant's argument is deliberately idiosyncratic insofar as it clearly distinguishes between the formula of universal law and the moral law proper. While the formula of universal law is devoid of any moral content, she contends, the moral law is not. Yet the reasoning we examined so far only intends to show that acting freely amounts to respecting the formula of universal law, and an additional argument must be furnished in order to bridge the gap between this formula and the moral law (Korsgaard 1996, 99–100).

As I suggested earlier, Korsgaard ultimately defends the idea that we must value humanity as an end in order to rationally value anything at all, and this view is more reminiscent of the second formula of the categorical imperative—the formula of humanity—than its first. Contrary to the formula of universal law, the formula of humanity—"act that you use humanity, whether in your own person or in the person of any other, always at the same time as an end, never merely as a means" (Kant 1996, 80)—clearly has substantive moral content. How is it then possible to move from the first formula to the second while remaining, as Kant wanted, within the confines of *a priori* philosophical reflection? It is in her discussion of this philosophical question that Korsgaard encounters the neo-Aristotelian teleological account of practical identities.

VALUING PRACTICAL IDENTITIES: THE KANTIAN CONSTRUCTIVIST PERSPECTIVE

According to the theory of agency I just sketched, a free action is an action committed according to one's own law the content of which remains indeterminate. Nothing, yet, precludes the agent from providing this law with any content of her choosing. A patriotic individual could consider, for instance, that the moral and social norms of her nation are more valuable than anything else and consequently give herself the following law: "Act only so that the results of your action contribute to the glory of your nation." It *befits* a patriot, she thinks, to act according to such a law. While it is true that she does not always respect the formula of humanity by acting in this manner—she fails to value, for instance, the humanity of agents who are not her compatriots—she nonetheless respects the principle according to which she must act according to her own law. The question we face, then, is to know whether the Kantian constructivist can demonstrate that our patriot fails to act rationally when she violates the second formula of the categorical imperative.

It is certainly Korsgaard's ambition to argue that she does. In her perspective, the patriot reasons like the neo-Aristotelian when she tries to achieve the end that is internal to her identity *qua* patriot, but doing so is not a sufficient condition of rational action. More precisely, the patriot's mistake is that she does not rationally assess the value of her practical identity *qua* patriot before attempting to achieve its internal end. In other words, Kantian constructivists accept that our identities have internal ends and that such identities are a source of reasons for action. As Korsgaard notes, "We may begin by accepting something like the communitarian's point. It is necessary to have *some* conception of your practical identity, for without it you cannot have reasons to act" (Korsgaard 1996, 120). Such a claim, however, is only the beginning of the philosophical reflection on morality, which neo-Aristotelians like MacIntyre and Descombes do not carry to its conclusion. Surely nobody would object to the idea that physicians have reasons to cure their patients, maybe even that it befits a Nazi to commit genocidal actions, but the important enquiry begins when I try to assess the moral value of such practical identities.

To be fair, neo-Aristotelians do not ignore this idea. On the one hand, communitarian Aristotelians like MacIntyre argue that valuable practical identities help us realize the ends internal to the philosophical tradition to which our community belongs. On the other hand, neo-Aristotelian naturalists contend that acting well amounts to pursuing the ends that are internal to my practical identity *qua* member of the human species. For the Kantian, such answers remain unsatisfying as they do not put an end to the philosophical query. What reasons do I have, indeed, to consider that my identity *qua* member of a specific community or *qua* member of the human species has value and that I can therefore consider it to be a source of moral reasons?

Korsgaard's transcendental argument about the value of humanity precisely aims to answer this question. Practical identities are a source of reasons for action, but the reasons that stem from a specific practical identity are not themselves reasons to accept or reject this identity. Being a fireman gives me reason to extinguish fires, but it does not give me reasons to become a fireman. How can I therefore rationally ground my choice to be or not to be a fireman? Are there properly moral reasons to decide in one way rather than the other?

The Kantian constructivist's answer is that the moral value of specific practical identities needs to be assessed from a standpoint external to those very identities, and more specifically from the standpoint of rational human agency. It is *qua* rational human agents that we must assess the value of being a father, rector, or Nazi. Without this standpoint, our decision to endorse specific dimensions of our practical identity will be unjustified. But what is so special about the standpoint of rational human agency? What makes my decision to determine what I morally ought to do from this standpoint less arbitrary than the neo-Aristotelian choice to do so by considering my identity *qua* member of this specific community or *qua* member of the human species?

As Korsgaard notes, most of our practical identities are contingent: "You are a mother of some particular children, a citizen of a particular country, an adherent of a particular religion, because of the way your life has fallen out" (Korsgaard 1996, 120). Because they are contingent, we may come to call the importance of such identities into question, and maybe even stop attributing any practical importance to them. If the members of my family never treated me well, I may simply reject claims that it is important for me to act *qua* son or brother or even consider that I am no longer, in a purely moral and non-biological way, the son or brother of person x. This practical identity will then stop having practical force: I will no longer consider it to be a source of reasons for action. There is, however, one dimension of my identity that is not contingent: my identity as rational human agent. Whatever I do, I cannot stop relying on my rational powers when I try to assess the value of my practical identities. This fundamental identity is *necessarily* mine: the one with which I will be left if I stop attributing importance to all my contingent practical identities. Rational human agency is the fundamental standpoint from which I assess their value, and Korsgaard believes that this makes it the identity from which the value and normativity of our contingent practical identities spring. It is, in her view, moral identity per se:

> Most of the time, our reasons for action spring from our more contingent and local identities. But part of the normative force of those reasons springs from the value we place on ourselves as human beings who need such identities. In this way all value depends on the value of humanity; other forms of practical identity matter in part because humanity requires them. Moral identity and the obligations it carries with it are therefore inescapable and pervasive. Not every

form of practical identity is contingent or relative *after* all: moral identity is necessary. (Korsgaard 1996, 121–22)

Here, Korsgaard is merely summarizing an argument of which I will offer a piecemeal reconstruction and critical discussion in the next section. Before I do so, however, note that such an argument does not ground the formula of humanity by itself. Indeed, what it intends to show is that I must value *my* humanity to also value my contingent practical identities, but the formula of humanity requires me to value my humanity *and* the humanity of others. Korsgaard is well aware of this fact and offers a second argument to support the conclusion that I must value the humanity of others if I value my own.

Imagine that a selfish individual agrees with Korsgaard that he must value his own humanity, but refuses to value the humanity of others. When others object to him that they deserve the same kind of respect he grants to himself, the selfish individual refuses to consider the reasons that others present to him as reasons that bind him. "These are not *my* reasons," he thinks to himself, "for they do not reflect my desires. They are *your* reasons for they reflect *your* desires. Yet, I do not value your desires and therefore do not recognize your reasons as binding." In Korsgaard's view, one problem with the selfish individual is that he fundamentally misunderstands the nature of reasons. Specifically, he considers that reasons amount to mental entities that can be private. According to this perspective, it makes perfect sense to speak of *reasons that are mine* and *reasons that are yours*, and to believe that the former might be radically different than the latter. I have reasons to value my own humanity, you have reasons to value yours, but my reasons to value my own humanity do not necessarily apply to your humanity, and vice versa.

In the next section, we'll see that there is at least one contemporary French Kantian who also envisions reasons in this very way. For the moment, let me point out that Korsgaard believes that this picture is deeply mistaken and that there are no such things as *private* reasons. In her view, all reasons expressed through language are intersubjective, that is, public rather than private. As she explains, "The space of linguistic consciousness—the space in which meanings and reasons exist—is a space that we occupy together." In other words, reasons are not the kind of things that can be rejected by people on the grounds that they are not *theirs*, but only apply to others. If I truly have a reason to value my humanity, then this reason will also apply to you. In fact, it will apply to all rational beings. Like me, you (and all rational beings) will have a reason to value my humanity. And if everyone has reasons to value their own humanity, then everyone will have reasons to value the humanity of everyone else.

At first sight, this reasoning seems to entail absurd conclusions. For instance, if I have a reason to visit my sick mother on her hospital bed, does the intersubjective character or reasons imply that everyone else also has a reason to visit her? This is not so. Indeed, not everyone has the same relationship with my mother as I do. If there are rational beings who have the same relationship with my mother as I do, however, then they also have a reason to visit her in the hospital. Although people's life circumstances are undeniably different, we have the same reasons to do the same things when we find ourselves in similar situations. What is more, if I reflect upon my own humanity, then I will find that it is the same as the humanity of others. Our everyday actions typically reveal that we recognize this fact. When we engage in discussion with others, for instance, we do so because we recognize them as the same kind of beings that we are. Like us, they have the capacity to think and to express thoughts through language, which is why it makes sense to discuss with them in the first place. Like us, they consider that they have reasons to do certain things and avoid doing others, which is why we find it appropriate to reason with them. In the end, other people's humanity is in no way different than *my* humanity, and attributing value to the latter without attributing value to the former would be incoherent, or so does Korsgaard suggest.

Let us take stock. While the first part of Korsgaard's argument aims to demonstrate that we must value our own humanity if we are to value anything at all, we have just seen that its second part is meant to establish a slightly different conclusion (i.e., that we cannot value our own humanity without valuing the humanity of others). In the next section, my objective will not be to evaluate both parts of this argument. Less ambitiously, my suggestion will be that the *first* part of this argument fails. Even if we admit that I must value the humanity of others if I am to value my own, I contend, we need not accept the claim that I must value my own humanity to value my contingent practical identities. Let us unpack this thought.

TWO OBJECTIONS AGAINST KORSGAARD'S TRANSCENDENTAL ARGUMENT

I propose the following reconstruction of Korsgaard's transcendental argument regarding the value of rational human agency:

P1. In order to rationally value anything at all, I must have reasons to do so.
P2. In order to have reasons to value anything at all, I must value a specific practical identity from which these reasons will spring.
P3. In order to rationally value a specific practical identity, I must have reasons to do so.

P4. In order to have reasons to rationally value a specific practical identity, I must value my identity *qua* rational human agent from which those reasons will spring.

C. In order to value anything at all, I must value my identity *qua* rational human agent.

Such a reconstruction helps us understand why Korsgaard is inclined to describe her reasoning as a transcendental argument; each premise establishes a necessary condition of a specific form of valuing and the resulting conclusion is that valuing my identity *qua* rational human agent is the necessary condition of all forms of valuing.[4]

To assess the validity of Korsgaard's argument, let us first examine the premises. The least controversial of the four premises are P1 and P3. Surely, in order to Φ rationally, I must have reasons to Φ, at least if we understand rationality as the cognitive power to respond to reasons. More contentious are premises P2 and P4. While P2 expresses the neo-Aristotelian idea that reasons for actions spring from contingent practical identities, P4 more radically asserts that my reasons to endorse those very identities necessarily spring from a more fundamental identity: my identity *qua* rational human agent. Yet it remains possible to accept P2 while rejecting P4. In other words, one can admit that contingent practical identities are a source of reasons without accepting that such identities can themselves only be rationally endorsed from the standpoint of rational human agency.[5]

More specifically, my suggestion is that an individual can rationally assess the value of one of his contingent identities by using the reasons that spring from the other contingent identities he bears. Let me clarify this idea with an example:

> On a Sunday morning, Miguel, a physician who is also a patriot and a Catholic, joins the other members of his parish for Mass as he does every week. During Mass, a very conservative newly appointed priest gives an inflammatory discourse against euthanasia and nationalism (which diverts believers from divine authority). Shaken by this experience, Miguel concludes that his practical identity as a member of the Catholic Church is in tension with the other dimensions of his identity. Not only is he a patriot, but he strongly believes that his duties *qua* physician occasionally require him to discontinue painful life-sustaining treatments. He already feels his religious fervour diminish. Six months later, it is completely extinct.

In this case, Miguel rationally assessed the value of a specific practical identity he bears—his identity *qua* Catholic—without relying on his identity *qua* rational human agent as such. It is not *qua* rational human being that Miguel cannot accept the priest's conservative discourse, but rather *qua* patriot and *qua* physician. If it is *possible* for us to behave like Miguel, then this fact will undermine Korsgaard's claim that I *must* rely on the standpoint of humanity to rationally assess the value of my contingent practical identities. Of course, one could object that Miguel's strategy of rational evaluation is not a very good one and that it would be *desirable* that he also rely on his identity *qua* rational human agent to perform this task. Miguel could wonder, for instance, whether the priest's discourse respects the humanity of others as an end.[6] Note, however, that, in order for Korsgaard's transcendental argument to succeed, Miguel's behaviour must be *impossible*, not merely *undesirable*. As I suggested, Korsgaard's transcendental argument portrays reliance on the standpoint of humanity as a *necessary* condition of valuing my contingent identities. Yet a coherentist reasoning about the value of his practical identities is available to Miguel, who *need* not rely on the standpoint of humanity.

There is nevertheless a second manner in which one can criticize Korsgaard's reasoning without, this time, contesting the validity of P4. For the sake of discussion, let us concede that the standpoint of rational human agency really is inescapable, that is, that we cannot rationally assess the value of our contingent practical identities without relying on it. Let us also grant that whoever relies on the standpoint of humanity attributes *some* value to it. It would be a curious decision, after all, to rely on the standpoint of humanity if we envisioned it as devoid of any value. What we must now determine is how the value of humanity compares with the value I attribute to my other practical identities. Does the fact that my identity *qua* human is inescapable necessarily entail that it is *more* valuable than my contingent identities?

Korsgaard seems to assume that it does, but she does not offer a detailed explanation of why this is so. In her view, if I find myself in a situation where the obligations tied to my identity *qua* rational human being conflict with the obligations that stem from my contingent identities, I will have to prioritize the former over the latter. Let us consider, for instance, G. A. Cohen's case of an idealized Mafioso who lives by a code of strength and honour and "does not believe in doing unto others as you would have them do unto you" (Cohen 1996, 183). In fact, he correctly believes that it befits a Mafioso to commit certain actions contrary to the formula of humanity. As a result, his identity *qua* human conflicts with his identity *qua* Mafioso and he will often have to choose between the two. Korsgaard believes that if the Mafioso is reflective and actively tries to rationally assess the value of his practical identities, he will unavoidably conclude that complying with his obligation as human is more valuable than fulfilling his Mafioso duties. As Korsgaard (1996, 258) states, "His obligation to be a good person is [. . .] *deeper* than his obligation to stick to his code."

Yet even on the assumption that my identity *qua* human is rationally inescapable, it remains unclear why its inescapability entails that it has more value than my other identities. Why is it so, indeed, that such an identity is the most valuable of all *just because* I must rely on it to assess the value of my contingent identities? Does inescapability have by itself the power to confer the greatest value on things? My suggestion is that it does not. Even if I admit that humanity has value, I can still believe that my contingent practical identities are more valuable than my identity *qua* rational human agent. If I am right, it will then be possible for me to rationally prioritize my obligations *qua* father, professor, physician, best friend, over my duty to comply with the formula of humanity.

Imagine, for instance, that Teresa, a paramedic, recognizes the value of humanity, but is inclined to prioritize her obligations as paramedic over her duty *qua* human being. By way of example, she often lies to individuals she assists *qua* paramedic by telling them that their injuries are not serious. This keeps them calmer, she finds, and facilitates her work. If Kant was right about lying, Teresa does not fully respect the humanity of the individuals she assists, and thereby violates the formula of humanity. Note, however, that her actions promote the well-being of the people it is her professional duty to help.

Is Teresa making a moral mistake? Possibly, but there remains a missing link between the outcome of Korsgaard's transcendental argument—that is, the idea that humanity is necessarily valuable—and the claim that would allow us to establish that she did make such mistake. Indeed, the conclusion that I *must* attribute value to my identity *qua* rational human agent does not entail that I must also believe that it is the most valuable of all identities, and that the obligations that spring from it systematically trump the obligations tied to my contingent practical identities.

If these remarks are plausible, then I can, like Miguel, assess the value of one of my contingent practical identities by relying solely on my other contingent practical identities. Like Teresa, I can also recognize the value of humanity without considering that the obligations which stem from it override all my other duties. While the first case shows that my identity *qua* human being is not rationally inescapable, the second suggests that it is not necessarily more valuable than all contingent practical identities even if we assume that it is, indeed, inescapable. If these conclusions are plausible, we have grounds to (i) reject Korsgaard's transcendental argument that aims to establish humanity as the source from which the normativity of all contingent practical identities ultimately derives, and (ii) abandon the claim that our identity as rational human agent bears more value than any other conceivable contingent practical identity.

We have come full circle and yet, this is philosophically troubling. More specifically, we are still looking for a satisfying account of the normativity of practical identities. As we have seen, neo-Aristotelian thinkers like MacIntyre or Descombes assume that practical identities are normative, but do not provide us with a detailed explanation of why this is so. Moreover, their view is vulnerable to a problem illustrated by Anscombe's rational Nazi scenario; if we simply assert that practical identities provide us with reasons to pursue ends that teleologically belong to them, we will be forced to admit that the bearers of problematic identities have reasons to pursue morally reprehensible ends. It *befits* a Mafioso or a Nazi to commit actions we deem unacceptable, so we need an account of why individuals should not be Mafiosi or Nazis in the first place. In other words, we need a point of view from which we can determine which practical identities it is morally appropriate for us to bear and which ends it is acceptable to pursue. The strength of Korsgaard's proposal is to acknowledge that we need such a point of view, but I ultimately found her philosophical defence of the standpoint of rational human agency to be lacking.

Still, drawing attention to the fact that practical identities are normative remains an important philosophical achievement. Specifically, it reminds us that people with whom we discuss the value of particular moral decisions and judgements are not abstract individuals, but persons who bear concrete social responsibilities. Philosophical attempts to ground moral obligations often take the form of imaginary dialogues between people who are fundamentally dissimilar to those that we meet in real life. As we have seen in the last chapter, for instance, Habermas's ultimate enemy is an indeterminate fictional character who refuses to justify her actions through dialogue and, for this reason, need not recognize the normative presuppositions of argumentative discourse. Other than her refusal to argue, we know nothing about this imagined person. Who is she? What does she do daily? About what does she fundamentally care? None of these questions need to be answered in order for philosophers to keep directing objections against discourse ethics. Yet one problem with this approach to moral theory is that the fictional characters portrayed in philosophy books rarely resemble people with whom we interact in real life. Unlike our friends, relatives, and acquaintances—who all bear concrete multidimensional practical identities—they are faceless and forgettable. Because of this, it is often quite hard for us to determine how we should respond to their arguments and objections.

By way of contrast, philosophers who—like Korsgaard and Descombes—argue that the concrete dimensions of our identity create moral obligations incite us to imagine characters that resemble those that populate our world. Like Miguel and Teresa, people with whom we interact typically recognize that their practical identities are normative. In fact, practical identities provide a dimension of objectivity to our arguments when we engage in moral discussion. While reading philosophy, I have witnessed many indeterminate imagined characters deny that they have any moral obligation at all. Yet I have never met parents, teachers or paramedics who straightforwardly deny that their practical identity (*qua* parent, teacher or paramedic) gives rise to moral obligations. In other words, people accept that some duties are intrinsically tied to the social roles they occupy, and their recognition of this fact often become the backbone of their ethical behaviour. "This is not how real friends behave" or "If I did not do *x*, I could not reasonably claim to be a teacher" are thoughts that often cross their mind. Yet people remain free to prioritize particular dimensions of their identity and, as was the case for Miguel, their sense of priority sometimes changes over the course of their lives.

In preceding paragraphs, I have also argued that Korsgaard fails to establish that there is a practical identity that we *must* value more than all others. In a sense, this conclusion is anxiety inducing for it raises what I call *the problem of reflexivity*: whichever dimension of my practical identity I have prioritized in the past, my rational capacities as a human being allows me to subject this decision to a continuous critical appraisal. I have been *such* or *such person*, but is this really the person that I should keep being? As we have seen, neo-Aristotelians seek to eliminate this anxiety by pointing out to communities and traditions which, in their view, can serve as moral beacons. Yet the fact that communities and traditions value particular ways of life does not relieve me from the task of using my own cognitive capacities to decide how *I* should live *mine*. When adults witness teenagers develop this capacity for self-reflection—one which often leads young people to rebel against existing social norms—they often look at them with mockery. They envision their child's "teenage rebellion" as a sign of her immaturity and long for the moment when she will finally endorse dominant social practices. Yet rebellious teenagers are often rebellious because they have grasped an important fact about human existence: no one else can make choices in their place, but a lot of people seem to pretend that this is not so by uncritically endorsing social norms. "Mock me as you want," the teenager will always be able to reply, "but refusals to question social norms have led to disastrous consequences in the past." In other words, rebellious teenagers are right that we are only fooling ourselves when we willfully and conveniently forget that we have the rational capacity to critically assess the value of traditional norms and identities. Between rebellious teenagers and conformists, who is really being immature? From a historical point of view, it seems to be the latter. Indeed, moral communities have more often been plagued by too little questioning than by too much.

If we accept the view that obligations stem from the social roles we endorse, then the fact that I can give more value to particular dimensions of my practical identity also entails that I am free to prioritize certain obligations over others. The practical importance of this *freedom to prioritize* manifests itself in situations where a particular course of action would allow us to fulfill *some* of our obligations, but not all. In these situations, we must choose who we truly want to be, just like Miguel had to choose between being a good physician and a good religious practitioner. And when we must make difficult but impactful moral choices, our reflection is often plagued by doubt, or even fear. Is this truly how I should act? Am I behaving like the person I want to be? Our moral lives are characterized by freedom, but also replete with hesitation and uncertainty.

Now, philosophical reflection on identity, freedom and ambiguity is not the prerogative of contemporary Kantian or Aristotelian moral philosophers. In fact, it is more frequently associated with European existentialism, a philosophical movement which heavily emphasized the idea that *no one but you can ultimately decide which dimension(s) of your practical identity you will value over others*. In my view, there are many overlapping ideas between contemporary Kantian constructivism and twentieth-century French existentialism, and perhaps the best way to demonstrate this is to examine some philosophical claims about the relationship between practical rationality and freedom made by contemporary French Kantian philosopher Alain Renaut. As we will see, Renaut is deeply familiar with the thought of a well-known existentialist: Jean-Paul Sartre.

MORAL AGENCY AND RADICAL FREEDOM: EXISTENTIAL KANTIANISM IN CONTEMPORARY FRENCH PHILOSOPHY

In his magnum opus *Being and Nothingness*, Sartre famously comments on the behaviour of a café waiter:

> Let us consider this waiter in the cafe. His movement is quick and forward, a little too precise, a little too rapid. He comes toward the patrons with a step a little too quick. He bends forward a little too eagerly; his voice, his eyes express an interest a little too solicitous for the order of the customer. Finally there he returns, trying to imitate in his walk the inflexible stiffness of some kind of automaton while carrying his tray with the recklessness of a tight-rope-walker by putting it in a perpetually unstable, perpetually broken equilibrium which he perpetually re-establishes by a light movement of the arm and hand. All his behaviour seems to us a game. He applies himself to chaining his movements as if they were mechanisms, the one regulating the other; his gestures and even his voice seem to be mechanisms; he gives himself the quickness and pitiless rapidity of things. He is playing, he is amusing himself. But what is he playing?

We need not watch long before we can explain it: he is playing at *being* a waiter in a café. (Sartre 1969, 59)

For a reader unacquainted with Sartre's philosophy, it might not be immediately obvious that his appraisal of the waiter's behaviour is thoroughly critical. In fact, the waiter is but one of the characters discussed in *Being and Nothingness* whom Sartre accuses of acting in *bad faith*, which amounts to pretending that *who one is* is not the result of a radically free decision on their part. If we pay close attention to the text, however, we find clues which reveal that Sartre's appraisal of the waiter is anything but flattering. First, the waiter is described as bending "forward a little too eagerly" and his eyes are described as expressing, "an interest a little too solicitous for the order of the customer." In other words, the waiter attempts to convince patrons that he revels in his employment, but he does so in an awkward manner which discloses that this might not be the case. In fact, from Sartre's perspective, what patrons notice first is that the waiter is trying hard to convince others—and most importantly himself—that he is indeed a waiter. "Look at me," we can imagine him thinking, "I'm doing all the things that waiters do!" Sartre also portrays the waiter as imitating, "in his walk the inflexible stiffness of some kind of automaton," which again reveals that there is something artificial and maybe even insincere about his behaviour. Third, the waiter gives himself "the quickness and pitiless rapidity of things" and "his gestures and even his voice seem to be mechanisms." These expressions suggest that the waiter is behaving as if he were something that he is not, that is, a *thing* instead of a *human being*. Lastly, Sartre summarizes his observations by writing that the waiter is "playing at *being* a waiter in a café." Interestingly, the game he is playing is a very particular one: what the waiter ultimately attempts to do is to convince himself of others that he simply *is* a café waiter. Yet this is not the case.

Existentialist thinkers argue that being true to oneself requires one to recognize one's freedom to endorse or reject social roles as well as the rights and duties which accompany them. According to Sartre, this is the fault committed by the waiter. When he understands himself as simply *being* a waiter, he willfully forgets that he *freely chooses* to be a waiter every time he walks into the café and starts serving patrons. What is more, the waiter could stop serving patrons at any given time. All things considered, nothing prevents him from throwing his towel and tray on the floor, lighting a cigarette, calmly walking out of the building and spending the rest of his day enjoying Paris. Importantly, that he probably will not do so changes nothing to the fact that he could. At any point in his life, the waiter could choose to stop being what he has chosen to be so far and instead become someone else. This is a distinctive feature of what he *actually* is: a free human being who, unlike *things*, has the power to transform himself through acts of his own will. This is what Sartre (1969, 59) means when he writes that "from within, the waiter in the cafe cannot be immediately a cafe waiter in the sense that this inkwell is an inkwell, or the glass is a glass." Humans are not objects, but free beings who can "transcend" situations in which they find themselves and choose to place themselves in different ones.

What is more, our freedom to choose who we are occasionally gives rise to anxiety. Because we are not things, we *must* make our own choices and take responsibility for them. However hard he tries, the waiter will never make it so that he simply *is* a waiter instead of a free man who, every day, freely chooses to continue to be waiter. As we have seen, all that he can do is *play* at being a waiter and momentarily forget that he remains free not to be one. For minutes, hours, or even days, he can avoid taking responsibility for his decision to wait tables for a living. In Sartre's perspective, this amounts to a form of voluntary blindness—a refusal to acknowledge one's freedom—in which we are *all* tempted to engage in order to appease the anxiety that freedom so often creates. In fact, it is quite telling that, in the midst of his commentary on the waiter's behaviour, Sartre begins to write in the first person and imagines *himself* as automaton-waiter:

> What I attempt to realize is a being-in-itself of the cafe waiter, as if it were not just in my power to confer their value and their urgency upon my duties and the right of my position, as if it were not my free choice to get up each morning at five o'clock or to remain in bed, even though it meant getting fired. As if from the very fact that I sustain this role in existence I did not transcend it on every side, as if I did not constitute myself as one beyond my condition. (Sartre 1969, 60)

As it turns out, acting in bad faith—playing at *being* someone that we *freely choose* to be—remains a temptation for philosophers too.

Now, how do Sartre's considerations on freedom relate to neo-Aristotelian and contemporary Kantian theories of moral judgement? After all, this is the topic of this book, and it might appear to the reader that I have suddenly lost track of it. Yet note that existentialism adds nuance to neo-Aristotelian traditionalist conceptions of the foundations of moral judgement. In the first part of this book, we have seen that thinkers like MacIntyre and Bubner argue that moral agents should use traditional norms as guiding principles when they face moral decisions. In their view, these traditional norms can also serve as a justificatory framework that agents can use to defend their moral choices. By way of contrast, existentialism reminds us that traditional norms are not *given* to us in a way that would make it impossible for us to question their value. In Sartrian terms, we can say that we never *are* the member of a particular community or tradition, we freely choose to be, and our choice could be otherwise. As free rational agents, we have the capacity to reject or endorse traditional norms, and people can legitimately hold us accountable for doing so. Like the café waiter, I can pretend that I *am* a professor, Québécois, friend, husband and father. In reality, I freely choose to act like ones, that is, to value these roles and accept the obligations that come with them. When the dimensions of my practical identity conflict and I prioritize certain obligations over others, this is also the result of a free decision and, according to Sartre, arguing otherwise would amount to acting in bad faith. In a nutshell, there is no such thing as a practical identity that I *must* endorse. I remain radically free not to do so.

Existentialism also had a significant impact on contemporary French Kantianism. While Korsgaard's transcendental argument aims to demonstrate that we must attribute value to our identity as a human being, one French Kantian influenced by Sartre's philosophy contends that valuing anything at all is necessarily the object of a free choice. According to his perspective, the very act of valuing cannot possibly be the object of an obligation. Here, I am thinking of Alain Renaut and his ethics of autonomy, the key affirmation of which is that the moral law cannot possibly bind agents until they freely decide to ratify it.[7] Renaut makes this point in a reflection on the nature of moral reasons in which he underlines that an important part of our ethical life amounts to assessing the strength of reasons which count in favour or against acting in certain ways. For instance, let me return once more to a previous example and say that my schedule allows me to *either* help my friend move *or* spend time with my anxious brother, who just had a panic attack. Then, I will have to engage in moral reasoning to decide if my reason to spend time with my brother is "weightier" than my reason to help my friend move, or vice versa.[8] For his part, Renaut considers that moral reasons are not *intrinsically weighty*. In fact, the comparative strength of reasons essentially depends on the weight that we give to them. In his view, moral reasons do not bind us unless we freely choose to endorse them. Whatever reason I am reflecting upon, indeed, I remain free not to give it any weight at all.

In other words, Renaut argues that agents individually ground the authority of moral reasons that apply to them through a free act of their will. In a book in which he debates the nature of moral reasons with American philosopher Charles Larmore, Renaut explains that "in order for the presence of reasons to lead me to act in one way over another, *I* must recognize them as *good* reasons. That is to say that I—and no one else in my place—must adhere to them, recognize myself in them" (Renaut and Larmore 2004, 100–1). If a moral agent does not recognize herself in a particular set of reasons, then she is free to consider that these are not *hers*. These might be reasons for others, but they are not *her reasons*. While commenting on discourse ethics,

Renaut similarly contends that moral prescriptions which are the outcome of Habermassian discussions are not *ipso facto* binding on discussants. Let us say that, after a long debate, my interlocutors and I finally agree on the validity of particular moral principles. In Renaut's view, I must still endorse these principles through an act of my will in order for them to bind me. As he underlines, I must envision these norms as ones that were created "by my autonomous freedom—otherwise I would receive them, so to speak, from the outside" and "experience them in a heteronomous manner" (Renaut 2003, 14). Ultimately, I can freely choose to adhere or not to adhere to a given moral principle; its authority depends on the relationship that I have with myself, that is, on my own personal commitments. Here, the Kantian language of autonomy blends with the existentialist conception of freedom. According to Sartre, the café waiter could choose to become anyone else at any time. Within Renaut's philosophy, agents are similarly free to stop recognizing the authority of a particular set of moral reasons and choose to respond to a different one. In both cases, moral life is an experiment in inner freedom, one in which no one can force anything upon us, not even a single moral reason.

One problem with Renaut's ethical outlook is that it runs into a problem that I have already sketched in this chapter. If moral agents truly have the power to make it so that some reasons bind them and some others do not through an act of their will, then it seems that nothing prevents me from deciding that I am only bound by reasons to which it is advantageous for me to respond. Simply put, it seems that I can freely choose to become a scoundrel and justify this decision with the claim that all reasons not to be a scoundrel are not *mine*. Curiously, this is the very objection that Renaut ultimately directs against Sartre's existentialism. As we have seen, to avoid bad faith and be *authentic*, Sartre argues that I must be aware that *I am who I freely decide to be* and avoid pretending that my current life circumstances define who I am. I may be a waiter, but I am not *essentially* a waiter; I can freely decide to stop being one at any time. In general, moral agents freely choose to endorse (and keep endorsing) certain dimensions of their practical identity as well as the obligations that come with them.

Now, being authentic and avoiding bad faith in Sartre's sense seems perfectly compatible with being a scoundrel. As long as I know that I freely *choose* to be a scoundrel—that I never simply *am* a scoundrel—then I am not acting in bad faith. This objection can also be directed against Renaut's ethics of autonomy. If individual moral agents have the power to ground the authority of reasons through an act of their will, then nothing prevents scoundrels not to endorse reasons that would lead them to care for the well-being of others. More precisely, my suggestion is that Renaut forebodes this objection, but never successfully answers it. Certainly, the French Kantian frequently invites his readers to reject individualism and treat others as equal *subjects*, that is, as human beings who deserve the same amount of care and consideration. This is what makes Renaut a Kantian. In his view, the most important moral choice agents must make amounts to deciding whether they will give the same moral weight to the needs of others as they give to their own, and the best way of doing so is to respect Kant's categorical imperative. Yet there remains a fundamental difference between Kant's philosophy and Renaut's existential interpretation of it. According to the former, philosophical reflection brings us to the conclusion that the moral law binds all rational agents regardless of the moral commitments they freely choose to make. There is simply no way to avoid this conclusion. In contrast, Renaut's philosophy entails that the categorical imperative cannot be binding on individuals who make the free decision not to recognize the moral law as their own.

For his part, Charles Larmore raises a different objection against Renaut's existential Kantianism. According to his perspective, the idea that moral agents can ground the authority of moral reasons makes no sense at all. By their very nature, Larmore, argues, reasons have intrinsic authority. We can even say that they impose themselves on us. As he writes while debating the metaphysical nature of moral reasons with Renaut: "There is a normative order to which thought is called upon to respond, an objective order of reasons of which we are not ourselves the authors, but the authority of which it is appropriate for us to *recognize* (not to *ground*)." More radically, Larmore argues that moral reasons are not located in our minds but exist in the world. They are "out there," and the very purpose of moral reasoning is to grasp them.[9] Certainly, agents can freely choose not to care for others, but they still have a moral reason to do so, one that exists independently of their ability to recognize it. In this sense, moral reasons are mind-independent entities. What is more, according to Larmore, the very fact that they are allows us to understand what moral mistakes are. From a moral point of view, agents often act wrongly precisely because they fail to recognize (or give proper weight to) the reasons they have to behave in certain ways. By way of contrast, it seems that scoundrels will be able to skirt moral objections if Renaut is right about the nature of reasons. As soon as someone accuses them of making a moral mistake, they can counter this accusation by claiming that reasons to behave in a different way than they do are not *their* reasons.

In response to Larmore, Renaut argues against the claim that moral reasons are "out there in the world." Even if moral reasons are truly part of the stuff of the world, he contends, we only have access to our own *experience* of the world, not to the world itself. In Kantian terms, we can say that we never perceive *things in themselves*. Although there might be such things as reasons which exist outside the sphere of representation—that is, outside of our subjective experience—we cannot grasp them, and it therefore makes little sense to claim that moral reasoning amounts to the task of identifying them. We only have access to *reasons we think we have* to do certain things, and discussing the putative existence of mind-independent reasons serves no purpose in the reflection on moral judgement. As Renaut explains (2003, 118), the philosophical perspective defended by Larmore "amounts to envisioning truth as the correspondence of a statement to reality in itself." Yet conceiving truth in this way amounts to asking the knowing subject for the impossible, that is, to "come out of herself in order to coincide with the in-itself." Although there might be a gap between *how things are in the world* and how *we represent those things to ourselves*, we will never know whether this is the case. Human beings cannot jump outside the sphere of representation to verify whether things they represent to themselves really match things-in-themselves.

What should we think of Renaut's rebuttal? My suggestion is that it does not demonstrate what Renaut hopes it will. Even if we grant Renaut that the only reasons that matter for moral judgement are those which exist within the sphere of representation, this claim does not entail that moral agents have the power to freely ground (or abolish) the authority of reasons through an act of their will. Let us say that I recognize that I have a reason to care for others (instead of behaving in a purely selfish manner), I agree with Larmore that I do not need to do anything with my will for this reason to bind me. Moral reasons bind us whether we like it or not. Once I realize that I have moral reasons to care for the well-being of others, I cannot abolish their authority by thinking things such as "I do not freely choose to endorse the authority of these reasons!" If this were the case, then I would have to ask myself, "What reasons do I have to endorse or reject the authority of reasons to care for others?" By doing so, however, I would quickly fall into an infinite regress. If there are reasons to care for others, and reasons to endorse reasons to care for others, are there also reasons to endorse reasons to endorse reasons to care for others? Of course, one way to avoid this regress amounts to considering that my choice to endorse and reject the authority of *such* or *such* reason is itself irrational.[10] If this is so, however, then it seems that morality loses power over us for no one could demonstrate that agents are *rationally obligated* to care for others. Scoundrels and Nazis could do as they please, and no one would have the means to establish that they *ought not to be scoundrels or Nazis*. In other words, Anscombe's rational Nazi challenge could simply not be met.

To sum up, neo-Aristotelians like Descombes argue that practical identities are normative as they come with ends and obligations that are internal to them. Yet it seems that moral agents can prioritize certain dimensions of their identity over others when these dimensions conflict. They can also question the value of their practical identities and, by extension, of the duties and obligations to which they give rise. Unlike moral reasons, it seems that practical identities do not impose themselves on us. If I am free to endorse *such* or *such* practical identity, then it seems that I can endorse one that will ultimately lead me to behave in immoral ways (Mafioso, Nazi, scoundrel, etc.). For instance, I can decide to only care about the well-being of the members of my crime family or, alternatively, to act in a purely self-interested manner. Now, to avoid this problem, Korsgaard offers a transcendental argument the aim of which is to demonstrate that in order to value anything at all, I must value my identity *qua* rational human agent. As we have seen, if such an argument succeeds, then the moral law is on a firm footing (provided, of course, that we grant her that valuing one's identity *qua* rational agent amounts to following the formula of universal law). Yet the hypothetical examples featuring Miguel and Teresa suggest the following: (i) *pace* Korsgaard, I can value things without valuing my identity *qua* human rational agent and (ii) I can value my identity *qua* rational agent without giving priority to my obligations *qua* rational agent over those that stem from other dimensions of my practical identity. If this is so, then Korsgaard's transcendental argument is ultimately unsuccessful.

We have also seen that the claim according to which humans are free to uphold or modify dimensions of their practical identity is deeply rooted in existentialism and continues to influence contemporary French Kantianism. To defend this claim, I have offered a critical discussion of the ethics of autonomy developed by French philosopher Alain Renaut, who portrays moral agents as having the power to endorse or reject the authority of the moral law through an act of their will. Drawing from Larmore's criticism of Renaut, however, I have suggested that Renaut's ethics is undergirded by a mistaken appreciation of the nature of moral reasons. Where does this leave us? Perhaps the most important insight is the following: even if our practical identities are unstable as moral agents can reject old ones, develop new ones and prioritize some over others, focusing our reflection on the obligations that stem from these identities creates a sphere of objectivity in moral discourse. As a romantic partner, friend, father and philosophy professor, there truly are obligations that I ought to fulfill. Of course, like Sartre's café waiter, I remain free to relinquish at least some of my practical identities. For instance, I could decide to quit my job as a philosophy professor tomorrow. If I did, then it would be morally acceptable for me to stop fulfilling some of the professional obligations I currently have. Yet we should not underestimate how complicated it is for moral agents to relinquish their practical identities and liberate themselves from the moral obligations they entail. By way of example, like most people, I have cultivated long-term friendships over the course of my life. While these friendships are the result of free decisions I have made, the view according to which I would no longer be obligated towards my friends if I suddenly stopped valuing my practical identity *qua* friend through an act of my will is mistaken. After all, my previous actions make it reasonable for my friends to count on my support, and this incites me to believe that suddenly withdrawing this support would amount to breaking an implicit promise I have made to them. Caring about each other is what good friends do, and friendships which were built over the course of many years cannot be destroyed through a spontaneous act of the will. Certainly, friendships can be lost, and past friends can stop being obligated towards one another, but this process usually takes time. Like most obligations which stem from my practical identities, my obligations as a friend of *such* or *such* person will bind me for quite some time, that is, until I have clearly signalled to them that I am no longer interested in offering them my support. By way of contrast, some practical identities can arguably never truly be relinquished. At some point in my life, I made the free decision to bring a child into this world. As I result, I will forever be obligated to help her live a good life.

To consider that it is reasonable for me to act as a scoundrel, it seems that I would have to detach myself from the concreteness of who I am as a person. Indeed, I would have to picture myself as an abstract reasoner devoid of practical identities, one who resembles the imaginary foes so often portrayed by philosophers who reflect upon the grounds of moral judgement. As we have seen, Descombes's critique of Anscombe amounts to the claim that, outside of thought experiments, no one has a unidimensional practical identity. Concretely put, no scoundrel is solely a scoundrel. If we take an honest look at who we are—i.e., people enmeshed in various social, familial and professional relationships—then we will quickly come to realize that moral duties fall upon us. For philosophers who aim to ground the objectivity of ethics, this conclusion might be a disappointing one. After all, arguing that our practical identities are normative is not the same as demonstrating that some obligations bind all humans regardless of who they are. Although I will limit myself to defending the first of these claims, I cannot reasonably contend that the philosophical project which amounts to rationally grounding ethics is doomed to fail. At this stage of my reflection, this conclusion would be premature. This is because Kantian constructivists are not the only philosophers who believe that there exists a fundamental normative identity from which we can derive moral obligations which are binding for all humans. In fact, some neo-Aristotelians also contend that this is the case. Unlike the ones we have encountered so far, these neo-Aristotelians are moral universalists. In contrast with Kantian constructivists, however, they do not invite us to primarily conceive of ourselves as rational agents, but rather as human animals.

Chapter 6

Contemporary Aristotelianism and the Normativity of Nature

One longstanding objection against Aristotelian perspectives on moral judgement amounts to the claim that Aristotle's practical philosophy rests on an outdated conception of nature. Since Aristotle's ancient account of the natural world has been invalidated by modern science, the objection goes, any ethics based on it must necessarily be obsolete. As Bernard Williams (1985, 204) explains, "Aristotle saw a certain kind of ethical, cultural and indeed political life as a harmonious culmination of human potentialities, recoverable from an absolute understanding of nature. We have no reason to believe in that" (2011, 59). In Williams's view, this is because Aristotle's account of nature is a teleological one; unlike modern science, it assumes that both living and non-living beings have a natural end. In the first book of his *Nicomachean Ethics*, indeed, Aristotle (1984, 1735–1736) famously argues that human beings are the only species who have a rational soul, and that the natural end of man consists in activity of the rational part of the soul in accordance with virtue. If human beings attain this natural end, then they will reach happiness (*eudaimonia*), which is the goal of ethics understood as the science of living well. According to Williams, however, the modern scientific worldview is incompatible with the claim that living beings have a natural end (from which Aristotle's entire ethics is derived). As a result, contemporary neo-Aristotelians must find new foundations for their ethical thought, that is, show that it need not rest on a premodern teleological conception of nature.

In chapters 1 and 4, we have seen that this is precisely what Alasdair MacIntyre attempts to do in *After Virtue* and *Whose Justice? Which Rationality?* Yet I have also argued that MacIntyre's philosophy is haunted by the spectre of historical relativism. For this reason, the present chapter focuses on a second neo-Aristotelian attempt to overcome Williams's objection, one which has been carried out by philosophers whom I call neo-Aristotelian naturalists. Contrary to neo-Aristotelian traditionalists, such philosophers do not base their conception of moral judgement on a defence of the value of traditional norms and customs. Instead, they propose to build a philosophical account of *natural goodness* which, in their view, is perfectly compatible with a contemporary scientific worldview. This is the perspective defended by the late Philippa Foot, a British Aristotelian virtue ethicist who has had a lasting impact on twentieth- and twenty-first-century ethics. Before I turn to Foot's philosophy, however, I wish the show that some neo-Aristotelian traditionalists were themselves tempted to embrace a naturalist and universalist version of Aristotelianism, one that might allow us to overcome the problem of historical relativism. The clearest illustration of this temptation can be found in MacIntyre's last major work—*Dependent Rational Animal*—of which I have said nothing so far.

More specifically, my reflection will proceed as follows. First, I offer a critical assessment of MacIntyre's own defence of Aristotelian naturalism in *Dependent Rational Animals*. I then turn to Foot's philosophy of natural goodness and argue that it is not immune to the problem I have sketched in chapter 5: the *problem of reflexivity*. To do so, I rely on philosophical objections directed against Foot by John McDowell. In general, I hope to show that Aristotelian naturalists face the challenge of answering a similar question than the one I pressed against Kantian constructivists such as Christine Korsgaard. Even if we admit that moral agents can pursue natural goodness and behave as good members of the human species, I contend, this does not entail that we ought to prioritize our moral obligations *qua* human specimens over those that stem from other dimensions of our practical identity. I end with a discussion of McDowell's interpretation of Aristotle's ethics, which rests on the claim that moral agents can come to *see* how they ought to behave if they have been properly educated.

HUMAN BEINGS AS VULNERABLE ANIMALS

Published in 1999, *Dependent Rational Animals* marks a turning point in MacIntyre's philosophy. In all of his earlier works, the Scottish philosopher avoided relying on what he calls "Aristotle's metaphysical biology," that is, on the claim that all living beings have a natural end. Yet he now believes like Aristotle that moral philosophers should reflect upon the biological constitution of human beings in order to better identity the virtues that they ought to acquire. This is not to say that MacIntyre fully endorses Aristotle's ancient philosophical conception of nature. In fact, the former criticizes the latter for paying insufficient attention to the fact that human beings are dependent and vulnerable animals by nature, and to the virtues that they must acquire to overcome their natural condition. As a result, the catalogue of virtues that

Aristotle defended in his *Nicomachean Ethics* remains incomplete, or so MacIntyre argues. One clear illustration of this is that Aristotle frowned upon people who publicly acknowledged their vulnerability and dependence in ancient Athens and described them as lacking in virtue. Consider for instance his remarks on magnanimous men, whom he describes as possessing perfect virtue. In his view, these men hate it when others recognize their need for help. They are also inclined to forget the help that others have given to them as receiving help is a source of shame in their view. By way of contrast, the magnanimous person likes to be reminded of the help he has given to others; he is "the sort of man to confer benefits, but he is ashamed of receiving them; for the one is the mark of a superior, the other of an inferior" (Aristotle 1984, 1774).

For his part, MacIntyre (1999, 127) considers that Aristotle's depiction of dependence and vulnerability as sources of shame results from "an illusion of self-sufficiency" that is "all too characteristic of the rich and powerful in many times and places." This illusion of self-sufficiency is itself caused by the view that human beings are less vulnerable to natural hazards than the other animals as they are capable of rational thought, a power which they can use to overcome their biological limitations. Although its origin can be traced back to Aristotle, the claim that human beings are the sole possessors of reason has had a lasting impact on the Western philosophical tradition. Throughout the twentieth century, it was defended by eminent representatives of both the continental and analytical schools of Western philosophical thinking. Within the analytic tradition, for instance, Donald Davidson argues that animals are incapable of *thought* as they do not communicate with one another through concepts. Within the continental tradition, Martin Heidegger similarly contends that non-human animals are *weltarm*—a German word which directly translates as *lacking-in-world*. This because they do not possess what Heidegger names the "As-structure" (*Als-Struktur*). Put simply, the idea at play is that non-human animals do not have the capacity to envision *individual* things as belonging to *kinds of things*. For instance, they do not see a particular house *as* a house, that is, as a specimen which exemplifies a more general concept. In the German philosopher's view, such a capacity can only be acquired through conceptual language.[1]

In response, MacIntyre argues that myriad contemporary scientific studies suggest that highly intelligent animals do in fact possess conceptual thought (or, at least, something akin to it). For example, bottlenose dolphins live in groups structured by complex hierarchies, have developed a complex communication system, experience emotions such as stress, and engage daily in joint cooperative action. They can also distinguish between claims that resemble each other such as "take the flying disc to the surfboard" and "take the surfboard to the flying disc." For this reason, the view according to which they do not engage in conceptual thinking turns out to be much weaker than appears at first sight. *Pace* Davidson, the fact that animals do not speak words that we can understand is not a sufficient reason to refrain from ascribing desires, beliefs, thoughts and reasons to them. For example, McIntyre contends that a dog who stops barking because a cat is no longer in a tree truly *believes* (or *thinks*) that the cat is gone. Furthermore, we can say that bottlenose dolphins hunt in groups because they understand that they have a *reason* to do so. As a rule, we tend to oversimplify the mental life of non-human animals by portraying them as *automata* who unreflectively respond to sensory data. When we pay close attention, however, we realize that their behaviour is nearly as reflective as our own. As a result, we should envision the difference between human intelligence and that possessed by non-human animals as a difference in degree, not in kind. Note also that speaking of human intelligence as if all human beings possessed the same degree of it is misleading. Like highly intelligent non-human animals, human children possess the power of conceptual thought even if they have not yet acquired the ability to express their thoughts through language. Like all animals, they are also vulnerable, dependent on others and essentially moved by the desire to fulfill their basic needs.

Yet MacIntyre (1999, 69) does consider that *some* cognitive capacities can only be possessed by human beings, most important of which is the capacity to evaluate reasons. According to his perspective, doing so not only requires animals to possess conceptual language, but also to be capable of distancing themselves from their immediate desires. While human beings frequently do so, non-human animals typically do not. For instance, it is only *qua* human being that I can ask myself questions such as, "Is it at this time and in these circumstances best to act so as to satisfy this particular desire?" When I evaluate my desires in this way, MacIntyre underlines, "I stand back from them, I put some distance between them and myself *qua* practical reasoner." In fact, I invite "the question, both from myself and from others, of whether it is in fact good for me to act on this particular desire here and now," and my very capacity to do so marks me as a human. Through the acquisition of conceptual language, human animals transition from a childish stage in which they only act to satisfy their most pressing desires to a mature one in which they have the power to answer the question, "What is best for me to do here and now?" Too often, however, the capacity to rationally distance ourselves from our immediate desires incites us to believe that human reason is almighty. If we can use our reason to control ourselves, we think, then perhaps we can also use it to control nature and all other living beings. Even more perniciously, human beings' excessive confidence in their own rational capacities can give them the mistaken impression that they can fulfill all their needs without relying on the help of others. In Macintyre's view, a brief reflection on childhood suffices to correct the misconception according to which practical rationality turns human animals into independent beings. Although children can use their own reason to resist some of their pressing desires, they also require constant assistance from their parents and other relatives in order to survive. Moreover, biological growth only leads them to *partially* overcome their vulnerability and dependence. One indication of this is that adult human beings still need to live in groups to face the vagaries of life and surmount the obstacles that will inevitably mark the course of their existence. To overcome obstacles such as physical illness, mental disorders or old age, we have no choice but to rely on the help of others (MacIntyre 1999, 155).

Beyond his account of moral judgement as rooted in philosophical traditions, MacIntyre thus came to develop a naturalist account of human vulnerability the central claim of which is that human animals are not omnipotent reasoners, but living beings whose existence is characterized by dependence and need.[2] Interestingly, this naturalist turn in his thinking does not lead him to reject Thomism as a philosophical framework.[3] Unlike Aristotle, he argues, Christian thinkers like Aquinas did not succumb to the illusion of self-sufficiency discussed above. Instead, they rightly underlined that human development depends on myriad forms of outside assistance, some of which are provided by other human beings and some of which are provided by God. In fact, MacIntyre believes that Aquinas's philosophy can help us pinpoint two distinct kinds of virtues that we must acquire for the very reason that we are dependent rational animals. First, there are virtues which help us gain some level of independence from others in our practical reasoning. As mentioned, a mature human being should be able to assess the moral value of actions which would lead her to satisfy these desires instead of immediately and unreflectively responding to them. She should also represent the multiple courses of action that are available to her and make a rational judgement about which course of action is best. Ideally, moral agents should be able to make such judgements even when advice from others is unavailable to them. By way of contrast, the second kind of virtues that humans beings ought to acquire incite their possessors to acknowledge their vulnerability and dependence. More specifically, these virtues can help moral agents minimize the negative impact that vulnerability can have on human well-being by creating relationships of mutual help with others. For instance, being grateful for the help that one has received is laudable as it typically strengthens relationship of trust between agents. Another virtue which belongs to this second kind is *misericordia* (or mercy), a virtue which leads moral agents to give without measure, that is, without expecting any benefit in return. According to MacIntyre, being merciful not only requires one to pay attention to the distress of others, but also to envision it as their own. For the merciful individual, the very fact that another human is in distress is a sufficient reason to offer help. What is more, the negative assessments that others frequently make when describing those in need—"Don't give to him; he's a drunk!"; "If she finds themselves without a home, that's because she made irresponsible decisions!"—are not good reasons not to help them.

Now, let us pause to wonder what philosophical status we should give to the ethics of vulnerability and assistance that MacIntyre develops in *Dependent Rational Animal*. As we have seen, this ethics is rooted in a reflection on the biological constitution of human animals. Considering that all human specimens are fundamentally vulnerable by nature, one possible interpretation is that MacIntyre's naturalist ethics is universal in scope. Arguably, any intellectual tradition which does not acknowledge human vulnerability and dependence will be flawed. Moreover, it seems that the truth value of the statement on which MacIntyre's ethics is now based—i.e., that human beings are dependent vulnerable animals—can be assessed regardless of one's commitment to a particular philosophical tradition. Simply put, human vulnerability is a fact of nature. This itself raises the question of knowing whether MacIntyre's naturalist ethics is compatible some of his previous philosophical commitments, for instance the view that there is no supra-traditional standpoint from which the truth value of moral claims can be established. I believe that it is. Certainly, the claim that human beings are vulnerable and dependent on others is universally true, but it is an empirically verifiable descriptive claim, not a moral claim about how human beings ought to act. By way of contrast, the decision to pay attention to this fact and conceptualize virtues which can help humans overcome the challenges posed by their vulnerability is a feature of some traditions, not all of them. Furthermore, MacIntyre considers that his own choice to emphasize the value of virtues such as gratitude and mercy is one that philosophers have often rejected throughout history. If we look outside of the Aristotelian-Thomist tradition which shapes MacIntyre's understanding of the human good, we can easily find philosophies which conceive of such good in a radically different manner. For instance, influential liberal thinkers have argued that collective human flourishing is the spontaneous result of interactions between individuals who are essentially concerned about *their own well-being* as opposed to the well-being of others. Economic transactions are illustrations of this as they allow self-interested parties to indirectly promote the interests of others by pursing their own. In his *Fable of the Bees* (1989), eighteenth-century philosopher Bernard Mandeville goes as far as to portray private vices like selfishness as yielding public benefits through this kind of exchange. By way of example, a prodigal man who likes to spend his money on luxury goods might end up helping small business owners thrive even though his actions are solely motivated by the prospect of his own pleasure. Of course, this conception of how moral agents ought to act is in stark contrast with MacIntyre's approach to ethics, which emphasizes the importance of giving without expecting benefits in return.

Note also that a moral agent's choice to conceive of themselves as an Aristotelian-Thomist virtue ethicist or a proponent of liberalism partly depends on the philosophical questions that they are inclined to ask in the first place. While virtue ethicists ask themselves, "What virtues should I acquire to reach human happiness and contribute to the flourishing of my community?," liberals are more inclined to raise the question of knowing how social and political institutions should be structured so that the pursuit of self-interest by all community members yields the common good. Can virtue ethicists convince liberals that they should focus their reflection on the acquisition of moral and civic virtues instead of reflecting upon the best way to coordinate public vices. As we have seen, MacIntyre believes that a fruitful dialogue between philosophical traditions is possible, but he also considers that there is no neutral way for advocates of a philosophical tradition to convince their rivals that their intellectual point of departure is best. As he explains:

> If one begins by posing one's questions in Aristotelian terms, as I have done, then naturally enough, the attempt to formulate answers to them will develop along Aristotelian lines. But to begin as I did is, it will be said, question-begging. It is to take for granted rather than to show that some version of Aristotelianism is superior to other relevant philosophical traditions. And this charge must be conceded [. . .] every starting point for philosophical enquiry is initially question-begging in just this way. There is no presuppositionless point of departure. (MacIntyre 1999, 77)

If there is no presuppositionless of departure, should we conclude that the truth value of any moral or political statement depends on philosophical assumptions that cannot themselves be shown to be true? If so, it seems that the spectre of relativism continues to haunt us considering that historical philosophical doctrines are based on radically different (and sometimes incompatible) assumptions. Interestingly, the preceding quote suggests that, although his reflection is now much more focused on biology, MacIntyre is still committed to the critique of universalism that he developed in the 1980s. Ultimately, the Scottish philosopher still envisions the quest for a neutral philosophical standpoint as a pipe dream. According to his perspective, the biological makeup of human beings entails that they must acquire a particular set of virtues in order to flourish. Yet he is also committed to the view that his particular conception of virtues derives from his prior endorsement of an Aristotelian-Thomist worldview. As a result, the naturalist discourse on human vulnerability and dependence that he develops in *Dependent Rational Animals* should not be envisioned as one produced from an Archimedean standpoint. As he stresses, such a discourse is part of a broader philosophical tradition which is not itself presuppositionless. This leads me to believe that, within contemporary Aristotelianism, there remains a fundamental disagreement between anti-universalist thinkers like MacIntyre and Bubner and Aristotelian universalists who more clearly argue that reflecting upon the biological features of human beings can lead us to conceive of a form of *natural goodness* to which all of its specimens should aspire. As I would now like to show, indeed, the hope of these universalist Aristotelians is to demonstrate that no human being can rationally reject the claim that they ought to be good in this natural sense regardless of the particular philosophical tradition to which they subscribe.

FROM THE GRAMMAR OF "GOOD" TO NATURAL GOODNESS

In 2001, philosopher Philippa Foot published an influential neo-Aristotelian work in which she attempts to provide a foundation for moral judgement by developing the concept of *natural goodness*. Alongside Elizabeth Anscombe and Peter Geach, Foot belongs to a group of British neo-Aristotelian thinkers born in the 1910s and 1920s who were deeply influenced by the philosophy of ordinary language put forward by Austrian philosopher Ludwig Wittgenstein. In fact, Foot's discourse on natural goodness is itself based on Geach's grammatical reflection on the ways in which the adjective "good" is used in everyday language. In his article "Good and Evil," for instance, Geach draws a distinction between two kinds of adjectives which he names logically *predicative* adjectives and logically *attributive* adjectives. As he writes (1956, 33) "in a phrase 'an A B' ('A' being an adjective and 'B' being a noun) 'A' is a (logically) predicative adjective if the predication 'is an A B' splits up logically into a pair of predications 'is a B' and 'is A.'" Consider the statement, "x is a red car." It makes perfect sense to divide this statement into two simpler ones by saying that "x is a car" and "x is red." Because of this, we can safely conclude that "red" is a logically predicative adjective. Now, if an adjective is *not* predicative, it is necessarily *attributive*. To see this, consider the statement, "x is a small elephant." Here, it would be misleading to claim that this statement can split up into the two following statements: "x is an elephant" and "x is small." Although x might be small *compared to other elephants*, no elephant is a small thing all things considered. In fact, because it is an elephant, it makes sense to claim that x is a pretty big thing overall! Like "small," attributive objectives are those that only apply to things in this comparative manner. Although things are red *in general*, they are only small or big compared with other things which belong to the same class. When describing a car as red, I can ignore the *kind of thing* to which it belongs as well as the features that things of this kind typically possess. I am not trying to say that the car is red *for a car*, but rather that it is red in absolute terms. By way of contrast, when I describe an elephant as small, I do need to pay attention to the features typically possessed by elephants for my description to be accurate. What I am really saying is that *this elephant* is small *for an elephant*, not that it is small in absolute terms.

Perhaps the easiest way to see that one needs to pay attention to *kinds* when using attributive adjectives is to reflect upon category errors. Let us say that I am observing a mouse. Upon closer inspection, I realize that the mouse is actually a rat. This might provoke a change in the adjectives I will be inclined to use to describe it. "I thought this animal was a *big* mouse, I might say to myself, but it is actually a *small* rat." After all, I know that the size of a normal rat is not the same as the size of a normal mouse. In this case, my choice of an attributive adjective not only depends on what I am seeing, but also on my *expectation* of what I will see when I observe mice and rats. In other words, it depends on my representation of the features typically possessed by an animal of *such* or *such* kind.

Now, the important point for our reflection on moral judgement is the following: both Geach and Foot argue that the adjectives "good" and "bad" are always attributive, and therefore never predicative. This means that, in order to determine whether a thing x is good, we must consider the *kind* of things to which it belongs as well as the features typically possessed by things of that kind. More specifically, Foot argues that we must consider the *function* normally fulfilled by things of x's kind. To see how typical features relate to functions, consider the following example. When I describe a philosophy book as being a "very bad philosophy book," I imply that it is not fulfilling its function, which is roughly to teach us something true about the world using the tools and methods of philosophy as a discipline. This is a typical feature of philosophy books, and it is also what they are for. Of course, the very bad philosophy book might accidentally fulfill another function—for instance, it might be a good *soporific*—but this is not what we have in mind when we speak of good and bad philosophy books. Philosophy books are meant to provide you with answers to important questions about human existence and the nature of reality, not to help you fall asleep.

As Foot (2001, 2–3) summarizes:

A colour word operates in independence of any noun to which it is attached, but whether a particular F is a good F depends radically on what we substitute for "F." As "large" must change to "small" when we find that what we thought was a mouse was a rat, so "bad" may change to "good" when we consider a certain book of philosophy first as a book of philosophy and then as a soporific.

In general, human socialization allows us to understand what functions artifacts like cars or houses are supposed to fulfill (help us commute, serve as shelter, etc.). Furthermore, this understanding of functions itself enables us to confidently speak of bad books and good houses. At this stage, however, why this point matters in a reflection on moral judgement is far from obvious. In fact, Foot's reflection only acquires a properly moral dimension when she suggests that, like artifacts, *living beings* should also be evaluated from a functionalist point of view. By way of example, saying that Tanya has good vision amounts to saying that she possesses a vision which allows her to see well. Vision is for seeing things, and a vision which does not fulfill its function is undoubtedly a *bad* one. Now, the most controversial ethical view defended by neo-Aristotelian naturalists such as Foot is that, like all other things, human beings are good or bad because they fulfill or fail to fulfill the function that they are meant to fulfill.

Of course, we frequently use the adjective "good" in a moral sense without thinking about functions at all. Imagine that I am currently going through an episode of depression. During this hard time, I am lucky enough to be surrounded by good friends who help me regain my mental health. When I say this, it is not obvious that what I mean is that my friends have fulfilled their function *qua* friends or, more generally, their function *qua* human beings. Even if this thought is not at the forefront of my reflection, however, it might still be the case that this is what "good" means. As I understand it, this is precisely Foot's suggestion. At the most fundamental level, the meaning of "good friend" compares to that of "good vision." When we use such expression, we are really assessing whether *this* friend or *this* vision accomplishes what *friends in general* or *vision in general* are meant to accomplish. In fact, claiming that "good" has a special meaning when we use it in moral discourse creates unnecessary philosophical confusion. Simply put, there is no special moral meaning of "good," and people are good or bad in the same way as all things are. As virtue ethicist Rosalind Hursthouse (2001, 195) points out, Foot ultimately argues that, "what goes for 'good cactus,' 'good knife,' 'good rider,' also goes for 'good human being' even when we use that phrase in ethics."

In which sense is this philosophical perspective naturalistic? According to Foot, identifying the function that human beings ought to fulfill requires us to envision humanity as a natural specie, and then to reflect upon the features that human specimens must possess to be well adapted to their environment. In fact, a core idea shared by neo-Aristotelian naturalists like Foot is that our very representation of life is normative. If we pay close attention to natural species, we will come to understand what features specimens of a particular species must possess as well as how these specimens must behave to *live well*. In other words, the descriptive study of the biological constitution and behaviour of "life-forms" sheds light on how members of a particular life-form can lead good lives.[4]

To help her readers grasp this point, Foot relies on the work of American philosopher Michael Thompson and, more specifically, on his reflection upon what he names "Aristotelian categoricals." In a nutshell, Aristotelian categoricals which are judgements pertaining to natural history of the sort that can be found in Aristotle's *History of Animals* (Thompson 2008, 63–67). Yet one need not be familiar with Aristotle's treatises on animals to understand what kind of judgement Thomson has in mind. Indeed, anyone who has watched a wildlife documentary such as BBC's *Planet Earth* can easily do so. In these documentaries, narrators—David Attenborough being the most famous—typically say things like "the beaver uses its tail to alert others to the presence of a predator" or "the wolverine jumps from tree to tree to surprise its prey." Those statements are Aristotelian categoricals, and—perhaps surprisingly—they are the very heart of neo-Aristotelian naturalists' reflection on the foundations of moral judgement. How so?

Note first that Aristotelian categoricals pertain to both physical attributes possessed by members of natural species (e.g., "the human being has thirty-two teeth") and their behaviour (e.g., "the bee stings when it senses a threat"). Moreover, although they appear to describe a particular specimen of a natural specie, they in fact apply to *species as such*. When David Attenborough utters, "the wolverine jumps from tree to tree to better surprise its prey," what he means is not that only *this* wolverine captured on film by the crew of *Planet Earth* jumps from tree to tree to better surprise its prey. Instead, he is saying that *all* wolverines typically do this. Lastly, Aristotelian categoricals are not statistical judgements. To see this, imagine that an eccentric academic calculated the total number of human teeth attached to human jaws that currently exist in the world, and then divided this number by the total number of human jaws which currently exist in the world. Because of lost teeth, perhaps the eccentric scientist would find that, on average, a human jaw contains 28.9 teeth. Still, people would understand what David Attenborough is truly saying when he explains that "the human being has thirty-two teeth." What this statement means is that, regardless of the number of human teeth and jaws which currently exist in the world, a human being has the biological potential to grow thirty-two teeth.

To sum up, Aristotelian categoricals can be distinguished from both judgements which pertain to a particular specimen (e.g., "This lion is sick") and statistical judgements (e.g., "currently, the average number of human teeth per jaw is 28.9"). Because of this, Thompson and Foot contend that Aristotelian categoricals belong to their own logical category. For Foot's ethical naturalism, however, the most important feature of Aristotelian categoricals is that they are simultaneously descriptive and normative. At first sight, the statement "the bee stings when it senses a threat" might appear to be purely descriptive. Upon closer inspection, however, this statement allows us to understand what bees must do to thrive. If the bee did not sting when it senses a threat, then the hive could not effectively defend itself against predators. Now, statements according to which members of natural species must possess certain features or behave in particular ways to thrive are not devoid of ethical significance, or so do neo-Aristotelian naturalists argue. Indeed, Aristotelian categoricals help us grasp "Aristotelian necessities," that is, things on which the well-being of living beings depends. As Aristotle (1984, 1603) writes in the *Metaphysics*:

> We call the necessary (1) that without which, as a condition, a thing cannot live, e.g., breathing and food are necessary for an animal; for it is incapable of existing without these.—(2) The conditions without which good cannot be or come to be, or without which we cannot get rid or be freed of evil.

According to Foot, Aristotle's remarks on the meaning of the adjective "necessary" remind us of a truth of which most modern moral philosophers have lost sight; the simple description of natural phenomena often involves a form of evaluation. This is because our apprehension of facts relating to the biological features and behaviour of specimens is intertwined with a representation of what is good for them. Whenever we describe life-forms with recourse to Aristotelian categoricals, we invariably picture a form of *natural goodness*. For instance, not only do we notice that wolverines jump from tree to tree, but we situate this observation against the backdrop of our general representation of what it is for a wolverine to live well. We understand that jumping facilitates hunting, that hunting allows for nourishment, and that nourishment is itself a precondition of flourishing. This normativity inherent in the representation of life also incites us to believe that a wolverine who does not have claws for hunting or cannot jump from tree to tree possesses a natural defect which threatens its well-being. Yet the very idea that a specimen possesses a natural defect presupposes that we represent ends that this specimen must reach to live well. Put differently, it presupposes that we represent Aristotelian necessities. Natural defects are only defects insofar as they prevent living beings from achieving natural ends such as staying alive, reproducing, avoiding injury or engaging in cooperative behaviour with other members of their species. What is more, the representation of a particular form of behaviour as being good or bad for a specimen depends on the species to which this specimen belongs. A particular form of behaviour can be good for members of a particular life-form, but bad for members of a different one. By way of example, a wolf who refuses to hunt with its pack can be seen as naturally defective, but a tiger who behaves in the very same way is not. This is because wolves are pack animals, but tigers are not. As Foot (2001, 26–27) underlines:

> "natural" goodness, as I define it, which is attributable only to living things themselves and to their parts, characteristics, and operations, is intrinsic or "autonomous" goodness in that it depends directly on the relation of an individual to the "life form" of its species.

Let us take stock. In preceding paragraphs, we have seen that Foot's philosophical perspective is rooted in a grammatical reflection on the meaning of "good." This reflection quickly develops into a discourse on the representation of life which, in her view, is not purely descriptive, but also normative insofar as it contains insights about natural goodness. At this stage of our reflection, what remains unclear is how natural goodness bears on ethics, that is, on the way human beings ought to relate to one another and non-human animals as moral agents. Considering the problem of reflexivity, that members of my specie must engage in particular forms of behaviour in order to live well does not immediately entail that, as a moral agent, *I* ought to engage in this form of behaviour. Nevertheless, Foot attempts to bypass this objection by arguing that moral defects are nothing more than a particular subset of natural defects. In her view, a "moral defect is a form of natural defect not as different as is generally supposed from defect in sub-rational living things" (Foot 2001, 27). If this is so, then we should picture a human being who succumbs to vices such as greed and selfishness as being defective in the same sense as a wolf who refuses to hunt with its pack. Like that of MacIntyre, Foot's philosophy is based on the idea that differences between human beings and non-human animals have been overstated in the history of Western philosophy. *Pace* Davidson and Heidegger, MacIntyre argues that some non-human animals are truly capable of thought. For her part, Foot contends that we should refrain from thinking that subjecting the actions of human beings to an ethical assessment amounts to doing something entirely different than evaluating animal behaviour from the point of view of natural goodness. Philosophical reflection on morality should not lead us to the conclusion that the meaning of statements such as "it is bad for human beings to lie" is different from the meaning of statements such as "it is bad for wolves not to hunt with their pack."

Now, the project of applying natural goodness to human morality comes with the risk of conflating biology with ethics. Such a conflation might in turn lead us to pass all kinds of wrong judgements such as "Martha acts badly when she chooses not to reproduce" or, even worse, "Sam is bad given that they are differently abled and cannot access this building in the same way as I do." According to this reading, Foot's naturalistic Aristotelianism would ultimately lead us to legitimize ableist discourse and arbitrarily discriminate against people who do not wish to have children. In response, Foot argues that this reading of her practical philosophy is deeply mistaken, and that Aristotelian naturalists can avoid biologizing ethics in this way. Certainly, natural ends like the survival of the human species are valuable. In fact, some of our most common moral judgements are motivated by our specie's desire to survive (e.g., "We ought to fight climate change and safeguard life on Earth!"; "If the human specie disappeared, that would be very bad!"). If we consider that humanity currently faces problems such as climate change and overpopulation, however, we will quickly come to realize that people who choose not to have children do not hinder the flourishing of our specie. Quite the contrary, their behaviour seems to be morally laudable for having children directly leads to an increase in carbon emissions (Wynes and Nicholas 2017). Similarly, there is absolutely no reason to believe that differently abled people cannot contribute to the well-being of the human specie if we care to include them in all parts of social life. Discrimination (as opposed to the fact that they possess different types of bodies) is what typically prevents them from doing so.

Foot also contends that natural goodness does not apply to human beings in *exactly* the same way as it applies to non-human animals insofar as human beings possess the capacities to *will* and *reason* in a way that non-human animals cannot. This means that, unlike non-human animals, human beings can be good or bad at willing and reasoning. Again, this claim does not entail that "good" and "bad" acquires a novel meaning when we apply these concepts to acts of the will or reasoning; "There is no change in the meaning of 'good' between the word as it appears in 'good roots' and as it appears in 'good dispositions of the human will'" (Foot 2001, 39). Instead, it simply means that, for human beings, natural goodness implies an *excellency of the will* and an *excellency of reason*. To see what these excellencies amount to, note first that we can formulate Aristotelian categoricals which apply to human beings. As Foot (2001, 51) explains, "there are truths such as 'Humans make clothes and build houses' that are to be compared with 'Birds grow feathers and build nests'." In both cases, the formulation of these categoricals is linked to the representation of Aristotelian necessities such as "human beings must protect themselves from cold weather to live well." Now, when reflecting upon human life, we also formulate categoricals which are the basis of complex moral judgements. For instance, to make collective life possible, "Humans establish rules of conduct and recognize rights" (2001, 51). According to Foot, the construction of houses, the establishment of rules and the recognition of rights are all valuable for the same reason, that is, because they contribute to the flourishing of the human specie by helping its members fulfill their fundamental needs. While houses protect us from cold weather, rules and rights allow us to engage in complex forms of joint action. For instance, rules of consent enable us to obtain medical assistance and foster intimate relationships while maintaining bodily integrity and psychological well-being.

As Elizabeth Anscombe (1969) pointed out, perhaps the best example of a rule of conduct that directly contributes to the flourishing of the human species is one that relates to promising. Foot (2001, 45) summarizes Anscombe's views on the subject by writing that:

> Much human good hangs on the possibility of one person being able to bind another's will by something in the nature of a promise or other contract (. . .) it is easy to see how much good hangs on the trustworthiness involved if one thinks, for instance, of the long dependency of the human young and what it means to parents to be able to rely on a promise securing the future of their children in case of their death. It would be different if human beings were different, and could bind the wills of others through some kind of future-related mind-control device. But we have not got such powers, any more than animals who depend on cooperative hunting have the power of catching their prey as tigers do, by solitary stalk and pounce.

Here, Anscombe's thoughts allow us to formulate the following Aristotelian categorical: "Human beings keep their promises to facilitate social cooperation." Interestingly, once we begin conceiving of Aristotelian categoricals that relate to complex forms of social interaction like keeping or breaking one's promise, it becomes much easier to grasp how these categoricals pertain to excellencies of the will and reason, that is, to moral virtues. A person who typically keeps her promise is one that we describe as possessing the virtue of honesty. In fact, within an Aristotelian naturalist framework, all virtues are laudable precisely because they help their possessors contribute to the flourishing of the human specie. For example, courage enables parents to protect the life of their children and, as we have seen, charity motivates moral agents to care for those in need. Like wolves who hunt with their pack or bees who sting predators, human beings perform actions that help other members of their specie live well when they behave in an honest, courageous or charitable manner. Borrowing a phrase from Peter Geach (1977, 83), we can say that "Men need virtues as bees need stings." Without stings, bees could not defend the hive. Without courage, human beings would not live as safely as they can. Ultimately, Foot's concept of natural goodness thus applies to a wide range of human behaviours some of which have little to do with human biology. According to her, a pathological liar has a bad will insofar as his lies hinder the pursuit of natural goodness. Regardless of his biological constitution, his lack of honesty counts as a natural defect insofar as it negatively impacts the well-being of the human specie.

If we attempt to translate the insights of neo-Aristotelian naturalists in Kantian language, then we can say that moral agents ought to respect the following imperatives: "act in such a way as to make it easier for all human beings to live well" and "acquire character traits that will help you contribute to the flourishing of the human specie." However, when Anscombe, Geach and Foot draw parallels between the behaviour of human and non-human animals, can we not object that they willfully ignore that, unlike non-human animals, human beings have the rational capacity to critically assess the value of their actions? As MacIntyre points out in *Dependent Rational Animals*, we human beings are *reflexive* animals who possess the power of raising questions such as "Is this really the best way for me to behave in this particular situation?" As we have seen in the previous chapter, we also have the capacity to formulate questions of the kind, "Should I prioritize my identity *qua* x over all other practical dimensions of my identity?" In my view, the problem of reflexivity is not only faced by contemporary Kantians like Korsgaard, but also haunts neo-Aristotelian naturalists. To see this, let us consider one of the most influential criticisms of Foot's philosophy, that put forward by John McDowell.

RATIONAL WOLVES AND REASONS FOR ACTION: MCDOWELL'S CRITIQUE OF NATURAL GOODNESS

To grasp the crux of his central objection against Foot's naturalism, McDowell (1998, 169) asks us to engage in a thought experiment and "suppose that some wolves acquire reason." More specifically, imagine that these wolves acquire what ancient Greek philosophers named *logos*, that is, the power to speak, use concepts just as humans do and reflect upon reasons for action. Suppose now that one of these rational wolves wonders whether it ought to hunt with its pack. Given that this wolf now possesses the same rational capacities as we do, it will, of course, be aware that hunting with its pack is but one possible action amongst myriad possible ones (taking a nap, playing with other wolves, hunting on its own, and so on). For rational beings, the awareness that they can choose to perform many different actions *hic et nunc* raises the following question: "Why should I commit *such* or *such* action instead of another?" Now, let us push our thought experiment one step further and imagine that an Aristotelian naturalist philosopher engages in dialogue with our wolf in order to convince it that it should indeed hunt with its pack. "It is naturally good for wolves to hunt with their pack!" the naturalist philosopher exclaims. Unimpressed, the rational wolf responds: "Who cares? Why should I not do as I please? Currently, I really feel like taking a nap."

McDowell's thought experiment is meant to illustrate that Aristotelian categoricals do not support the conclusion that all specimens who choose not to contribute to the flourishing of their species act in an irrational manner. From the statement "The wolf hunts with its pack to acquire food in an efficient manner," we cannot rationally derive the affirmation that "*This* wolf ought to hunt with its pack." It remains possible to imagine a rational wolf who would behave as a free rider and try to benefit from its pack's hunting booty without shouldering the costs of joint action. Of course, McDowell's rational wolf is but a fictional character. In the real world, wolves do not possess the same rational capacities as we do, and they are instinctively led to hunt with their pack. Yet the point of McDowell's thought is not to teach us about wolves, but to shed light on the human condition considering that human beings are, like the rational wolf, animals endowed with *logos*. Like French novelist Gustave Flaubert identified with the main character of his famous work *Madame Bovary*—"Madame Bovary, c'est moi!"—we can imagine McDowell exclaiming, "The rational wolf, c'est moi!" And from the moment we realize this, it will no longer be possible for us to act as if natural goodness immediately provides us with compelling reasons for action:

> Reason does not just open our eyes to our nature, as members of the animal species we belong to; it also enables and even obliges us to step back from it, in a way that puts its bearing on our practical problems into question. With the onset of reason, then, the nature of the species abdicates from a previously unquestionable authority over the behaviour of the individual animal. (McDowell 1998, 172)

Like the rational wolf, *I* have the capacity to question whether natural goodness perfectly coincides with *my* good. Ultimately, the main objection that McDowell formulate against Foot's neo-Aristotelian naturalism is similar to the one that I have directed against Korsgaard in chapter 5. Even if we admit that our practical identities create moral obligations, I have argued, reflective moral agents have the capacity to question the value of these identities.[5] In certain cases, they might even come to abandon them entirely (e.g., "I used to be friends with x, but we have not talked for years"). Yet if moral agents can question the value of their identity *qua* friends, philosophy professors, café waiters, members of a particular church or mosque, and rational agents *tout court*, then they can doubt the value of their identity *qua* members of the human species in the same way. Certainly, we happen to be human animals, but this does not entail that I should primarily behave as a good human animal as opposed to, say, a good father or philosophy professor. In cases where natural goodness conflict with my obligations as father (or other dimensions of my practical identity), why should I prioritize natural goodness over these obligations? For instance, why not be dishonest if that ultimately allows me to better pursue my family's interests? Here, my claim is not that I should, but rather that Foot's discourse on natural goodness does not clearly entail that I should not. In the end, the problem of reflexivity haunts both Kantian constructivism and Aristotelian naturalism. As McDowell (1998, 173) explains:

> Even if we grant that human beings have a naturally based need for the virtues, in a sense parallel to the sense in which wolves have a naturally based need for co-operativeness in their hunting, that need not cut any ice with someone who questions whether virtuous behaviour is genuinely required by reason.

How can an Aristotelian naturalist respond to such an objection? The rational wolf thought experiment is undergirded by the idea that rational agents can question the value of natural goodness and virtuous behaviour from the point of view of their own subjective desires and reasons for action. If I can benefit from social cooperation without having to suffer the costs of cooperating with others, it seems that I have a reason not to do so. After all, what is generally good for my specie is not necessarily *good for me*. In response, Foot rejects the claim that moral agents can determine what is good for them by identifying the desires they have to behave in certain ways (e.g., "I wish to nap instead of hunting; therefore it is better for me to nap"). If we proceed in this way, then we will necessarily be led to embrace a purely instrumental conception of practical rationality according to which the selfish individual truly has reasons to commit evil deeds if doing so is in her interest. Yet if embracing evil can be portrayed as rational behaviour, then this is the sign that our attempt to define practical rationality has gone astray, or so Foot argues. According to her perspective, a conception of practical rationality which leads its proponents to depict evil actions as rational is devoid of any interest for philosophers who are interested in reflecting upon the demands of morality. If we defend such a conception, then "rational" will no longer relate to "morally good" in any meaningful way. To safeguard a morally relevant conception of practical rationality, we should accept the postulate that the actions we have reasons to perform are those that are conducive to the good. Methodologically speaking, the first step of our reflection on practical rationality should amount to defining the Good—for instance by equating it with natural goodness—and then conceive of practical rationality as an instrument which enables us to pursue the Good. Then, the relationship between "rational" and "morally good" will be restored and we will avoid the conclusion the doing evil can be rational.[6]

Does Foot's response to McDowell's objection solve the problem of reflexivity? I doubt it. First, it seems that her considerations on the relationship between practical rationality and the Good beg the question. One fundamental puzzle about the nature of practical rationality is that of whether our reasons to pursue the Good are overriding, that is, stronger than our reasons to fulfill our subjective desires when these desires conflict with the pursuit of the Good. Foot does not truly answer this puzzle. Instead, her answer to McDowell suggests that there are no such things as reasons to fulfill our desires unless doing so simultaneously allows us the pursue the Good or, at least, does not run contrary to this pursuit. Yet this claim leads us to counterintuitive conclusions. For the sake of the discussion, let us suppose that it is bad for me to smoke cigarettes, but that I enjoy doing so. All things considered, I might have an overriding reason to refrain from smoking cigarettes (for instance, because doing so comes with the risk of dying from lung cancer, which would itself prevent me from spending quality years with my loved ones). That said, it seems strange to consider that, because smoking is bad for me, I have absolutely no reason whatsoever to smoke cigarettes even if I very strongly desire to do so. In fact, it seems preferable to claim that, although I do have a reason to smoke cigarettes, this reason is not as strong (or "weighty") as the ones I have not to do so. Yet Foot's philosophy appears to be incompatible with this line of reasoning. If the only actions I have reasons to perform are those that allow me to pursue the Good, then how strongly I desire to ϕ has no bearing on whether I have a reason to ϕ. But such a claim does violence to our everyday experience of the world, and this itself counts against Foot's proposal.

That said, Foot's response to McDowell raises an important worry about the latter's approach to practical rationality. As we have seen, her concern is that refusing to equate actions that we have a reason to pursue with actions that are morally good will force us to defend a purely instrumental conception of rationality according to which doing evil is rational for actors that desire to do so. However, McDowell believes that this is not the case. To see this, let us take a step back and consider how the debate that the present chapter aims to reconstruct has unfolded so far. First, we have considered Bernard Williams's claim that Aristotle attempted to ground moral judgement on "an absolute understanding of nature" that contemporary philosophers should reject as it rests on an obsolete teleological conception of nature. Then, we have seen that, in reaction to this claim, neo-Aristotelian naturalists like Foot attempt to ground moral judgement in a conception of natural goodness which, in their view, is perfectly compatible with contemporary science. According to neo-Aristotelian naturalists, a careful observation of the natural world helps us understand that certain forms of behaviour are good for the members of a given specie, and this claim bears no relation to pre-Modern teleological accounts of nature. For his part, McDowell argues that Williams and Foot make a similar philosophical mistake. Despite their disagreement about the viability of neo-Aristotelian naturalism, both philosophers consider that moral judgements must ultimately be grounded in a normative conception of nature.[7] Unlike Williams, Foot believes that it is still possible for contemporary moral philosophers to do so, but both of them agree that the problem of rational grounding is in need of a solution. As for McDowell, one of his central philosophical claims is that moral judgements need not be rationally grounded in anything at all. In his view, the belief that individual moral judgements can only be justified through the demonstration that they allow agents to pursue natural ends is fundamentally un-Aristotelian:

> By my lights, Williams's reading is a historical monstrosity; it attributes to Aristotle a felt need for foundations, and a conception of nature as where the foundations must be, that make sense only as a product of modern philosophy, and then represents him as trying to satisfy the need with an archaic picture of nature. According to Williams, modernity has lost a foundation for ethics that Aristotle was still able to believe in. But what has happened to modernity is rather that it has fallen into a temptation, which we can escape, to wish for a foundation for ethics [. . .] that it never occurred to Aristotle to supply it with. (McDowell 1998, 195)

To support this reading, McDowell (2009, 27) draws our attention to Aristotle's claim, in his *Nicomachean Ethics*, that a good moral agent commits a virtuous action for its own sake (*di'auto*). In the Stagirite's perspective, virtuous action is an end in itself, not a means to further ends. For instance, a courageous woman behaves courageously because she knows that courage is a virtue; she does not need any further explanation of why she ought to act in this way. By way of contrast, the concept of natural goodness incites us to envision virtuous actions as means to natural ends (e.g., cooperation, reproduction, survival). As we have seen, neo-Aristotelian naturalists argue that keeping one's promise is *instrumentally good* for humans as it supports the social institution of promising, which itself allows human beings to engage in sophisticated forms of cooperative behaviour. Yet this is not the same as arguing that human beings should keep their promises for the simple reason that honesty is an intrinsically valuable virtue. In fact, those two distinct justifications might yield different courses of action. Imagine a situation in which I break one of my promises without anyone realizing that I have. For instance, let us say that a few minutes before he passed, I promised my late father that I would scatter his ashes in the Pacific Ocean. No one witnessed this conversation, which makes it easy for me to break my promise without anyone knowing. If breaking one's promise is only wrong because doing so risks damaging the social institution of promising, I can reasonably justify my action by thinking that, in this specific case, I am not damaging this institution in any way. Arguably, what philosophers mean when they claim that breaking promises damages the social institution of promising is that people will stop trusting the promises they make to each other if they witness too many of them being broken. Yet if no one knows that I broke my promise to my father, my action will not have any negative consequences. According to philosophers who believe that keeping one's promise is good because honesty is an intrinsically valuable virtue, however, I still behaved badly by betraying my father's last wishes.

To sum up, McDowell argues that neo-Aristotelian naturalism is based on a distorted conception of the value of virtuous actions. In his view, virtuous agents understand that virtues such as courage, honesty or temperance should be sought *di'auto*. One need not argue further that these virtues contribute to the flourishing of the human specie to convince them that they should cultivate them. Still, this raises the question of knowing what Aristotle would say in response to people who, unlike virtuous agents, do not immediately see virtuous actions as intrinsically valuable. For instance, imagine an objector who exclaims: "You have not demonstrated that virtues are intrinsically valuable; you just assume that they are! No argument has been offered to support this claim!" According to McDowell's interpretation, Aristotle would not be troubled by this objection for his intention was never to convince sceptics that virtuous action is desirable. In the *Nicomachean Ethics*, he explains that his lectures on ethics are prepared for an audience of people who "have been brought up in good habits" and "can easily get starting-points" (Aristotle 1984, 1731). In other words, Aristotle seems to be addressing listeners who have already received a moral education and need not be convinced that it is good for them to act virtuously. To those who have not received such an education, there might not be anything to say that will convince them otherwise. According to McDowell, this is not a reason to sound the alarm. To be true Aristotelians, we must "stop supposing the rationality of virtue needs a foundation outside the formed evaluative outlook of a virtuous person" (McDowell 1998, 174). Instead of attempting to convince moral sceptics that it is good for them to act virtuously, we should reflect upon how people typically come to believe that it is. Aristotle's answer to this question is that habit leads to the formation of a good character. Similarly, McDowell (1998, 188) suggests that moral education leads human beings to acquire a "second nature" which shapes their "practical *logos*," that is, their understanding of how they ought to act as well as their motivation to do so. It also influences the emotions they feel when they act virtuously (e.g., pride, relief, pleasure). Once they have acquired this second nature, it will become clear to them that acting in accordance with virtue is a noble end which should be pursued for its own sake. As McDowell (1998, 192) underlines:

> The point of a particular courageous action lies not in the fact that human beings in general need courage [. . .] but in the fact that this action counts as worthwhile in its own right, by the lights of a conceptual scheme that is second nature to a courageous person.

Importantly, the acquisition of a second nature is not the result of a sound philosophical demonstration, but of a gradual shift in perspective which enables us to see the world in a new light. As children, we are essentially preoccupied with the satisfaction of our own desires. By the time we reach adulthood, we have come to understand that the needs of others are as worthy of moral attention as our own. In fact, when we interact with deeply selfish individuals who show no consideration for others, we cannot help but think that something has gone wrong in their moral education. "Perhaps they did not have the right role models," we think, or "perhaps they were so neglected while growing up that they cannot help but focus on their own needs." That said, most moral agents rule out purely selfish behaviour as an option. While growing up, we come to understand that acting virtuously is good for us. When this happens, we begin to treat others fairly and with respect. The sovereignty of our instinct or "first nature" has been replaced by the authority of our second nature. Unlike other animals, we are not immediately moved by our natural desires, but we have the capacity to ask ourselves, "How should I act?" While many worry that our capacity for reflection will unavoidably lead to "a *coup d'État* from self-interest," McDowell (1998, 188) calmly reassures us by underlining that properly socialized and educated human beings usually take morality seriously. Of course, we all know people who do not treat others fairly. Once again, neither Aristotle nor McDowell are especially troubled by this fact. While moral education typically succeeds, it sometimes fails. As a result, not all moral agents will acquire a second nature which leads them to act virtuously. Yet this itself does not make the claim that human beings ought to behave virtuously any less binding: "What is distinctive about virtue, in the Aristotelian view, is that the reasons a virtuous person takes himself to discern really are reasons; a virtuous person gets this kind of thing right" (McDowell 1998, 189).

Is this philosophical framework naïve? Certainly, McDowell appears to be a moral quietist. Moral education allows agents to grasp objective reasons to act virtuously, and the fact some people perform immoral actions is not a sufficient reason to believe that these reasons are not binding. Given that some people will fail to acquire a proper second nature, we should not be surprised by immoral actions. What is more, arguing with those who stubbornly believe that they have no reason to behave virtuously is pointless. Still, one worry with McDowell's Aristotelianism is that it fails to do justice to the complexity of everyday moral disagreements. In fact, it can incite us to treat our interlocutors contemptuously by claiming that they only disagree with us about moral matters because they have not been properly educated and, as a result, have not acquired the right second nature. Yet people who take morality seriously and have developed sophisticated ethical outlooks often disagree about how they ought to act. Think, for instance, of the disagreement on the moral value of lying. While deontologists consider that it is always wrong to lie as it amounts to a form of disrespect for the rational capacities of others, consequentialists believe that is it morally permissible to lie when it does not negatively impact the well-being of others. In this case, claiming that either deontologists or consequentialists do not possess an adequately shaped practical *logos* would be unfair. Doing so does not amount to offering a good argument in favour of or against lying, but rather to engage in an *ad hominem* attack. Furthermore, even if we grant that moral agents sometimes have overriding reasons to lie, it seems that ordinary moral education does not enable all agents to grasp those reasons and weight them properly (or else we would have to admit that no deontologist who believes that lying is always wrong has been properly educated). If this is so, then such an education will not allow moral agents to act rightly in cases where the best course of action is not obvious. In these cases, two moral agents who have received a similar moral education might end up weighing reasons differently and choose dissimilar courses of action. When it comes to identifying the best course of action, it seems that moral education and the acquisition of a second nature cannot be the whole story.

To rephrase this objection, I worry that McDowell does not pay sufficient attention to the importance of dialogue for moral change. The philosophical theory he puts forward amounts to a moral perceptualism according to which the natural and value of virtuous behaviour is not primarily understood through philosophical discussion or argumentation, but through the gradual shaping of one's *logos*. By defending this theory, McDowell remains true to Aristotle's idea that virtue is primarily acquired through observation, imitation and habit. Once we have been educated in this way, we will simply *see* that acting in *such* or *such* way is the right thing to do. Yet our moral lives are replete with situations in which we disagree with people whom we consider to be moral peers, that is, people who have the same moral capacities as we do. When this happens, we rarely think that our disagreement can be explained away by the fact that some of us are better than others at perceiving objective reasons for action. This is at least how *I* feel when I engage in philosophical discussion with others. In the face of disagreement, the thought that my interlocutors might not agree with me because they have not been properly educated never crosses my mind. In fact, I usually consider that they make important and valid points. Of course, this might be because I have failed to acquire the second nature discussed by McDowell. If I had, then perhaps the correct solution to all moral problems would come to me more naturally.

Nevertheless, there is no doubt that the vocabulary of perception is a central feature of contemporary Aristotelianism, not a peculiarity of McDowell's own moral theory. This can be explained by the fact that Aristotle (1984, 1803) himself describes practical wisdom as "concerned with the ultimate particular, which is the object not of knowledge but of perception." This very idea underpins the second main objection directed by neo-Aristotelians against contemporary Kantians discussed in the first part this book. In addition to arguing that contemporary Kantians like Habermas and Korsgaard are unable to formulate universal moral principles that could serve as the foundation for particular moral judgements, neo-Aristotelians like Descombes contend that Kantians cannot explain how we come to determine what the best way to act in concrete situations is. While some Kantian moral principles tell us what *not* to do (e.g., lying), others are so broad that they leave many courses of action open (e.g., "you ought to develop your natural talents"). In chapter 3, I offered a detailed reconstruction of this objection, but I have yet to examine Kantian responses to it. Once more, doing so will allow me to compare German and Anglo-American perspectives on the nature of moral judgement.

PART III

Principles, Skills and Actions

Chapter 7

From Principles to Actions

One central thesis defended by neo-Aristotelians amounts to the claim that moral agents must be practically wise to act rightly. To grasp the morally salient facts of the case at hand, one must possess the virtue of practical wisdom (*phronesis*). By way of contrast, Kantians tend to neglect *phronesis* when they portray moral judgement as a matter of applying general moral principles to individual cases. Even if philosophy could ground universally binding moral principles, neo-Aristotelians argue, such principles would still be too general to guide action. What is more, principles often conflict with each another. When this happens, moral agents face the task of deciding to which principle they should give priority, which itself requires them to possess practical wisdom.

This chapter aims to shatter the myth that contemporary Kantians never successfully responded to this objection. Instead, I wish to suggest that Kantians always took this neo-Aristotelian objection seriously, and that this incited them to reconceptualize judgement as something other than the application of "quasi-algorithmic" rules to cases (O'Neill 1996, 82). To make this claim plausible, I propose to assess three Kantian models of moral judgement. The first model—lexical ordering—assigns to philosophers the task of ranking moral principles in a way that would eliminate conflict between them. Once this is done, moral agents could use this ranking in order to determine what the best way to act in a given situation is. The second model—*Urteilskraft*—stems from contemporary German philosophy. Like the neo-Aristotelian discourse on *phronesis*, it aims to show that moral agents cannot solely rely on general principles to make good moral judgements. According to Hannah Arendt, for instance, Kant (1996, 279) himself recognizes that performing good actions implies an "act of judgment by which a practitioner distinguishes whether or not something is a case of the rule." Interestingly, the *Urteilskraft* model has recently been criticized by Anglo-American philosophers who propose a third model of judgement based on a different Kantian concept, that of "imperfect duty" (*unvollkommene Pflicht*). Examining these three models will help us see that Kantians need not reject the neo-Aristotelian idea that good judgement requires skill and, most importantly, that the interpretation according to which they do is a historical misconstruction. As it turns out, the claim that moral principles already contain the conditions of their correct application is neither defended by Kantians nor by Kant.

THEORY, PRACTICE AND LEXICAL ORDERING

Without a doubt, many contemporary philosophers inspired by Kant are quite hostile to the kind of neo-Aristotelian moral perceptualism discussed in chapter 6.[1] According to their perspective, Aristotle's (1984, 1752) observation that correct moral decisions often rest with perception is vague and unhelpful. Instead of claiming that virtuous people simply *see* how they ought to act, philosophers should provide agents with a ranking of principles on which they could then rely when they face difficult moral decisions. Within contemporary Anglo-American philosophy, such an idea was discussed by John Rawls in an attempt to overcome the moral theory put forward by David Ross. Indeed, Ross develops a pluralist version of deontological ethics according to which acting rightly amounts to fulfilling one's duties. Like Kant, he conceives of a list of moral duties that all agents ought to respect.[2] Unlike Kant, however, he refrains from arguing that all such duties can be derived from a single moral principle like the categorical imperative. In fact, Ross (1930, 21) simply proposes a list of seven basic moral duties which, in his view, summarize the obligations we have towards others and towards ourselves. These are:

(1a) Duties of fidelity (e.g., keeping one's promise and refraining from lying).
(1b) Duties of reparation (e.g., making up to your friend after you have wronged her in some way).
(2) Duties of gratitude (e.g., thanking one's parents after receiving a gift from them).
(3) Duties of justice (e.g., ensuring that a person who performs an essential and difficult job is sufficiently compensated).
(4) Duties of beneficence (e.g., donating to charity).
(5) Duties of self-improvement (e.g., trying to become a more agreeable co-worker).
(6) The general duty not to injure others.

Ross considers that this list of duties reflects our moral intuitions and need not be justified with recourse to arguments such as those provided by Kantian constructivists like Korsgaard or neo-Aristotelian naturalists like Foot. He also argues that we become intuitively aware of these duties as we move towards adulthood. Eventually, the proposition that we ought to fulfill these duties begins appearing to us as a self-evident truth. What is more Ross (1930, 29–30) compares basic moral statements to mathematical axioms.[3] As he explains:

> The moral order expressed in these propositions is just as much part of the fundamental nature of the universe (and, we may add, of any possible universe in which there were moral agents at all), as is the spatial or numerical structure expressed in the axioms of geometry or arithmetic.

In other words, general moral principles such as "you ought not to lie" are not any less "out there" than mathematical laws.

In addition, Ross argues there is no such thing as a moral duty which admits no exception. This is because all duties are such that they can conflict with one another.[4] For instance, we can easily imagine a situation in which my duties of beneficence conflict with my duties of fidelity (e.g., "I know that I promised you this money, but on second thought, I think that it is better to give it to charity"). For this reason, Ross explains that all duties contained in his list are what he calls *prima facie* duties, that is, duties which can be overridden by other duties.[5] As for moral judgement, it amounts to the task of determining which duty I should prioritize in concrete situations (or, to borrow Ross's own terminology, of identifying what my *duty proper* is). Unfortunately, this is a much harder task than defining a list of prima facie duties. Unlike prima facie duties, what my duty proper is in a particular case is *not* self-evident. As Ross (1930, 30–31) writes: "Our judgments about our actual duty in concrete situations have none of the certainty that attaches to our recognition of general principles of duty." Instead, particular moral judgements are "probable opinions which are not logically justified conclusions from the general principles that are recognized as self-evident." Interestingly, these remarks bring Ross's moral theory closer to the Aristotelian perceptualist position defended by John McDowell. According to this position, determining what the best way to act is in a concrete situation requires a trained moral vision. Certainly, philosophers can assist moral agents by formulating lists of general duties, but they cannot go further. When moral agents face difficult moral choices, they are ultimately on their own.

As mentioned, many contemporary philosophers disagree with Ross about this last idea. To see this, consider Rawls's characterization of Ross's position on "the priority problem" in his *Theory of Justice*. In Rawls's view, the priority problem is the task of determining which *prima facie* duty is weightier than others in the case at hand. As he notes, intuitionist moral theories like that of Ross have two fundamental features:

> First, they consist of a plurality of first principles which may conflict to give contrary directives in particular types of cases; and second, they include no explicit method, no priority rules, for weighing these principles against one another: we are simply to strike a balance by intuition, by what seems to us most nearly right. (Rawls 1999a, 30)

In other words, moral intuitionists believe that our moral experience is too complex for philosophers to provide moral agents with a decision procedure that would allow them to identify the best course of action in all possible situations. For his part, Rawls argues that philosophers can and should go further than this. If moral theorists merely formulate lists of prima facie duties, moral agents who agree on a list might still end up behaving very differently from one another. This is because they risk attributing an unequal weight to duties included on this list. As Rawls (1999a, 37) summarizes, these agents "cannot assume that their intuitive judgments of priority will in general be the same." For example, you might think that duties of fidelity are more important than all others, but I might prioritize duties of beneficence over them. To truly agree on moral matters, people must not only conceive of the same prima facie duties, but also rely on a common *ordering of duties*. This is where Rawls's concept of a *lexical ordering* comes into play:

> A second possibility is that we may be able to find principles which can be put in what I shall call a serial or lexical order [. . .] This is an order which requires us to satisfy the first principle in the ordering before we can move on to the second, the second before we consider the third, and so on. A principle does not come into play until those previous to it are either fully met or do not apply. A serial ordering avoids, then, having to balance principles at all; those earlier in the ordering have an absolute weight, so to speak, with respect to later ones, and hold without exception. (Rawls 1999a, 37–38)

Rawls famously applied the method of lexical ordering to the principles of justice he defends: the greatest equal liberty principle, the equal opportunity principle and the difference principle. Specifically, he argues that the greatest equal liberty principle takes precedence over both the equal opportunity principle and the difference principle.[6] This entails that political societies should never sacrifice the equal basic liberties of citizens in the name of socio-economic equality. Imagine for instance that denying anti-tax libertarians the right to assemble and discuss their ideas together was an effective way to achieve economic equality between citizens. The priority of basic liberties entails that depriving these libertarians of their right to freedom of association to bolster socio-economic equality would be unacceptable from the point of view of justice.

Importantly, Rawls's *Theory of Justice* only contains two core principles (the second of which is itself divided into the equal opportunity principle and the difference principle). In other words, it does not aim to define *all* obligations that fall upon moral agents. As a result, applying the method of lexical ordering to Rawls's political philosophy is considerably easier than using it to rank all moral duties theorized by Kant or Ross. In fact, one can doubt that using this method to rank all obligations which fall upon us as moral agents will help us make good moral judgements in all cases. Our moral lives are quite complex, and no particular situation in which we find ourselves is exactly the same as another. This is largely due to fact that people with whom we interact have distinct personalities, needs and desires. Throughout this book, I reflect upon moral judgement by using generic expressions such as "my duties towards my friends" or "your obligations to your relatives," but this always comes with a risk of oversimplification. How we ought to act often depends on the distinct features which make the people we know who they are. In the eyes of some of my relatives, cancelling a holiday trip because it has become inconvenient for me to travel might seem perfectly acceptable. According to others, it amounts to a great disappointment, perhaps even a small betrayal on my part. Here my point is not that we should never disappoint our loved ones, but simply that we should take their personalities and desires into account when deciding how best to act. An appropriate way of behaving towards one of my relatives or friends might be an inappropriate way of behaving towards another. Considering their generality, however, rankings of duties cannot possibly reflect the unique personalities, needs and desires which vary from person to person. This means that whichever lexical ordering philosophers endorse, moral agents are likely to encounter a situation in which *not respecting it* amounts to the best possible course of action.

A second worry with lexical ordering is that rankings of duties are still insufficiently precise to spare moral agents from having to rely on their own judgement. To see this, imagine the following lexical ordering of Rossian duties. In case of conflict, duties of fidelity are to override duties of reparation, duties of reparation are to override duties of gratitude, duties of gratitude are to override duties of justice, duties of justice are to override duties of beneficence, and duties of beneficence are to override duties of self-improvement. Even if we accept this ranking, many important moral questions remain answered. For instance, moral agents who endorse it will know that they have duties of self-improvement. They will also know that these duties can be overridden by duties of fidelity, reparation, gratitude, justice and beneficence. Yet they are still likely to wonder how, for instance, they ought to fulfill their duties of self-improvement. Should they do so by attempting to become empathetic, honest and charitable people? Is it sufficient for them to develop their natural talents? Even if they attempt to do both of these things, what precise state must they reach to consider that they have fulfilled their duties of self-improvement to a reasonable extent? And when self-improvement becomes tiresome and monotonous, is it acceptable for them to engage in more pleasurable activities instead? Regardless of how we order duties, how best to fulfill each of them remains an open question. With or without lexical ordering, moral theory leaves a gap between general deontic principles such as "you ought to improve yourself" or "you ought to show gratitude to others" and individual actions. Ultimately, Rawls (1999a, 39) himself recognizes this point when he explains that the purpose of lexical ordering is "that of reducing and not of eliminating entirely the reliance on intuitive judgements."

As we will see below, some Anglo-American Kantians—many of whom are deeply indebted to Rawls—have recently integrated this insight within their practical philosophy. These philosophers aim to build a Kantian theory of moral deliberation which builds on the idea that duties are indeterminate and that agents should have some leeway when making moral judgements. Before I turn to this idea, however, I want to consider a second Kantian perspective on the relationship between general moral principles and individual actions. More precisely, I want to examine the model of moral judgement famously defended by Hannah Arendt in her work on Kant's political philosophy. Unlike that of Anglo-American Kantians, this model focuses on a concept which Kant develops in his third *Critique*: that of *Urteilskraft*, which he defines as "the faculty for thinking of the particular as contained under the universal" (Kant 2000, 66).

KANTIAN *URTEILSKRAFT* IN HANNAH ARENDT'S PHILOSOPHY

Interpreting Arendt's reflections on the faculty of judgement is a complicated task.[7] In 1975, a few days after she finished writing the second volume of her major work *The Life of the Mind*—which was planned as a trilogy—the twentieth-century German political thinker passed away in her Manhattan apartment. Of the third volume of her planned trilogy—*Judging*—she only typed the title and two epigraphs on a piece of paper found on her typewriter. Needless to say, this third volume would have been the most relevant of all three parts of *The Life of Mind* for philosophers interested in moral judgement. Fortunately, Arendt's *Lectures on Kant's Political Philosophy*, which are composed of notes from a series of conferences that she gave at the *New School for Social Research* in 1970, contain many valuable insights on this topic. Yet, as Arendt never planned to publish these notes, it remains hard to tell if her reflection would have built on them in *Judging*. What is more, Arendt's philosophical project in the *Lectures* is quite idiosyncratic as she aims to construct a political philosophy out of Kant's reflections on *aesthetic* judgements, that is, judgements which relate to beauty as opposed to the Good. As she explains, this is because she believes that "judgment of the particular—*This* is beautiful, *This* is ugly; *This* is right, *This* is wrong—has no place in Kant's moral philosophy" (Arendt 1992, 12). To develop a Kantian theory of judgement, she argues, one must therefore turn to the *Critique of the Power of Judgement*, which is not a work of moral philosophy but rather contains Kant's reflections on beauty, the sublime and teleology.[8] More specifically, Arendt believes that she can build a theory of moral and political judgements by focusing on Kant's reflections on what he dubbed *reflective* judgement. As opposed to *determining* judgement, which amounts to the application of a general rule to a case, reflective judgement occurs when a thinker considers a particular case first, and then wonders under which general rule that case should be subsumed. One kind of determining judgements are judgements of cognition through which we subsume a particular thing under a concept. Consider the following example. If I visit your home and encounter a piece of furniture with four legs and a flat top, I might think to myself, "This thing is a table." When I do so, I attribute a predicate ("is a table") to a given object ("This thing"). Importantly, the fact that *this* thing is a table does not depend on me in any way. Even if I never visited your home, there would still be a table in it. By way of contrast, Arendt argues, making an aesthetic judgement such as "this flower is beautiful" does not amount to attributing the predicate "is beautiful" to a particular thing in the same way as in the table example. This is because, unlike "being a table," "being beautiful" is not a property that flowers possess independently of the effect that they have on us. If no one ever observed flowers, then they would not be beautiful. Kant (2000, 170) expresses this idea by writing that "beauty is not a concept of the object, and the judgment of taste is not a judgment of cognition."

If judgements of taste are of a different nature than judgements of cognition, what conditions must they meet to be considered valid? According to Kant's perspective, we cannot claim that such aesthetic judgements are *objective* like judgements of cognition. Yet they are also not purely subjective. When I say that something is beautiful, I am not merely claiming that such thing is pleasing *to me*. To see this, consider Arendt's claim that judgements of taste involve two distinct mental operations. The first operation is that of imagination, "in which one judges objects that are no longer present, that are removed from immediate sense perception and therefore no longer affect one directly" (Arendt 1992, 68). In other words, imagination allows me to represent an object which I am not currently perceiving through sensory experience. Let us say that I visited your home yesterday, looked at your favourite painting, and then left. I can still use my imagination to represent this painting in my mind. When I do so, I can also decide whether I find it aesthetically pleasing by thinking "I like it" or "I don't like it" or, as Arendt puts it, "it-pleases" or "it-displeases." In Arendt's view, imagination prepares the object for a second operation, which she calls the operation of *reflection*. Unlike imagination, reflection amounts to "the actual activity of judging something" (69). Put simply, reflection is a process through which I subject my initial appraisal of an object to a critical assessment. As Arendt explains, my initial appraisal of the painting I saw in your home as pleasing or displeasing "is itself subject to still another choice." Indeed, I can "approve or disapprove of the very fact of *pleasing*." As any art snob knows, instead of simply thinking "I like this painting" or "I dislike this painting," I can wonder whether I *should* find it pleasing. If I believe that I should find it pleasing, then this means that I find the object *beautiful*. In other words, to call an object beautiful, I cannot solely perceive or imagine it; I must also reflect upon the experience that perceiving or imagining it provoked, that is, approve or disapprove of this experience.

Now, how can I decide whether I *should* or *should not* find an object pleasing? This amounts to raising the question of knowing how we can make valid aesthetic judgements. According to Arendt's interpretation of Kant, such judgements must be "generally communicable" (*allgemein mittheilbar*) to count as valid. To call something beautiful, I must in fact think that *everyone* would find it pleasing were they to perceive or imagine it. This is not a simple task for it requires me to follow what Kant calls the maxim of enlarged mentality and put myself in the shoes of everyone else. As Kant explains, a person of enlarged mentality "disregards the subjective private conditions of his own judgment, by which so many others are confined, and reflects upon it from a general standpoint (which he can only determine by placing himself at the standpoint of others)" (Arendt 1992, 71). This is made possible by *sensus communis*, a Latin concept used by Kant which Arendt translates as "community sense." In Kant's own words (2000, 173), *sensus communis* is a "faculty for judging that in its reflection takes account [. . .] of everyone else's way of representing in thought, in order as it were to hold its judgment up to human reason as a whole." In other words, humans have the capacity to go beyond their purely subjective appreciation of things. When I look at a beautiful vista, not only can I think that I find it pleasing, but I can also judge that everyone would. Although beauty is not a mind-independent property that belongs to objects independently of our appreciation of them, aesthetic judgements are *intersubjective* to the extent that calling something beautiful amounts to saying that it is pleasing from the standpoint of human reason *in general*.

This *excursus* on Kant's aesthetics allows us to understand an analogy which is at the core of Arendt's political philosophy. Ultimately, Arendt argues that moral and political judgements have the same structure as aesthetic judgements; they, too, require us to follow the maxim of enlarged mentality:

> That the capacity to judge is a specifically political ability in exactly the sense denoted by Kant, namely, the ability to see things not only from one's own point of view but in the perspective of all those who happen to be present; even that judgement may be one of the fundamental abilities of man as a political being insofar as it enables him to orient himself in the public realm, in the common world—these are insights that are virtually as old as articulated political experience. The Greeks called this ability *phronesis*, or insight, and they considered it the principal virtue or excellence of the statesman in distinction from the wisdom of the philosopher. (Arendt 1961, 221)

The central claims of Arendt's theory of judgement I have examined so far are derived from her interpretation of Kant's considerations on aesthetic judgement. When discussing moral and political judgement, however, Arendt not only draws inspiration from Kant, but also from ancient Greek political science. As she notes, "the ability to see things not only from one's own point of view but in the perspective of all those who happen to be present"—which Kant named *sensus communis*—is the same as what Greeks called *phronesis* and considered to be "the principal virtue or excellence of statesman in distinction from wisdom of the philosopher." Like the hiker who encounters a vista and thinks, "This view is so beautiful that everyone would find it pleasing," wise people commit actions with which everyone would agree. This is at least what Arendt's proposed analogy between *sensus communis* and *phronesis* suggests.

Is such an analogy convincing? To answer this question, we must understand what it means, precisely, to make moral and political judgements that are "generally communicable." This expression is quite ambiguous and can be interpreted in many ways. When I make a moral judgement about how I ought to act or a political judgement about a law that the state should enact, must I ensure that *all human beings* would agree with these judgements to consider that they are valid? Perhaps not. As we have seen, Arendt sometimes speaks of the "perspective of all of those who *happen to be present*," which is arguably not the same as the perspective of human reason as a whole. As Ronald Beiner notes, part of the ambiguity comes from the fact that the German expression "allgemein mittheilbar"—which Kant frequently uses in his discussion of *sensus communis*—can be rendered as both "*generally* communicable" and "*universally* communicable." Arendt herself prefers the former translation, and this could incite some readers to offer an anti-universalist interpretation of her theory of judgement. According to this interpretation, following the maxim of enlarged mentality when making moral and political judgements only requires me to compare my opinions to those of other members of my political community (as opposed to those of *all* human beings). If we choose this interpretation, however, then Arendt's theory of judgement will be vulnerable to same objections as those that contemporary Kantians direct against communitarian neo-Aristotelian thinkers. Making good judgements will essentially amount to applying communal norms to individual cases, but nothing will guarantee that these communal norms are valid.

For his part, Beiner believes that this communitarian interpretation of Arendt's theory of judgement is mistaken. In his view, Arendt was "resolutely anti-communitarian in her own praxis as a theoretical spectator and critic" and systematically refused to regard communal ideologies as the ultimate benchmark of the validity of political judgements (Beiner 1997, 30). How could she have, as a Jewish thinker who had to flee her home and native land to avoid being persecuted by proponents of a racist ideology? What is more, her most famous work—*Eichmann in Jerusalem*—is a thorough critique of a high-ranking Nazi officer who sent hundreds of Jewish people to their death and attempted to justify his actions by arguing that he was simply following orders. Covering Eichmann's trial for the *New Yorker* in 1963, Arendt argued that the desire to obey orders and follow community standards can incite banal men like him to perform atrocious actions.[9] In fact, one of Arendt's central claims is that Eichmann committed horrendous crimes through lack of thinking in a Kantian sense. If the Nazi officer followed the maxim of enlarged mentality, he would have been able to put himself in the shoes of those whom he persecuted; to stop thinking qua Nazi and realize that the norms he was asked to obey were radically unjust. In other words, what Eichmann primarily lacked is *sensus communis*.

If Arendt was resolutely anti-communitarian, perhaps we can offer a universalist interpretation of her theory of judgement, one that does not read too much into her decision to render "allgemein mittheilbar" by "*generally* communicable" instead of "universally communicable." This is Beiner's preferred reading, but it unfortunately comes with its own set of problems, the most important of which is that assessing one's moral and political judgements from the perspective of humanity as a whole might be impossible. According to this objection, whichever judgement I choose to make, I can never truly ensure that all other human beings would agree with it. The problem is twofold. First, there might not be any moral or political judgement on which all of humanity would agree. Second, even if there were, moral agents are not in an epistemological position to know what these are. As I have argued in my discussion of Habermas's discourse ethics, people can only discuss with humanity as a whole in a metaphorical sense. Certainly, they can engage in thought experiments and attempt to predict how others would evaluate their own judgements. When they do, however, nothing guarantees that they will reach the right conclusions. In fact, for those of us plagued by self-doubt, claiming that everyone else would agree with one's moral and political judgements is the mark of brashness and overconfidence in one's critical abilities. To add to this worry, it seems that the principle of enlarged mentality interpreted in a universalist manner will be even harder to follow when moral agents must take quick decisions about how they ought to act. Arguably, identifying judgements with which everyone else would agree takes time, but when we interact with others, we often do not have the luxury of engaging in a quasi-divinatory reflection about what others would do if they were in our place. If this is what Arendt's theory of judgement requires us to do, then it seems that she is demanding the impossible.

Yet there are reasons to believe that Arendt does not truly expect moral agents to compare their actual judgements to the hypothetical judgments of all other human beings each time they make a moral or political decision. At the very end of her *Lectures on Kant's Political Philosophy*, she recognizes the need for agents to rely on general criteria that serve as moral beacons when they judge particular cases. Ultimately, agents need better guiding devices than a vague principle which stipulate that we should "make judgements that everyone else would also make if they found themselves in similar circumstances." Unlike the Kantian philosophers we have encountered so far, however, Arendt believes that the general criteria on which agents should rely when they engaged in practical deliberation are not *principles*, but *examplars*:

> Every particular object—for instance, a table—has a corresponding concept by which we recognize the table as a table. This can be conceived of as a "Platonic" idea or Kantian schema; that is, one has before the eyes of one's mind a schematic or merely formal table shape to which every table somehow must conform. Or one proceeds, conversely, from the many tables one has seen in one's life, strips them of all secondary qualities, and the remainder is a table-in-general, containing the minimum properties common to all tables: the abstract table. One more possibility is left, and this enters into judgments that are not cognitions: one may encounter or think of some table that one judges to be the best possible table and take this table as the example of how tables actually should be: the exemplary table ("example" comes from *eximere*, "to single out some particular"). This exemplar is and remains a particular that in its very particularity reveals the generality that otherwise could not be defined. Courage is like Achilles. Etc. (Arendt 1992, 76–77)

In this important paragraph of her Kant *Lectures*, Arendt develops the concept of "exemplary validity" and stresses its importance for moral and political judgement. In our daily life, we are often struck be the exemplary moral behaviour of others. When reading Homer's *Iliad*, for instance, many readers are struck by the courage Achilles exhibits in his military exploits (or so does Arendt suggest in the very last sentence of the passage quoted above). Of course, we are not solely impressed by fictional characters like Achilles, but also by real people. Consider the following example. During a trip to Berlin, Isaac, the son of my close friends Julia and Maurits, expressed an interest in wearing nail polish. Doing so is traditionally coded as feminine in Western societies and, throughout my life, I have unfortunately met many parents who would have straightforwardly denied this request. This did not happen to Isaac. In fact, I was struck by the kindness and open-mindedness with which Julia reacted to the expression of his desire. The idea that a boy wearing nail polish could pose a problem in any way did not even cross her mind. It seemed completely obvious to her that, when rearing children, one should set gender norms aside and let their inner beauty shine. Although I am well aware that gender norms have led to marginalization and oppression, I was still impressed by Julia's parenting. "If I am ever a parent," I thought to myself, "I want to raise my child like she raises her son." By treating Isaac with love and respect, Julia appeared to me as a moral exemplar. She exhibited character traits that I find admirable and made me want to become more like her.

Although Arendt's remarks on exemplary validity are scarce, they are also quite profound. Books on moral theory are full of general statements such as "doing x is good" or "you ought to do x," and yet deliberately choosing to follow well-articulated moral rules is only a part of our moral lives. Often, our reactions to other people's behaviour are spontaneous and emotional ("Julia is good; I want to be more like her"). As we have seen in the last chapter, neo-Aristotelian virtue ethicists do justice to this idea when they argue that we primarily become virtuous people by observing and imitating others instead of attempting to apply general principles to particular cases. What is more, we are not immediately aware of *why* we have the spontaneous emotional reactions that we have. When Julia reacted to Isaac's behaviour with kindness, her response simply struck me as good. A few hours later, I reflected on her interaction with her son, and only then did I start using abstract concepts such as "gender norms" to describe her behaviour. In this case, it seems that moral principles like "one ought to be open-minded" and "one ought to resist gender norms which contribute to the marginalization of others" played a central role in my reflection when I attempted to *understand* and *justify* my own reaction to Julia's interaction with Isaac. At the time of observation, however, such general statements did not cross my mind. I was simply impressed and inspired.

Does this example warrant the claim that we should refrain from portraying moral judgement as the application of general statements to individual cases? Not necessarily. Even if well-articulated moral principles did not immediately play a role in my reflection when I observed Julia, my spontaneous emotional reaction to her behaviour was likely shaped by such principles. Had I not already believed that "one ought to resist gender norms which lead to marginalization and oppression," I probably would not have reacted so positively to Julia's decision to embrace Isaac's desire. This supports the claim that I did in fact evaluate Julia's behaviour—perhaps unconsciously—in light of some moral principles. Indeed, one could argue that it is precisely because Julia's reaction to Isaac counts as an application of the principle according to which "one ought to resist gender norms which lead to marginalization and oppression" that it struck me as good. This is an important point to keep in mind when discussing Arendt's theory of exemplary validity, which suggests that we do not judge particular actions in light of moral principles, but rather by comparing these actions to those of moral exemplars. For instance, in the aforementioned example, instead of thinking "you ought to x," I would simply have thought, "be more like Julia." Yet, if I thought "be more like Julia" precisely *because* Julia correctly applied a principle of the form "you ought to x," then Julia's behaviour is not itself the criterion of moral judgement on which I relied when evaluating her actions. This criterion is still a principle of the form "you ought to x," which Julia happened to respect when interacting with Isaac. If this is so, then exemplary actions do not truly replace general principles in moral reasoning. In fact, these actions seem to be exemplary in the sense that they amount to particularly good applications of general moral principles. Kant (1996, 63) himself recognizes this point in the *Groundwork of the Metaphysics of Morals*:

> Nor could one give worse advice to morality than by wanting to derive it from examples. For, every example of it represented to me must itself first be appraised in accordance with principles of morality, as to whether it is also worthy to serve as an original example, that is, as a model; it can by no means authoritatively provide the concept of morality.

Here, Kant is making a subtle but important point. Whichever action I consider to be an *exemplary action*, this action is an example of *something good*. According to Kant, this "something good" is derived from the principles of morality. If Achilles's actions or Julia's actions did not amount to applications of moral principles, then they would not truly be exemplary actions. In the end, actions are only exemplary insofar as they comply with the demands of morality.

To see this, consider a second example. Imagine that nineteen-year-old Tyrone deeply admires his best friend Jake, who is quite skilled at seducing women. When Jake flirts with women, he often feigns interests in what they have to say, and this works well for him. Tyrone is amazed at the effectiveness of Jake's strategy. "I want to be more like Jake," he often thinks to himself. In this case, Jake's behaviour is sexist and deceitful. Instead of treating women with respect by engaging in real conversation with them, he manipulates them into thinking that he is someone who he is not (that is, someone who is actually interested in what women have to say). In other words, Jake treats women as objects of sexual gratification as opposed to equal subjects. This is hardly surprising. In contemporary culture, treating women as semi-rational beings that can be tricked into sleeping with you is often portrayed as something that "real men" do or, at least, as a morally permissible move in the game of seduction.

Beyond "Don't be like Jake," the point of this second example is that exemplary validity can easily lead people astray. When Tyrone thinks, "I want to be more like Jake," he is making a moral mistake. Now, imagine that you have to convince Tyrone that he should not attempt to be more like Jake. It is unlikely that you would successfully do so without engaging in moral discourse and using concepts such as "respect," "deceit," "manipulation" and "equality." For instance, you might tell Jake that he should treat women with equal respect. If you do so, then it seems that you are appealing to a general moral principle. In fact, it seems that we *must* appeal to general moral principles to determine whether actions truly are exemplary. From a moral point of view, we cannot live well by simply thinking "be more like Julia" or "be less like Jake." Instead, we need to take moral reflection one step further and have thoughts such as "be a person who respects principle p."

Let us direct a final objection against Arendt's remarks on exemplary validity. Simply put, it is far from obvious that a theory of judgement based on this concept is any more action guiding than one based on general moral principles. Certainly, moral agents can observe the actions of people they admire and try to imitate them. They can think things like, "Courage is like Achilles," or "Love and respect are like Julia." Yet being more like Achilles or Julia is not a simple task. After all, my own life is singular and the situations in which I find myself are not the same as the ones they faced. If I choose to be more like them, I will therefore have to ask myself questions such as, "What would Julia do in *this* situation in which I find myself?" However, my answer to this question will often be "I don't know!" Even if they know them quite well, there are myriad situations in which moral agents will be unable to tell how the people they admire would react if they were in their place. I do not know what Julia would do, for instance, if she taught university courses as I do and had to react to a student who just made a very inappropriate comment in class. In this case, it might make more sense for me to reflect upon how my best colleagues (instead of Julia) would handle this situation, but the answer to this question might still elude me. As professors know all too well, they only have a few seconds to respond to inappropriate comments during a class meeting. With regard to time, asking themselves, "What would person x do?" might not be the best strategy. Nevertheless, the important point is that determining how I can be more like people I admire in *such* or *such* situation is as hard—if not harder—than following general moral principles such as "Always tell the truth!" or "Treat others with respect!" If this is so, then Arendt's thought does not allow us to answer the neo-Aristotelian objection according to which Kantian theories of moral judgement are too imprecise to guide action. In my view, this can be explained by the fact that, as a political theorist, Arendt was always more interested in reflecting upon *thought* than upon *action*. To be fair, this might be because she did not have time to write *Judging* before her death. As for her remarks on enlarged mentality, *sensus communis* and exemplary validity, their primary aim is not to shed light on real-time moral deliberation. By her own admission, the maxim of enlarged mentality is one that can be followed by *spectators* who evaluate actions as opposed to *actors* who must perform them. As she explains, the standpoint of enlarged mentality is:

> A viewpoint from which to look upon, to watch, to form judgments, or, as Kant himself says, to reflect upon human affairs. *It does not tell one how to act*. It does not even tell one how to apply the wisdom, found by virtue of occupying a "general standpoint," to the particulars of political life. (Arendt 1992, 44)

This is an interesting claim, but I always found it puzzling. While Arendt may be right that Kant did not develop a theory of moral deliberation in his *Critique of the Power of Judgement*, he very clearly did so in other works. For instance, the *Metaphysics of Morals* contain some of Kant's most important remarks on the nature of moral judgement. For this reason, it remains hard not to question Arendt's methodological decision to build a Kantian theory of judgement out of a book devoted to aesthetics and teleology. By way of contrast, Anglo-American Kantians such as Onora O'Neill, Barbara Herman and Nancy Sherman all argue that Kant's theory of moral deliberation is mainly contained in his *Doctrine of Virtue*. Let us then see how.

MORAL DELIBERATION AND IMPERFECT DUTIES IN KANT'S *DOCTRINE OF VIRTUE*

In spite of the objections formulated above, one of Arendt's major accomplishments is to have drawn our attention to the role that reflective judgement plays in moral deliberation. Remember that Kant conceives of *Urteilskraft* as the faculty for subsumption of the particular under the universal. More precisely, Kant believes that all acts of subsumption can be *determining* or *reflective*. In the case of determining judgements, the universal is given, and the task of judgement is to find a particular which can be subsumed under it. For instance, your judgement will be determining if I present to you a general rule like the formula of universal law and your task is to find a particular action which conforms to it. In the case of reflective judgement, however, a particular is given and the task of judgement is to find a universal under which it can be subsumed. Now, Arendt's remarks help us see that reflective judgements play a central role in our daily moral experience in at least three ways. First, when we face a difficult moral decision, we envision the situation in which we find ourselves as a *hard case*, that is, as a situation in which we will need to deliberate as the best course of action is not at all obvious. As Otfried Höffe (1990) points out, reflective judgement is already at play when we do so. Indeed, conceptualizing *this* situation as belonging to the *kind* of situations which require deliberation amounts to subsuming a particular (i.e., *this* situation) under a universal (i.e., the kind of situation which amounts to a hard moral case). Second, reflective judgement is also at play when we reflect upon which moral principles apply to the situation in which we find ourselves. Consider Peter Singer's (1972) famous drowning child scenario and imagine that you encounter a child which appears to be drowning in a pond while you are on your way to work. Hopefully, you will understand that your moral duty is to rescue the child. If you do so, then you have recognized this situation as one in which your duties to help others (or "duties of beneficence") apply. In other words, this situation represents an *occasion* for you to help others. Once again, this amounts to making a reflective judgement. When you decide to help the child, you conceive of a particular situation as belonging to the kind of situation in which *such* or *such* moral duty comes into play. Not all situations belong to this kind. In many cases, there is no real risk for us to fail to fulfill our duties of beneficence to the same extent, for instance when we sit alone at home reading. When we interact with others as we often do, however, things are more complicated.[10] Lastly, when duties conflict, we must also decide which duty should have priority over others. In such cases, reflective judgement is once again at play. When I decide to give money to charity instead of repaying my debts, for instance, I conceptualize the case at hand as one in which my duties of beneficence take priority over my duties of fidelity. This still amounts to subsuming a particular (*this* situation) under a universal (this *kind* of situation in which this duty should take priority).

Of course, conceptualizing situations as hard moral cases or as ones in which a given duty takes priority over others is not all there is to moral judgement. Whenever I decide to fulfill a moral duty, I must still choose between many possible courses of actions that will allow me to do so. When I encounter a drowning child on my way to the office, for instance, I must decide whether I should immediately jump in the pond or call emergency services first. Now, that some cognitive tasks involved in moral deliberation are *not* reflective judgements incites neo-Aristotelian philosophers to argue that, contrary to Arendt's suggestion, *phronesis* is not the same as *Urteilskraft*. Even if we grant Kantians that the latter allows moral agents to correctly categorize situations, virtuous agents must possess the former to choose the best possible course of action amongst a set of possible ones. As we have seen in the last chapter, however, one disadvantage of the neo-Aristotelian discourse about practical wisdom is that it remains quite vague. Neo-Aristotelians are quick to explain what *phronesis* is, but not so quick at telling us who are the practically wise. To agree that *such* or *such* person is practically wise, we must first agree that this person frequently acts in the best way possible when they face difficult moral decisions. Yet, to agree about this, we must also agree on the course of action which counts as the best possible one. In other words, it seems that agreeing on best possible courses of action is a precondition of identifying the practically wise. If this so, then claiming—as neo-Aristotelians often do—that good moral actions are those committed by the practically wise amounts to putting the cart before the horse.

For this reason, many contemporary Kantian philosophers have deliberately avoided developing a theory of moral judgement which relies on the concept of practical wisdom. Yet some of them agree with neo-Aristotelians that filling the gap between principles and actions is an important philosophical task. For instance, Onora O'Neill (2001, 5) underlines that:

> The ethical principles that received most attention are highly indeterminate rather than quasi-algorithmic. They may constrain but do not regiment action; they are more likely to recommend types of action, policy, and attitude than to offer detailed instructions for living.

One possible way to fill this gap amounts to developing a Kantian version of the neo-Aristotelian discourse on *phronesis*. Like neo-Aristotelians contend that some moral agents possess the virtue of practical wisdom, Kantians could argue that people who act rightly are endowed with a sophisticated *Urteilskraft*. As we have seen, Arendt herself chooses this option when she compares *Urteilskraft* to Aristotelian practical wisdom. That said, the Kantian discourse on *Urteilskraft* poses the same inconveniences as the neo-Aristotelian discourse on *phronesis*. The idea that some moral agents possess a more sophisticated *Urteilskraft* than others is equally vague as the neo-Aristotelian claim that practically wise agents simply *see* what the best course of action is when they face difficult decisions. As I have argued above, identifying practically wise agents—those who possess practical wisdom or a sophisticated power of judgement—also seems to presuppose that we can agree on what counts as the best possible course of action.

For her part, O'Neill believes that building on the Kantian concept of *Urteilskraft* amounts to taking the wrong philosophical path. In fact, she criticizes Arendt for confusing moral judgement with reflective judgment. As we have seen, reflective judgement is a mental operation which allows agents to categorize the case at hand as (i) one that requires deliberation and (ii) one in which specific moral duties come into play. Once this is done, moral agents still need to determine how, precisely, they ought to act, and this does not amount to finding a universal under which a particular can be subsumed. When they engage in moral deliberation, moral agents do not already know what particular action they ought to commit (or else there would be no need to deliberate in the first place). Such an action is not given, but it must be found. In O'Neill's view (2007, 404), this warrants the conclusion that moral judgements—ones through which agents decide to commit *this* action instead of another—are not reflective judgements:

> When we act we may as a preliminary matter have to decide how to view the situation in which we already find ourselves, and in which we seek to act: here reflective judgement may indeed be needed. But even when reflective judging is completed, and we have determined how to view the situation, we will still need to decide what to do: and that is where practical judgement does its work. A focus on reflective judging will not reveal [. . .] how practical judging works. (O'Neill 2007, 404)

Interestingly, O'Neill also avoids describing moral judgement as a cognitive operation through which moral agents *prioritize* certain duties over others. In her view, deliberation is best described as the task of identifying actions which allows *me* to simultaneously respect *all* of my duties. Let us say for instance that I promise to help you with your philosophy homework, and then do so. It seems that I have simultaneously respected my duty of beneficence and my duty of fidelity. Not only have I provided you with assistance, but I have also avoided breaking my promise. In this sense, "Practical judgement is an aspect of practical reasoning because it aims to *integrate* rather than to *prioritize* [. . .] a plurality of norms" (O'Neill 2007, 404).

This is an interesting suggestion, but it has some flaws. Certainly, morally best actions are often such that they allow us to respect all of our moral duties. As O'Neill points out, making good moral judgements is often akin to building a house. Like builders must ensure that the houses they build meet a multitude of construction standards, moral agents should take decisions which allow them to avoid flouting any moral duty which falls upon them. Yet, throughout this book, I have given several examples of situations in which moral duties conflict. When this happens, it will be impossible for moral agents to simultaneously respect all of their duties. In such cases, how should moral agents deliberate? One Anglo-American Kantian philosopher who has extensively reflected upon this question is Barbara Herman. In general, Herman's work aims to destroy two myths about Kant's practical philosophy. The first myth—*formalism*—amounts to the claim that Kant's thought solely contains moral principles which are too general to guide action. As we have seen, this myth is very popular amongst neo-Aristotelians. The second myth—*rigorism*—is the idea that Kantian duties are so strict that they do not provide moral agents with any leeway when they face difficult moral decisions (e.g., "Whatever you do, *never lie!*"). To help combat these myths, Herman (1993, 73) offers a "normative reconstruction of Kantian ethics" which directly addresses the neo-Aristotelian objections that I have examined in the first part of this book. In fact, Herman is perhaps the contemporary Kantian philosopher whose work has been the most influenced by these objections. In her view, "The pressures on Kantian moral theory arising from the challenges of the virtue theorists have been entirely salutary" (Herman 2007, 28).

According to Herman, one important lesson that can be drawn from the neo-Aristotelian critique of Kantian models of moral judgement is that good moral deliberation is made possible through moral education. To see this, consider Herman's response to the problem of the tailoring of maxims which famously plagues Kant's formula of universal law.[11] In a nutshell, one serious objection against Kant's universalization test amounts to the claim that agents can tailor the maxims that they submit to it in order to justify acting as they please. For instance, if I realize that the maxim "I will always lie to get out of trouble" cannot become a universal law and cannot be universalized. I can still reformulate this maxim in a way that will make it seemingly acceptable for me to lie *in certain cases*. Let us say that I lie to my best friend by telling him that his hideous new pants look really good on him. Then, I can easily justify my action by telling myself (or others) that the maxim on which I act is not "I will always lie when this gets me out of trouble" but rather "I will only lie to my best friend when he asks me about his hideous new pants." Although a world in which all people lie to get out of trouble would be worse than the one in which we currently live, a world in which people only lie to their best friends about the look of their new pants is arguably not. Of course, the problem of the tailoring of maxims does not solely apply to lies which relate to fashion or aesthetics. The worry is rather that, whenever an agent is presented with the idea that "φ-ing" is wrong, they will be able to justify φ-ing by claiming that the maxim of their action is not "I will φ," but "I will only φ *in these very specific circumstances.*"

In response to this problem, Herman argues that moral agents do not possess an innate capacity to formulate adequate maxims for their actions. According to her perspective, neo-Aristotelians are right to argue that this capacity is acquired through moral education. More precisely, Herman contends that education allows people to learn what she calls rules of moral salience, which enable agents to distinguish between morally relevant and morally irrelevant features of situations.[12] Consider the example discussed above once more. When I lie to my friend about the look of his new pants, the fact that I am lying to a friend is morally relevant. Strong friendships are based on honesty and trust and, as a result, my choice to hide the truth undercuts the bond that unites us. If I understand this point but still choose to lie, I prioritize the avoidance of embarrassment or awkwardness over the protection of our friendship. The maxim of my action resembles the following: "I will lie to my close friends to avoid embarrassment even if this damages our friendship." This maxim is not truly universalizable, and in a Kantian perspective, acting on it is morally wrong.[13] Now, the difference between the situation in which I tell myself that "I will only lie to my best friend when he asks me about his hideous new pants" and the one in which I realize that it is wrong to damage friendships to avoid embarrassment is but a shift of perspective. In other words, recognizing the maxim on which I truly act is essentially a matter of *moral perception*, or so Herman argues. In her view, Kantians can perfectly accommodate this neo-Aristotelian idea:

> Those who have emphasized the importance of perception relative to matters of principle and moral decision-making have been right to do so. I think they have not seen the place of moral perception in Kantian ethics because they have assumed that all of the Kantian agent's moral knowledge resides in rules of duty or in the CI. (Herman 1993, 83)

To correct this misperception, Herman underlines that moral perception plays a central role in moral reasoning *before deliberation happens*. In fact, it amounts to a pre-deliberative moral knowledge which helps moral agents grasp the relevant features of the case at hand and formulate maxims that will then be submitted to the universalization test. When maxims pass this test, they become what Herman names *deliberative presumptions*. For instance, if I find that the maxim "I will always keep my promises" is universalizable, then this provides me with a moral reason to keep my promises. That said, deliberative presumptions are not deliberative conclusions. The fact that there is a deliberative presumption in favour of keeping my promises does not mean that I should never break them. According to Herman's interpretation (1993, 148), indeed, the categorical imperative is a procedure which constrains moral deliberation by providing moral agents with *pro tanto* reasons to commit certain actions and refrain from performing others, but a deliberative presumption can still "be rebutted by reasons [. . .] of a different sort."

Imagine that I find myself in a situation in which I consider that I should break one of my promises. To consider that it is morally permissible for me to do so, I must establish whether the deliberative presumption in favour of keeping one's promises is overridden by other considerations. For example, if breaking a promise enables me to assist someone who urgently needs my help, then I can arguably justify my decision to depart from the moral principle according to which I should never break my promises. Herman (1993, 149) provides us with a useful example to illustrate this claim:

> Let me give you an example. In order to help A, who is my friend, I must make a deceitful promise to B. Suppose there is a deliberative presumption against deceitful promising in pursuit of one's interests per se [. . .] But if the deception of B were for the purpose of saving A's life, something of value independent of its value to me (say because saving A's life is called for by duty of mutual aid), then there is a legitimate deliberative question.

Herman's concept of deliberative presumption enables her to avoid rigorism. If the Categorical Imperative only grounds deliberative presumptions, there is still room for deliberation once moral agents know whether a particular maxim passes the universalization test. As we have seen, the fact that a particular maxim passes this test does not entail that it should *always* be followed. Yet, I worry that Herman's theory of deliberation will not satisfy neo-Aristotelians who press the objection of formalism against Kantians. When deliberative presumptions compete with one another, moral agents might reasonably disagree about how they ought to act. Consider once more the example in which I consider lying to my best friend about the look of his new pants. As mentioned above, I personally believe that doing so would be a moral mistake as even benign lies have the capacity the undercut the bonds of trust which make friendship possible. In this scenario, I consider that the deliberative presumption against lying is not overridden by other moral considerations. Yet it would also be unreasonable for me not to engage with the views and arguments of those who believe that it is in fact morally acceptable to lie to your best friend about the look of his new pants. Indeed, I can easily imagine a serious and sincere interlocutor who would grant me the claim that repeatedly lying to my friend would hurt our friendship, but still argue that one very specific benign lie will not negatively impact it in any way. Of course, things would be different if my friend asked me for my opinion about a more important matter (e.g., "Do you think that my current partner is the right person for me?"). In the ugly pants example, however, people might weight moral reasons differently. If this is so, neo-Aristotelians will be quick to argue that Herman's theory of deliberation does not provide us with a procedure that clearly allows us to determine if a given deliberative presumption is overridden by other considerations. As we have seen, they are also likely to argue that only agents who have acquired the virtues will properly weigh deliberative presumptions against other moral reasons.

Interestingly, Kantian theories of deliberation which provide moral agents with flexibility in judgement might not be incompatible with the neo-Aristotelian discourse on *phronesis*. This is one of the central conclusions drawn by Nancy Sherman, who argues that we should make room for practical wisdom in Kantian ethics. Specifically, Sherman (1997) contends that Kant was well aware of the problem of indeterminacy in the application of moral principles and, like Aristotle, understood that identifying the best possible course of action in a given situation is often a difficult enterprise. This is especially clear when Kant discusses imperfect duties in the *Doctrine of Virtue*. There, he writes:

> If the law can prescribe only the maxim of actions, not actions themselves, this is a sign that it leaves a playroom (*latitudo*) for free choice in following (complying with) the law, that is, that the law cannot specify precisely in what way one is to act and how much one is to do by the action for an end that is also a duty. (Kant 1996, 521)

According to Sherman, these remarks relate to Aristotle's thoughts on practical wisdom. If, as Kant explains, the moral "law cannot specify *precisely* in what way one is to act," then moral agents will have to rely on their own judgement to take good decisions. What is more, this passage allows us to conceive of a Kantian version of Aristotle's practical syllogism. First, moral agents formulate the first premise of their practical reasoning by determining the general aim of their action (e.g., "I will fulfill my duty of beneficence by helping this person in distress"). Second, they formulate the second premise by identifying a particular action which allows them to fulfill this aim (e.g., "I will help this person by buying her a meal *hic et nunc*"). Importantly, Kant underlines that moral agents have some leeway when doing so. Certainly, there are many ways of helping people in distress, but choosing a particular way of helping others is at the helper's discretion within reasonable limits. Lastly, the third and final step of moral reasoning amounts to performing the action identified at the second step. Often, the justifiability of a particular action will depend on the agent's identity, capacity and needs. Aristotle (1984, 50–51) seemed to have had this idea in mind when he explained that the appropriateness of generous actions partly depends on the assets possessed by those who commit them. When the billionaires of Silicon Valley transfer assets to offshore accounts to avoid taxation, they act immorally by refusing to contribute to the common good. By way of contrast, no one should blame a single mother of three who recently lost her job for deciding not to give any money to charity this year. Interestingly, such an idea is also at the heart of Kant's philosophical reflection in the *Metaphysics of Morals*. Consider the following passage in which he discusses our duty to promote the happiness of others:

> I ought to sacrifice a part of my welfare to others without hope of return, because this is a duty, and it is impossible to assign determinate limits to the extent of this sacrifice. How far it should extend depends, in large part, on what each person's true needs are in view of his sensibilities, and it must be left to each to decide this for himself. (Kant 1996, 524)

Like Aristotle, Kant therefore defends the view that the rightness of actions depends on the situation in which those who perform them find themselves. He also suggests that no one can ultimately decide for us what actions we ought to commit. Our moral lives are complex, and they often require us to make judgement calls. This does not entail that moral theory cannot assist deliberation, but rather that the task of determining how moral principles should be applied to the case at hand is not itself a task that can be fulfilled by philosophers. When we face difficult moral decisions, we can refer to the insights of thinkers we admire or ask a friend for advice, but this does not relieve us from making our own decisions. After all, a suggestion made by a friend or a philosopher is still a suggestion that I am free to endorse or reject.

Having said this, some objections can be pressed against Sherman's claim that both Aristotle and Kant recognize that moral agents have some leeway when they must decide how they ought to act. First, as discussed in the last chapter, one important weakness of the neo-Aristotelian discourse on practical wisdom is its vagueness. Even if we accept that good decision-making is undergirded by *phronesis*, this view leaves some important questions about moral deliberation unanswered. Let us say that I ask you, "Why did you decide to act in this way?" Then, "I simply *saw* this was the right thing to do" is not a fully satisfying answer to my question. What I want to know is the reasons for which you think that it was right for you to act as you did. When we discuss morality with others, we usually demand sophisticated answers, and the claim that wise people possess some sort of moral vision which enables them to see things that we do not amounts to a refusal to provide us with such answers. When they emphasize Kant's remarks on leeway in judgement, are contemporary Kantians making the same mistake? One possible response to this objection amounts to the claim that Kant's thoughts on *latitudo* relate to freedom of choice more than to *phronesis*. Instead of arguing that, when moral agents face difficult moral decisions, only the wise will successfully identify the best possible course of action, Kantians can argue that there are in fact many excellent courses of action, and that agents remain free to choose one that suits them. This is an important point. When friends ask us for advice, we often think that there are myriad good ways for them to behave. For instance, imagine that a friend tells me that one of their closest relatives has died. How should I respond? Should I express empathy and tell them that I am available to talk whenever they feel the need to do so? Should I refrain from talking too much but do something which demonstrates that I care for them, perhaps by cooking them a meal or inviting them to spend a relaxing day by the Pacific Ocean in my company? Would it appropriate for me to cheer them up by attempting to make them laugh? Personally, I would not choose this last option, but I have friends who would. I have yet to master the art of making people laugh in challenging situations, but they have. This is not to say that their way of behaving is better or worse than mine; it simply makes sense for them to play to their strengths. In many cases, the best way to act depends on who you are, and what you do well. If we interpret them with charity, Kant's remarks on leeway remind us of this very idea.

A second possible objection to Sherman amounts to the claim Kant assign strict limits to *latitudo* by pointing out that agents should not use it to make exceptions to moral rules (e.g., "I will do my best to help others, just not *this* time"). Flexibility in judgement is only meant to "limit one maxim of duty by another" (Kant 1996, 521). Here, Kant's favoured example is that of a person who would limit "love of one's neighbour in general by love of one's parents." For instance, we can picture a person who tends to prioritize their duty to help members of their own family over their duty to help strangers. In this case, an agent allows themselves a margin of freedom when deciding how best to fulfill their duty of beneficence, but this is not the same as derogating from one's duty. While contemporary Kantians such as Herman or Sherman could easily accommodate this claim, Kant also stresses that not all duties count as "duties of wide obligation," that is, duties which provide moral agents with some flexibility in judgement when they seek to fulfill them. Only *imperfect* duties are of this kind. Beyond our duty to help and promote the happiness of others, the main example of an imperfect duty discussed by Kant in the *Metaphysics of Morals* is our duty to seek our own perfection by cultivating our natural talents. As he writes:

> This duty is a merely ethical one, that is, a duty of wide obligation. No rational principle prescribes specifically *how* far one should go in cultivating one's capacities (in enlarging or correcting one's capacity for understanding, i.e., in acquiring knowledge or skill). Then too, the different situations in which human beings may find themselves make a human being's choice of the occupation for which he should cultivate his talents very much a matter for him to decide as he chooses. (Kant 1996, 523)

By way of contrast, *perfect* duties—which include our duty never to lie—do not provide agents with the same leeway. Remember the case of the murderer at the door debated by Kant and Constant.[14] In short, Constant argues that we only have a duty to tell the truth to those who have a right to know the truth. Yet this excludes people who plan to use the truth to harm others. *Pace* Constant, Kant (1996, 613) argues that we have an unconditional duty—a "sacred command of reason"—never to lie. In other words, Kant considers that there is a wide range of duties which do not provide moral agents with any leeway when they reflect upon how they ought to act. Some rules of duty are unbendable, and Kant would presumably have rejected contemporary theories of moral deliberation which make too much of his own remarks on *latitudo*.

Unsurprisingly, the arguments put forward by Kant in his discussion of the case of the murderer at the door are often used by those who aim to show that his practical philosophy is misguided, and that orthodox Kantians who follow it strictly risk committing wrongful actions. During the Second World War, for instance, the consequences of systematically telling the truth to Nazi authorities were sometimes horrendous, and those who chose to do so arguably bear some responsibility for the Holocaust. Of course, we can only speculate about whether Kant himself would truly have condemned those who resisted genocide by hiding to truth from actual murderers. Some parts of his philosophy suggest that resistance to tyranny is in fact appropriate, and commentators have recently cast doubt on the traditional interpretation of his views on lying. For instance, Helga Varden (2010, 404) underlines that Nazi officers did not "represent a public authority on Kant's view and consequently there is no duty to abstain from lying to Nazis." Whether we side with Varden on this question, it is worth noting that contemporary Kantians are within their right to disagree with Kant that we ought never to lie and, more generally, that there are such things as perfect duties that leave no room for deliberation. In fact, there is little doubt that they in fact do. Building on Herman's proposed theory of deliberation, Sherman (1997, 321) writes that "a sympathetic interpretation [of the *Doctrine of Virtue*] would want to restore the lying prohibition to the status of a deliberative *presumption* rather than an absolute norm." Such a remark illustrates that building a contemporary Kantian theory of deliberation often comes at a historical cost. To avoid the rigorism objection, indeed, contemporary Kantians like Herman and Sherman must distance themselves from Kant's own claims in the *Metaphysics of Morals* and envision *all* Kantian duties as imperfect ones. If they do so, then they can argue that all duties only ground deliberative presumptions which can be overridden by other moral considerations in certain cases. From the point of view of contemporary moral theory, this is a viable strategy albeit one that clearly shows that contemporary Kantians have been moved by neo-Aristotelian objections. By paying attention to neo-Aristotelian virtue ethics, both Herman and Sherman saw the need to develop an unorthodox Kantian theory of deliberation according to which there are no such things as exceptionless moral principles. Within such theory, there might even be room for a contemporary Kantian virtue ethics.

Chapter 8

Kantian Virtues

How do people become competent moral agents? As we have seen, neo-Aristotelians argue that people do so by acquiring the virtues. They also argue that Kantians neglect this fact and, as a result, lack a satisfying theory of moral development. More precisely, this objection is twofold. First, some neo-Aristotelians argue that contemporary Kantians neglect the long process of socialization and education which provides moral agent with the capacity to make good judgements. Since the development of a person's capacity to take good decisions largely depends on the social environment in which they live, neo-Aristotelians emphasize, any theory of moral judgement should contain some insights about the type of training which enables them to do so. Perhaps unsurprisingly, many contemporary Kantians agree with this neo-Aristotelian claim. This is undoubtedly the case with Barbara Herman, who underlines (2007, 1) that neo-Aristotelian virtue ethicists have rightly argued that "the conditions for moral judgment involve the complexities of a developed moral character." The second part of the neo-Aristotelian objection I wish to examine in this chapter directly relates to the first. It amounts to the claim that neglecting education leads Kantians to oversee the need for agents to acquire moral virtues. Without acquiring these virtues, the objection goes, agents will be unable to feel the right emotions and grasp all relevant moral reasons. According to Rosalind Hursthouse (2001, 119), for instance:

> Where Aristotle, and thereby the Aristotelians, have an edge over Kant (and, indeed, Hume) with respect to the moral significance of the emotions is in the account Aristotle gives us of human rationality, an account that allows the emotions to participate in reason and thereby play their proper role in the specification of full virtue.

Do contemporary Kantians truly neglect moral education and the virtues? This is not so. As some historians of philosophy have pointed out, Kant himself wrote extensively about moral education, and contemporary Kantians often inherit his views about this topic (Sticker 2015). In fact, many contemporary Kantians have taken up the challenge of developing a Kantian theory of moral education—sometimes even a Kantian virtue ethics—which complements their conception of moral deliberation. In what follows, I assess attempts to do so by examining the claims of three philosophers whose work I have begun to discuss in the previous chapter: Barbara Herman, Nancy Sherman and Onora O'Neill. My central suggestion is that Kantian contributions to virtue theory are more significant than neo-Aristotelians customarily assume, and that the role played by virtues in reasoning can be accommodated within a Kantian theory of moral judgement. Contrary to Hursthouse, contemporary Kantians do not frown upon the participation of emotions in moral reasoning. They also allow emotions to participate in moral reasoning and their work is perfectly compatible with the claim that virtues support moral agents' ability to make good judgements by helping them grasp reasons for actions.

MORAL LITERACY AND AUTONOMOUS JUDGEMENT

Perhaps the most exhaustive attempt to develop a Kantian theory of moral education is that of Barbara Herman (2007, 106), who generally contends that Kantians are in a better position than neo-Aristotelians to explain how moral agents come to appreciate what she dubs "new moral facts." Before I turn to this concept, some remarks are in order. Herman explains that the first step moral education is that through which agents develop *moral literacy*. At this stage, moral agents come to understand that persons have a different moral status than inanimate things. Like all forms of literacy, the development of this capacity is not the result of normal physiological growth, but of socialization. Specifically, the transmission of moral literacy to young members of a community involves a deliberate effort on the part of older members to help the former understand that people have moral worth. When successful, it provokes a shift in perspective through which young moral agents actively use their cognitive capacities by thinking things such as "you have moral interests like I do" and "your moral interests are equally worthy as mine." Accordingly, it leads young agents to attribute dignity to other human beings on their own accord. For example, instead of systematically prioritizing their interests over that of others, moral agents begin treating others in the same way as they would like to be treated themselves. In Herman's view, moral literacy cannot be acquired through a system of rewards and punishment. It is not the result of behavioural conditioning, but of a conceptual educational process through which people come to freely choose to act on a particular set of maxims (e.g., "I will treat you the same as all other moral agents"). As Kant (2007, 468) explains in his *Lectures on Pedagogy*:

> Moral culture must be based on maxims, not on discipline. The latter prevents bad habits, the former forms the way of thinking. One must see to it that the child accustoms itself to act according to maxims and not according to certain incentives. Discipline leaves us only with a habit, which, after all, fades away over the years. The child should learn to act according to maxims whose fairness it itself understands.

Now, one possible objection to Herman's discourse on moral literacy is that this rudimentary form of moral education is unlikely to be sufficient for agents to make the best possible decisions when they face difficult moral decisions. This leads Herman to argue that moral literacy must be complemented by a second type of moral education through which agents learn rules of moral salience, a concept which I introduced in the previous chapter. While moral literacy incites agents to attribute equal moral worth to all human beings, rules of moral salience help them understand how they can fall short of their moral obligations in concrete situations. For instance, a moral agent who has mastered these rules will understand that not helping someone in distress amounts to failing to meet their duty of beneficence. Mastering rules of moral salience provides agents with a pre-deliberative intelligence that enables them to identify moral risks. If I know that lying is wrong and also recognize the situation in which I find myself as one in which it would be easiest for me to lie, then my moral radar will alert me to the fact that I must resist the urge to follow my inclination to lie. In this sense, "rules of moral salience constitute the structure of moral sensitivity" (Herman 1993, 78). When they are well internalized, "they cause the agent to be aware and attentive to the significance of 'moral danger.'"

Once they have developed moral literacy and mastered rules of moral salience, moral agents must learn to deliberate per se. This requires them to correctly prioritize some of their duties over others in case of conflict. Simply put, the properly educated agent usually knows when it is best to derogate from one duty to better satisfy another. As we have seen in the last chapter, this is not a simple task, and some contemporary Kantians grant some leeway to moral agents when it comes to deciding how precisely they ought to act to fulfill one or multiple obligations at the same time. Yet even moral agents who have gone through a complex educational process sometimes make mistakes. To see this, let us now return to the concept of new moral fact. According to Herman perspective, failing to grasp new moral facts is an important way in which agents make moral mistakes. As she explains (2007, 220):

> We expect a normal, or morally literate agent to be able to [. . .] respond to the moral facts of her world accurately. Access to the rationale of moral rules allows for the exercise of moral intelligence, giving an agent control over judgment and

a wider range of read and response. This is moral character working well. It may not, however, be enough to cope with new moral facts.

New moral facts are not an ontologically distinct class of facts, but normal facts of special moral significance. One subcategory of these are morally significant historical facts; for instance, political upheavals which abruptly interrupt the ordinary life of citizens and place new moral demands on them. One of Herman's favourite examples of a new moral fact is the end of the apartheid regime in South Africa, which raised the question of knowing how South Africans should reckon with their country's racist history. To do so, the South African people created a Truth and Reconciliation Commission the members of which shed light on past crimes, punished perpetrators, and provided reparations to victims. In Herman's view, this counts as a successful response to a new moral fact. An unjust regime ended, and South Africans seized the opportunity to account for injustice. However, we should also not underestimate how difficult it is for people to adequately respond to new moral facts. Keeping the example of racial segregation and oppression in mind, it is fair to say that many countries are still struggling to repair past injustices. By way of example, in 2021, the unmarked graves and more than a thousand indigenous children were found in my own country of Canada. Undoubtedly, this also counts as a new moral fact, that is, one which places new moral demands on the Canadian people. Whether Canadians will fulfill their moral obligation to repair historical wrongs by actively working towards indigenous self-determination remains to be seen, but indigenous thinkers have repeatedly criticized the Canadian government for celebrating the culture of First Nations without granting them political sovereignty (Coulthard 2014).

Herman also believes that philosophy has an important role to play in our collective response to new moral facts. Indeed, philosophical reflection has the power to shed a novel light on the status quo and transform "old" facts into new moral ones. In certain cases, the status quo is not upended by sudden historical change as was the case in the apartheid example, but by a philosophical reinterpretation of current social and political institutions. Like historical events, this reinterpretation sometimes places new moral demands on people. Here, let us take the example of feminist philosophers who have helped reveal that actions and discourses which were long envisioned as morally acceptable unjustly reinforce gender oppression. In the 1990s, feminist philosophers of language drew attention to the fact that pornography silences women by repeatedly portraying them as enjoying non-consensual sex (Langton 1993). Their reasoning is as follows: in many pornographical films, women initially refuse sexual advances, engage in sex nevertheless, and are then depicted as enjoying it. In real life, "no" always mean no, but in pornography, "no" often ends up meaning "yes." As a result, feminist philosophers argue that pornography weakens women's power to refuse sex in real life by making their utterances less effective. When men flirt with them, the former wrongly expect the later to eventually agree to sex even if they said "no" in the first place. Note that in this case, facts remain the same. Pornography is still widely available, and the depiction of women in pornographical films has not changed. Still, feminist philosophers have proposed a new interpretation of old facts. If we accept the preceding argument, this interpretation places new moral demands on us. Without condemning all forms of pornography, it seems morally right to avoid portraying women as enjoying unwanted sexual relations in works of fiction as this disempowers them in the real world.

These considerations lead Herman to object to neo-Aristotelian approaches to moral judgement. As we have seen in previous chapters, many neo-Aristotelians ground judgement in traditional norms. By doing so, Herman contends, they neglect the fact that political upheavals or shifts in perspective sometimes bring about a change in these norms. When this happens, moral agents lose the guidelines on which they previously relied to make decisions.[1] Then, they must engage in what Herman calls "moral improvisation." When South Africans decided to create the Truth and Reconciliation Commission, they did not merely rely on traditional norms (i.e., those that were socially dominant during apartheid). Instead, they had to move beyond such norms and ask themselves, "Given that previous traditional norms were oppressive and unjust, how should we act now?" Given that they tend to emphasize the value of communal norms, neo-Aristotelian traditionalists are ill-equipped to answer this question, or so Herman argues. As we have seen throughout this book, one of the most frequent objections directed by contemporary Kantians against neo-Aristotelians like Gadamer and MacIntyre amounts to the claim that only universalist moral theories have the power to protect agents from being complicit in historical injustice. This is because respecting traditions might lead moral agents to embrace social conservatism at a time when political transformations are needed, as was the case during apartheid. In a Kantian perspective, moral agents cannot live a good life without examining the value of social norms they have been encouraged to follow by relying on universal moral principles. For this reason, contemporary Kantians like Herman underline that moral education must ultimately be an education to autonomy, one which culminates in the acquisition of an ability to question traditional norms.[2] In fact, some Kantians go as far as describing Kantianism as a "radical ethics of permanent revolution with respect to social custom" (Wood 2011, 87). Undoubtedly, Herman subscribes to this anti-conservative conception of moral education which seeks to elevate agents to universality. Often, adequately responding to new moral facts requires agents to reject traditional norms on the grounds that these are incompatible with morality and justice as such.

To be fair to neo-Aristotelians, Herman's theory of moral education is sometimes imprecise. While its goals are quite clear, it remains hard to understand how, precisely, we can ensure that young moral agents will reach them. Granted, most people acquire moral literacy—the ability to pay attention to the interests of others—by adulthood, and usually much sooner. Yet how do people develop the capacity to respond to new moral facts while others do not? Does it suffice for moral educators to emphasize the importance of questioning the status quo in light of universal moral ideals? What makes it so that some people end up being complicit in historical injustice, and what pedagogical techniques (if any) can prevent this from happening? It may be that I am asking too much of a moral philosopher. In fact, I doubt that philosophers can successfully answer these questions without relying on empirical research. Yet Herman could at least explain—like neo-Aristotelians do—which character traits we should encourage moral agents to develop to minimize the likelihood that they will act wrongly. Of course, it remains possible to imagine what character traits Herman hopes that moral agents will acquire. Arguably, resisting historical injustice requires courage, empathy and a strong sense of justice. Nevertheless, some contemporary Kantians like Onora O'Neill and Nancy Sherman go much further than Herman on the neo-Aristotelian path to virtue theory. Specifically, they propose a Kantian virtue ethics which fulfills a similar function to that put forward by neo-Aristotelians. In addition to discussing the goals of moral education, they attempt to identify characterological dispositions that agents must develop if they are to reach these goals. Unsurprisingly, their reflection begins with an examination of the Kantian concept of virtue (*Tugend*) which I briefly examine in the following section.

KANT ON VIRTUE

Philosophers who wish to develop a Kantian virtue ethics must overcome a historiographical challenge. Throughout his life, Kant formulated several objections against ancient virtue ethics, and one could therefore argue that the project of developing a virtue ethics is decisively not Kantian in spirit. I propose the following reconstruction of Kant's critique of virtue, which is based on five claims.

(i) *The value of virtues depends on an agent's will.* In the first section of the *Groundwork for the Metaphysics of Morals*, Kant (1996, 49) famously argues that nothing can "be considered good without limitation except a good will." This remark is meant as an objection to virtue theories who emphasize the improvement of "talents of mind" or "qualities of temperament" without consideration for the moral law (50). "However unconditionally they were praised by the ancients," Kant explains, virtues like moderation and self-control are bad when they are not accompanied by the will to obey the moral law for they can easily be put to the service of evil ends. When agents pursue bad ends, we would prefer that they did not possess character traits which make it easier for them to do so. As Kant writes, "The coolness of a scoundrel makes him not only far more dangerous but also immediately more abominable in our eyes than we would have taken him to be without it." In a nutshell, virtues only have an instrumental value, not an intrinsic one.

(ii) *Eudemonistic virtues ethics rest on a contradiction.* In the *Doctrine of Virtue*, Kant further argues that practical philosophies centred on the concept of happiness (*eudaimonia*) often contain two contradictory claims. The first claim is that the central aim of the virtuous agent's actions is to reach happiness. As he explains (1996, 511), "The concept of duty does not determine his will *directly*," but "he is moved to do his duty only *by means of* the happiness he anticipates." The second claim is that happiness must be conceived of as a reward for good actions that virtuous agents commit for their own sake. Now, why does Kant consider that these two claims are contradictory? While the first claim suggests that virtuous agents act rightly because it will make them happy, the second implies that they perform good actions for their own sake (i.e., regardless of the effect that doing so will have on them). Yet both theses cannot be true at the same time (or so does Kant think):

> For on the one hand he ought to fulfill his duty without first asking what effect this will have on his happiness, and so on *moral* grounds; but on the other hand he can recognize that something is his duty only by whether he can count on gaining happiness by doing it, and so in accordance with a *pathological* principle, which is the direct opposite of the moral principle. (Kant 1996, 511)³

(iii) *Virtue is not a habit.* In book II of the *Nicomachean Ethics*, Aristotle explains that virtue is the result of habituation. Without explicitly mentioning the Stagirite, Kant takes issue with this claim in his *Doctrine of Virtue*. His worry is that portraying virtue as a habit will incite us to envision good agents as being fundamentally unreflective, that is, as people who do not make free and conscious decisions to act rightly. Specifically, Kant contends that, once it has become a habit, virtue is no longer a free aptitude. Yet aptitudes which are not free are not *moral* aptitudes proper:

> An *aptitude (habitus)* is a facility in acting and a subjective perfection of *choice.*—But not every such *facility* is a *free* aptitude *(habitus libertatis);* for if it is a *habit (assuetudo),* that is, a uniformity in action that has become a *necessity*

through frequent repetition, it is not one that proceeds from freedom, and therefore not a moral aptitude. Hence virtue cannot be *defined* as an aptitude for free actions. (Kant 1996, 535)

In Kant's view, people who act rightly do not do so out of habit, but out of a deliberate and reflective choice to fulfill their moral obligations. If one insists on defining virtue as a habit, then one should define it as the habit "to determine oneself to act through the thought of the law." In other words, Kant fears that representing virtuous agents as people who are habituated to act well will lead us to wrongly believe that people can act rightly without consciously thinking about the moral law and the duties it entails.

(iv) *Virtue is not a mean between extremes*. There is at least one objection that Kant explicitly directs against Aristotle in his *Metaphysics of Morals*: that according to which Aristotle's claim that virtue is a mean between two extremes is uninformative. In an Aristotelian perspective, acting rightly is matter of avoiding doing too little or too much of something, but such a thought is of no assistance to moral agents who must decide how they ought to act:

The proposition, one ought not to do too much or too little of anything, says in effect nothing, since it is a tautology. What does it mean "to do too much"? Answer: to do more than is good. What does it mean "to do too little"? Answer: to do less than is good. (Kant 1996, 556)

Here, Kant appears to worry that Aristotle and his followers argue in a circular manner. Let us picture a moral agent who aims to act courageously. To do so, they ask a virtuous person for advice. "Which actions count as courageous?" the agent asks. The virtuous person then replies: "Courageous actions are those that are neither timid nor reckless." "But which actions count as timid or reckless?" the agent continues. "Those that are not courageous," the virtuous person responds. Until the virtuous person gives a concrete example of an action which counts as timid, reckless or courageous, the agent who seeks to act courageously will not be able to take their advice. To help others act rightly, one cannot merely define "good" as a mean between two extremes, and then refuse to give any example of good or extreme actions.

(v) *Perfect virtue is an unattainable ideal.* Strictly speaking, this claim is not an objection directed by Kant against ancient virtue ethics, but it nonetheless marks an important difference between Aristotle and Kant's practical philosophies. Contrary to Aristotle, Kant believes that moral agents cannot become fully virtuous. As he writes (1996, 537), virtue "is always in progress because, considered objectively, it is an ideal and unattainable." In fact, acquiring it "surpasses man's power" (1996, 556). Accordingly, perfect virtue is not a requirement of good action, but an elusive standard that moral agents have a duty to approximate.

Now, some contemporary Kantians agree with Kant's criticism of ancient virtue ethics, but are still inclined to draw parallels between Aristotle's and Kant's moral philosophies. In their view, there exists an important similarity between Kant's claim that moral agents must willingly subordinate their inclinations to the moral law and the ancient Greek picture of virtuous people whose behaviour is steered by the rational part of their soul (as opposed to the desiring part). Here, the idea at play is that Kant and Aristotle share a common conception of the relationship between reason and emotions. Like the latter, the former believes that moral agents will systematically fail to fulfill their duty unless they have cultivated emotional dispositions which enable them to act rightly. According to both philosophers, people become virtuous by taming their inclinations through an education of their sentiments (Sherman 1997, 175).

To assess the plausibility of these claims, it will help to first clarify the meaning of "virtue" (Tugend) as Kant uses this concept throughout his works of moral philosophy. Note first that Kant usually speaks of "virtue" in the singular form and defines this term as "the moral strength of a human being's will in fulfilling his duty" (1996, 533). From a philosophical point of view, there is but one virtue, which amounts to "moral strength of one's maxims" (567). Yet, from a practical point of view, we can conceive of a multitude of virtues and vices like ancient Greek philosophers did (courage, moderation, wisdom, etc.). As for Kant's conception of the relationship between virtue and emotions, it remains hard to pin down. According to one reading, virtuous actions do not involve the emotions. While people who act on their inclinations are swayed by their emotions, those who act from duty are moved by reason alone. On this picture, people who act rightly do not follow a *desire* to do so, but rather understand that they ought to do so through a representation of the moral law which itself moves them to action. Some of Kant's most famous remarks support this reading. In the *Doctrine of Virtue*, for instance, he explains that "perfection consists subjectively in the *purity (puritas moralis)* of one's disposition to duty," that is, "in the law being by itself alone the incentive, even without the admixture of aims derived from sensibility" (1996, 566). In the *Groundwork*, he also writes that "inclinations themselves, as sources of needs, are so far from having an absolute worth" that it must be "the universal wish of every rational being to be altogether free from them" (79). At first sight, the virtuous agent thus appears to have freed themself from emotions and desires. Their will is pure to the extent that it is immediately moved by the representation of the moral law, not by inclinations.

Yet a tension arises if we compare these passages with other parts of Kant's works in which he seems to attribute a positive role to emotions in the exercise of moral judgement. In the section of the *Doctrine of Virtue* in which he discusses ethical ascetics, for instance, Kant (1996, 598) speaks highly of joy and underlines that "the training (discipline) that a human being practices on himself can become meritorious and exemplary only through the cheerfulness that accompanies it." There, he even mentions a duty for moral agents to put themselves in a cheerful mind. This implies that virtuous agents have not freed themselves from all emotions. Instead, they have subordinated them to reason to ensure that they will not lead them astray. This reading aligns with Kant's remarks according to which the goal of moral education is not to eliminate one's emotions, but simply to combat "natural impulses sufficiently to be able to master them when a situation comes up in which they threaten morality" (598). A few years before he wrote the *Doctrine of Virtue*, Kant also expressed a similar idea in his *Religion within the Bounds of Mere Reason*:

> The difference, whether the human being is good or evil, must not lie in the difference between the incentives that he incorporates into his maxim (not in the material of the maxim) but in their *subordination* (in the form of the maxim): *which of the two he makes the condition of the other*. (Kant 2001, 83)

There therefore seems to be a discrepancy between passages in which Kant contends that people who act from pure practical reason are free from inclinations, and those in which he more moderately suggests that obeying the moral law requires one to control one's passions and subordinate them to reason. This raises several questions. First, is there a way to reconcile these two readings? Second, if this is indeed the case, does cultivating emotional dispositions amount to acquiring virtues? Third, and lastly, what role do emotions and virtues play within moral judgement? As I would now like to show, these questions are at the core of the reflection of two contemporary philosophers who were strongly influenced by Kant's considerations on virtue: Nancy Sherman and Onora O'Neill.

KANTIAN VIRTUES ACCORDING TO SHERMAN: APATHY, SYMPATHY AND GRATITUDE

Sherman generally contends that the differences between Aristotle's and Kant's theories of virtue have been blown out of proportion by contemporary moral philosophers and historians of philosophy alike. According to her perspective (1997, 1):

> To cast Kant as the harsh "duty philosopher" unsympathetic to human emotions, and to see this as a Stoic inheritance would be misguided. For it has not been

adequately appreciated that Kant develops a complex anthropology of morals—a tailoring of morality to the contingent features of the human case—which at times brings him into surprising alliance with Aristotle.

To argue this claim, Sherman distinguishes between Kant's considerations on the *a priori* foundation of morality in the *Groundwork* and his remarks on virtue and emotions in the *Metaphysics of Morals*. In his later works, Kant is as interested in understanding how agents reach a cognitive and emotional state which enables them to act from duty as he is in discussing the nature of the moral law. Certainly, some of Kant's central philosophical ideas are absent from ancient virtue ethics (for instance, his claim that the moral value of actions only depends on an agent's will). Still, we should be careful not to "overstate the distance between Kant and the ancients" (Sherman 1997, 6). Indeed, both Aristotle and Kant believe that acting rightly requires "the positive transformation of our natures, including our emotional receptivities" (140). While Aristotle defends this idea in his *Nicomachean Ethics*, Kant primarily does so in his discussion of apathy, sympathy and gratitude, three character traits which Sherman envisions as Kantian virtues.

(i) *Apathy*. In the *Doctrine of Virtue*, Kant (1996, 536) describes moral apathy as an absence of affects experienced by "a *tranquil mind* with a considered and firm resolution to put the law of virtue into practice." Such tranquility is the mark of moral agents who have learned to discipline their passions. While apathetic agents feel emotions, they do not let them overpower their will. As Sherman (1997, 166) puts it, "In the truly tranquil mind there will be emotions, but none that are abject or lacking the sovereignty of reason." Importantly, Kant's remarks on apathy help us understand that he does not consider *all* inclinations (*Neigungen*) to be bad. Instead, he suggests that moral agents should free themselves of *particular kinds* of inclinations, namely affects (*Affekte*) and passions (*Leidenschaften*). By definition, an affect is a "surprise through sensation" which suspends the mind's composure, is rash, and "makes reflection impossible" (Kant 2007, 354). One example of affect is anger, which tends to be short-lived. In comparison, passions such as hatred are long-lasting. Unlike affects, they also involve maxims of actions which lead agents to deliberately act in a way that is prescribed by one's feelings as opposed to the moral law. Passions are more harmful than affects as they gradually corrupt people's will. As Kant writes, "Affect works like water that breaks through a dam; passion, like a river that digs itself deeper and deeper into its bed" (354).

In light of these remarks, we can understand apathy as the virtue possessed by agents who successfully resist the influence of affects and passions. Interestingly, Kant's thoughts on this topic are more Stoic than Aristotelian in character. In the *Anthropology*, he even describes apathy as "an entirely correct and sublime moral principle of the Stoic school" (2007, 355). As Sherman (1997, 136) underlines, what is absent in Kant's discussion of apathy is "the moral Aristotelian notion that fully mature virtue rests not merely in control, but in transforming desires so they no longer rebel." Unlike Aristotle, Kant portrays the virtuous agent's soul as involving a battle between reason and inclinations. By way of contrast, Aristotelians argue that the virtuous agent's desires have not only been tamed, but completely transformed to align with the demands of morality. In an Aristotelian perspective, virtuous people take pleasure in performing morally good actions.

(ii) *Sympathy*. More clearly Aristotelian in character is Kant's discussion of sympathy in the *Metaphysics of Morals*. There, he suggests that, depending on their character, people are naturally inclined to either feel pleasure or displeasure when they are confronted with the suffering of others. Taking delight in the misfortune of others (*Schadenfreude*) is common behaviour, but it is undeniably a vice. In contrast, sympathy is the name that Kant gives to the feeling of sadness experienced by virtuous agents who witness other people's pain. From a moral point of view, sympathy is a virtue as it generally incites people to perform benevolent actions. Specifically, Kant (1996, 575) contends that using sympathy "as a means to promoting active and rational benevolence" is a duty, but the passage of the *Doctrine of Virtue* devoted to this issue remains hard to interpret. On the one hand, Kant suggests that rational agents only have a duty to *act* in a sympathetic manner, not to *feel* sympathy itself. Imagine for instance that one of your friends is sick with an incurable disease. Many would consider that it is morally appropriate for you to be saddened by this fact. They might even blame you if you are not. After all, not being saddened by a friend's sickness is arguably a sign of coldheartedness. By way of contrast, Kant contends that it is *not* morally wrong for you not to feel sympathy for your friend. In his view, feeling sad is an ill, and "there cannot possibly be a duty to increase the ills in the world" (Kant 1996, 575). At the same time, Kant also argues that we have a duty to cultivate emotional dispositions—including sympathy—which make it more likely that we will perform morally good actions. Consider the following passage:

> But while it is not in itself a duty to share the sufferings (as well the joys) of others, it is a duty to sympathize actively in their fate; and to this end it is therefore an indirect duty to cultivate the compassionate natural (aesthetic) feelings in us. (Kant 1996, 575)

Here, Kant distinguishes between the direct duty to perform sympathetic actions (i.e., "sympathize actively") and the indirect duty to cultivate feelings which increase the likelihood that we will do so. One way to interpret these remarks is the following: strictly speaking, rational agents do not have a duty to feel sympathy, but they do have a duty to *attempt* to feel it as doing so will help them act benevolently. When I learn that my friend is plagued by an incurable disease, for instance, I can actively choose to think about how difficult this situation must be for them and their relatives. If I do so, then I might feel sadness, and this sadness might in turn lead me to offer help to my friend or their relatives. In this sense, a moral agent who feels sympathy is more likely to help others than one who is entirely indifferent to their misfortune or, worse, is prone to *Schadenfreude*. If this interpretation is plausible, then Kant truly contends that moral agents ought to cultivate emotions which facilitate right action, and this philosophical view aligns with that of Aristotle and contemporary virtue ethicists. As Sherman (1997, 134) summarizes:

> Kant argues that we have a duty to cultivate emotions so that they can become a pervasive part of the supportive structure of virtues. So, for example, by schooling our sympathy in certain ways rather than others, we use the receptivities of our nature to support the virtue of beneficence.

(iii) *Gratitude*. Kant's remarks on gratitude also support the view that rational agents ought to cultivate emotional dispositions which facilitate right action. In the *Doctrine of Virtue*, he explains that being grateful, that is, honouring a person because of a benefit they have rendered us, is a duty (1996, 573). Considering Kant's ambiguous remarks on sympathy, one might be inclined to believe that rational agents only have a duty to perform *actions* which express gratitude, not to *feel* gratitude itself. Yet this does not appear to be the case. Undoubtedly, the duty of gratitude requires us to perform actions which communicate to our benefactors the respect that we feel for them; this is what Kant calls *active gratitude*. However, he also describes *affective* gratitude as a duty. As he writes, "Even mere heartfelt *benevolence* on another's part, without physical results, deserves to be called a duty of virtue" (573). This raises the question of knowing why Kant believes that feeling sympathy is not a duty, but that feeling gratitude is one. One possible answer is that, unlike being saddened by another person's misfortune, feeling grateful is not an ill. For this reason, a duty to feel grateful is not a "duty to increase the ills in the world" (Kant 1996, 575). Kant's proposed distinction between *sensitivity* and *sentimentality* can also help us understand his ambivalence with regard to sympathy. Sensitivity (*Empfindsamkeit*) is "a power which either permits or prevents both the state of pleasure as well as displeasure from entering the mind" (Kant 2007, 339). This means that sensitive agents control the pleasure or displeasure they experience in a way that does not distract them from their moral obligations. In contrast, "Sentimentality (*Empfindelei*) is a weakness by which we can be affected, even against our will, by sympathy for others' condition who, so to speak, can play at will on the organ on the sentimentalist" (339). In Kant's view, sympathy has the power to transform us into sentimentalists who have lost control over their emotions. Although it can help us act benevolently, it therefore remains a dangerous emotion. In the soul of the sentimentalist, emotions and desires overpower reason. Ultimately, we should seek to become sensitive agents without turning into sentimentalists. In other words, we should cultivate emotional dispositions which move us to duty without ever letting emotions detract us from the moral law. Admittedly, this picture is strongly Aristotelian. If we understand virtues as dispositions to feel emotions that incite us to commit right actions, it becomes possible to make room for virtue within Kant's practical philosophy as Sherman intends to do. Interestingly, apathy, sympathy and gratitude are not the only Kantian virtues discussed by contemporary moral philosophers. So are solicitude, solidarity and tolerance.

KANTIAN VIRTUES ACCORDING TO O'NEILL: SOLICITUDE, SOLIDARITY AND TOLERANCE

Like Sherman, O'Neill contends that many prominent Anglo-American Kantians pay insufficient attention to the reflection on virtue that Kant develops in the *Metaphysics of Morals*. This includes John Rawls, who has exclusively focused his attention on the concept of justice. As she explains, "Some leading advocates of justice now take pride in remaining 'agnostic about the Good for Man' and many more are carefully minimal about the good life" (O'Neill 1996, 9). As a result, the concept of virtue—which is usually discussed in neo-Aristotelian works about the good life—is often depicted as being incompatible with Kantian justice. Indeed, it seems that justice and virtue have become "antagonists, whose philosophical champions skirmish over countless issues" (9). This calls for a new treatment of the relationship between justice and virtue within Kant's philosophy, one that erases the line that has artificially been drawn between them. As O'Neill reminds us, Kant envisioned the *Doctrine of Right*—in which he discusses duties of right and political justice—and the *Doctrine of Virtue* as the two central parts of a single book: *The Metaphysics of Morals*. This speaks to his desire for these doctrines to be read together. Unfortunately, this desire has been lost within the contemporary liberal philosophical tradition:

> Much contemporary writing on ethics, and especially on justice, builds on systematic deontic structures. A lot of this work is broadly liberal in orientation, and the majority of it treats the perspective of the subject or recipient as prior to that of [. . .] the agent, and accordingly treats *rights* rather than *obligations* or *duties* as the fundamental ethical notion. (O'Neill 1996, 127)

The neglect of obligations and duties as fundamental ethical notions has both practical and theoretical consequences. At the practical level, liberalism as a political philosophical doctrine has had a deep influence on international law. For instance, it has led to the drafting of charters which lists the rights that all people possess by virtue of being human. Yet these charters often stipulate neither whose responsibility it is to ensure that people's rights are respected nor what precise moral obligations they entail. If all human beings have a fundamental right to education, for instance, *who* should do *what* in situations where some of them are denied access to schooling? For agents whose human rights are violated, charters which merely proclaim the existence of human rights but have no practical influence can add insult to injury.

At the theoretical level, liberal writings on rights suggest that all moral obligations come with a corresponding right. If I am morally obligated not to lie to you, for instance, this means that you have a moral right not be lied to. According to O'Neill, this last suggestion is mistaken. In her view, every moral right comes with a corresponding duty. For instance, it does not make sense to claim that each human being has an inalienable right to bodily integrity without simultaneously asserting that all moral agents have a duty to respect the bodily integrity of others. Yet the reverse is not true; we can conceive of duties without corresponding rights. To see this, compare the two following parental duties. All parents have a duty (i) to ensure that their children's basic needs are met and (ii) to contribute to the full development of their children's abilities and talents. Accordingly, parents should not only ensure that their children are healthy, but also help them fulfill their life aspirations. If your daughter desires to learn how to swim, for instance, it is arguably wrong to deny her the opportunity to do so over the course of multiple years (provided, of course, that you have access to resources which make this project possible: a body of water, time, swimming lessons and the financial means for them, etc.) Interestingly, O'Neill contends that children have a *right* to have their basic needs met by their parents, but no right to demand that parents do everything in their power to help them fulfill all of their life aspirations. Our legal systems customarily reflect this thought. While states have the power to remove custody of children from parents when their basic needs are not met, they cannot do so on the grounds that a child has been denied swimming lessons. This suggests that the parental duty to help children fulfill their life aspirations is an obligation without a corresponding right.

In O'Neill's view, the fundamental concept of practical philosophy is that of duty, not that of right. As she (1996, 140) writes, "Practical reasoning that assigns priority to rights and to recipience rather than to obligation and to action is an unnecessary and damaging [. . .] feature of contemporary writing on ethics." In fact, liberal Kantians' focus on rights as opposed to other central concepts of Kant's practical philosophy—most importantly duty and virtue—created fertile grounds for the neo-Aristotelian critique of contemporary Kantian moral theory. When Kantians set the *Doctrine of Virtue* aside, neo-Aristotelians like MacIntyre are prompted to argue that contemporary Kantianism is an individualistic moral philosophy which overlooks our obligations towards others and, most importantly, the moral virtues which enable us to fulfill them. Like Sherman, O'Neill believes that developing a virtue ethics is perfectly consistent with the spirit of Kant's philosophy and contends that obedience to duty is generally facilitated by the cultivation of characterological traits. "Without some underlying orienting stance, without certain attitudes [. . .], in short without a *character*," she writes, "action would be unstable and erratic" (O'Neill, 1996, 186). Unlike Sherman, however, O'Neill does not derive her catalogue of Kantian virtues from a close reading of the sections of the *Doctrine of Virtue* in which Kant discusses apathy, sympathy and gratitude. Instead, she begins by formulating two Kantian moral principles, and then argues that these principles entail that moral agents ought to cultivate particular virtues.

O'Neill's proposed moral theory begins with a thought experiment in which a plurality of agents suspend judgement on the validity of all existing moral rules. Then, they attempt to lay out the fundamental principles of action which will allow them to live with one another in a coordinated fashion. If moral agents did not already live together but wanted to begin doing so, which moral principles would they implement? To answer this question, O'Neill argues, we must make three assumptions about them.[4] First, the very fact that there exists a plurality of moral agents should lead them to formulate principles that they can all follow. Second, moral agents are interconnected in the sense that some of their actions have an impact on the lives of others. Third, and lastly, moral agents are marked by *vulnerability* and *finitude*. This means that (i) the actions of others can set back their fundamental interests and (ii) their capacity to pursue these interests are limited by their life circumstances. In O'Neill's view, the first moral principle that a plurality of interconnected, vulnerable and finite agents would implement in order to make coordinated living possible is the principle of non-injury, which stipulates that no one should arbitrarily injure others.[5] This is because arbitrarily injuring others is not a rule that can be followed by everyone. In a typically Kantian fashion, indeed, O'Neill (1996, 164) argues that the universalization of injury entails a contradiction:

> Putting the matter simply, principles of action will not be universalizable if attempted universal adoption would foreseeably injure capacities and capabilities for action of some of those within the relevant domain of ethical concern, thereby ensuring that they cannot adopt those principles.[6]

Yet, if everyone arbitrarily decided to injure others, then some people's capacity to act would be diminished because of the injuries they have sustained. In other words, the universal adoption of the principle of injury would generally limit people's capacity for action, and O'Neill's suggestion is that adopting a principle of action which limits people's capacity for action is practically contradictory.

In addition to the principle of non-injury, vulnerable and finite agents who desire to make coordinated living possible would also implement a principle of non-indifference, which stipulates that all moral agents should offer help to those in need. Again, O'Neill's justification for this principle is that indifference cannot reasonably be universalized. In her view:

> No vulnerable agent can coherently accept that indifference and neglect should be universalized, for if they were nobody could rely on others' help; joint projects would tend to fail; vulnerable characters would be undermined; capacities and capabilities that need [. . .] nurturing would not emerge; personal relationships would wither; education and cultural life would decline. It follows that those with plans and projects, even of the most minimal sort, cannot regard indifference and neglect as universalizable. (O'Neill 1996, 194)

As it is the case with injury, universalizing indifference and neglect would impair human beings' capacity to act. To see this, consider that fulfilling our individual needs and aspirations typically requires us to engage in joint action. As I write these lines, my newborn daughter must constantly rely on the help of her parents to maintain a state of well-being. Of course, her capacity to act by herself will gradually improve over time, but she will never become a fully independent agent. When she reaches adolescence, engaging in activities with her friends is likely to be an important way in which she meets her emotional needs. When she reaches adulthood, her professional activities will involve forms of cooperative behaviour which will require her to pay attention to the needs of others (colleagues, supervisors, clients, etc.). If human beings did not choose to continuously engage in joint action—to help others and be helped in return—then it would be harder for them to be nourished, find shelter, stay safe, rest and forge meaningful relationships with others.

Importantly, O'Neill contends that effectively helping others necessitates the acquisition of a set of virtues which lead moral agents to pay close attention to one another's vulnerability, and thus reject indifference. One of these virtues is *solicitude*, which is a disposition to show loving care to our friends and relatives. By way of example, people who devote a substantial amount of their time to care for sick relatives undoubtedly possess the virtue of solicitude. Yet O'Neill also urges us to remind ourselves that our friends and relatives are not the only human beings who need our help. Strangers also do, but it is all too easy for moral agents to forget that they do, especially when they live far away from us. As the saying goes: out of sight, out of mind. To avoid being indifferent to strangers, moral agents need to acquire the virtue of *solidarity*, which is a disposition to offer help to vulnerable people whom they do not personally know. Displays of solidarity are easy to represent; they include assisting people in distress, donating to charity and actively helping people who stand against social and political injustice. During Black Lives Matters protests, for instance, those who are not negatively affected by structural racism but chose to protest by the side of those who are arguably displayed solidarity.

Although solicitude and solidarity are the two central virtues which lead moral agents to *directly* reject indifference, O'Neill also conceives of one additional virtue which incites them to *indirectly* do so. This virtue is tolerance, which O'Neill defines as a disposition to help maintain the social fabric of a divided political society.[7] Tolerant people do not feel hatred for their political adversaries. Despite their different views, they show concern for them by envisioning them as equal human beings whose basic needs deserve to be met like those of everyone else. While tolerant people might not directly offer help to their adversaries, they help create a climate in which all people who belong to a given society see one another as embarked on the same political journey. In short, they see their rivals as *co-citizens*.[8] Consider the following example. During the COVID-19 pandemic, many people have refused to be vaccinated against this disease. Compared with the vaccinated, the unvaccinated are more likely to transmit COVID to others, and not being vaccinated therefore strikes me as a morally bad decision. Yet people sick with COVID who show the same symptoms should be provided with the same healthcare services regardless of their vaccination status. Instead of hating the unvaccinated and discriminating against them, it helps to remind ourselves that our contingent life circumstances have an immense influence on the people we choose to trust. Had I been repeatedly disrespected by healthcare professionals—something that many citizens experience—I might have thought twice before deferring judgement to medical experts in a time of pandemic and refused to be vaccinated. This is not to say that, all things considered, people should not get vaccinated. My point is rather that, in certain cases, blaming the unvaccinated for refusing to get vaccinated is overly simplistic. What is more, it might have negative political consequences in the long run as it risks damaging the social fabric of contemporary democracies.[9]

Apathy, sympathy, gratitude, solicitude, solidarity and tolerance: these are the Kantian virtues that Sherman and O'Neill ultimately invite us to represent. Of course, this does not entail that Kantian virtues should *replace* traditional Greek virtues such as courage, moderation and justice. In fact, Kant himself would arguably have rejected this conclusion. In his *Lectures on Pedagogy*, he proposes a tripartite classification of virtues some of which directly relate to those discussed by Aristotle in the *Nicomachean Ethics*:

> The virtues are either virtues of *merit* or merely of *obligation* or *innocence*. To the first kind belong magnanimity (in self-conquest regarding revenge as well as ease and greed), beneficence, and self-mastery; to the second kind belong uprightness, decency, and peaceableness, to the third kind, finally, belong honesty, modesty, and frugality. (Kant 2007, 479)

While magnanimity is contained in Aristotle's catalogue of virtues, self-control is equivalent to the ancient Greek virtue of moderation (*sophrosune*). Granted, Kant does not discuss these virtues to the same extent as Aristotle does in his own works of practical philosophy. Nevertheless, the *Doctrine of Virtue*, *Anthropology* and *Lectures on Pedagogy* all suggest that Kantian approaches to moral judgement can make room for virtues. As we have seen, they are also compatible with the neo-Aristotelian claim that acting rightly requires moral agents to cultivate emotional dispositions which help them fulfill their obligations. As Sherman's commentary of Kant's *Metaphysics of Morals* demonstrates, the disciplining of emotional impulses creates fertile ground for good deliberation, which is itself a precondition of moral behaviour. In my view, virtues can also play a second role in moral reasoning. By way of conclusion, I wish to examine this claim in greater detail. Then, I will return to the problem of reflexivity and briefly explain how an influential French phenomenologist—Maurice Merleau-Ponty—can help us overcome it.

(A Merleau-Pontian) Conclusion

Which picture of moral judgement emerges from Kantian responses to the neo-Aristotelian critique? In the last chapter, we have seen how contemporary Kantians make room for virtues within their theory of moral deliberation. Like neo-Aristotelians, they argue that cultivating emotional dispositions can help agents fulfill the obligations that fall upon them. According to this perspective, the function of virtues is essentially *conative*; virtues either help agents keep their desires and negative emotions in check (e.g., apathy) or arise sentiments which bolster their motivation to act from duty (sympathy, gratitude, solicitude, solidarity and tolerance). The moral psychology which undergirds this discourse rests on the idea that human beings are not born with the desire to act rightly, but that the cultivation of virtues will gradually lead moral agents to acquire it. At an earlier time in my life, when my friends shared their worries with me, I use to tell them that they should "toughen up." This was an immature and unproductive attempt to help others feel better; by focusing on what people can *do* instead of how they *feel*, I thought, they are more likely to overcome the challenges they face. Over the years, however, I have come to understand that such a reaction was woefully inadequate as it prevented me from making others feel understood. To become a more empathetic person, I had to practice suppressing my callous reactions to expressions of worry and to remind myself that I, too, like being listened to when I am anxious. Nowadays, empathy comes more easily to me, and listening to others (sometimes) prompts me to offer help to my friends. I even take pleasure in the thought that I am there for them. Although I still frequently make moral mistakes, I have trained myself to feel an emotion that bolsters my desire to act rightly.

Such considerations allow us to grasp a second role that virtues can play within moral reasoning. To see this, note that the process which led me to become more empathetic was not purely conative. It was partly a *cognitive* process which required me to engage in rational reflection and discussion with those that I have wronged by suggesting that they "toughen up." Specifically, I had to understand why my spontaneous reaction was wrong and what my reasons to act differently were. For instance, I now *know* that feeling understood can help others reach an emotional state which will help them address their problems or—even more importantly—that simply being there for your friends is intrinsically valuable (even when it does not lead to change). This itself suggests that virtues fulfill an important cognitive function in moral reasoning. They transform the way in which moral agents understand the world and perceive facts as reasons for actions. If you have trained yourself to become an empathetic person, then you now pay special attention to the suffering of others and, most importantly, you envision the presence of suffering as a reason to offer help.

By way of contrast, we can conceive of three kinds of individuals who lack empathy. The first kind includes those who, in Aristotelian terms, suffer from *astheneia*; although they know how they ought to act, they cannot find the moral strength to do so. Like empathetic agents, these individuals envision the presence of suffering as a reason to offer their help to others, but they lack the motivation to do so. After all, helping others requires energy and effort, and satisfying one's own desires is sometimes much more tempting. The second type of individuals who lack empathy are those who suffer from *propeteia*.[1] When the time to deliberate comes, these individuals' passions are so strong that they prevent them from even understanding how they ought to act. Once they have acted in accordance with their selfish desires, however, they come to realize that they should have behaved differently and feel regret. "I should have offered help, they think, but I could not see this in the heat of the moment." The last kind of agents who lack empathy are the properly vicious individuals. Unlike agents who suffer from *astheneia* and *propeteia*; these individuals never envision other people's suffering as a reason to offer them their help. For instance, they might think that it is not their fault if other people live through difficult situations, and that their own responsibility is simply to care for themselves. Now, the contrast between the first and third kinds of individuals who lack empathy best allows us to pinpoint the cognitive dimension of virtues. In the agent who suffers from *astheneia*, lack of virtue provokes a failure of moral motivation. In the properly vicious individual, it provokes an error of moral *reasoning*. In this case, the problem is not that the agent's will is weak, but that the agent is unable to envision a fact ("x suffers") as a reason for action ("I should offer help to x"). Differently put, they fail to understand the practical significance of suffering. If these remarks are plausible, then we can say that virtues support moral judgement in two different ways. First, they bolster people's moral motivation to act rightly. Second, they enable them to correctly envision facts as reasons for action. For example, honest people not only find the moral strength to tell the truth in situations where they could easily get away with lying, but they also understand that lying damages relationships of trust, and that itself is a reason to refrain from lying. Like empathy, the virtue of honesty not only supports moral motivation, but it also assists moral reasoning and judgement by shaping our apprehension of reality.

Although neo-Aristotelian philosophers have repeatedly defended the role of virtue in moral reasoning, some contemporary Kantians now defend it with the same fervour. Are Kantians equally successful when it comes to answering the neo-Aristotelian objection according to which moral principles are too general to guide action? As we have seen, agents who engage in deliberation must often choose between many possible actions which are compatible with the same set of principles. This suggests that judgement involves a transition from a general statement which expresses a desire to act in a given way (e.g., "I wish to fulfill my duty of beneficence") to a proposition which identifies the precise action that will best allow me to do so (e.g., "Φ-ing would best allow me to fulfill my duty of beneficence"). Neo-Aristotelians typically consider that identifying the best action that one can perform in the case at hand requires moral agents to possess practical wisdom, a virtue which allows them to "see" what particular situations demand of them. Some contemporary Kantians attempt to accommodate this insight by emphasizing the role played by *Urteilskraft* in moral judgement. As they describe it, *Urteilskraft* is an aptitude which enables moral agents to envision situations in which they find themselves as belonging to a specific kind. For instance, it helps them answer questions such as "Does the situation in which I find myself poses a moral risk?" and "If so, which moral obligation am I in risk of flouting here and now?" In other words, moral agents who possess a sophisticated sense of *Urteilskraft* successfully distinguish between normal situations in which they can allow themselves to act spontaneously and those that require them to carefully deliberate and make difficult moral decisions.

Moved by the neo-Aristotelian critique, contemporary Kantians also ask themselves the following question: considering that the same moral end can be achieved through a multitude of actions, how can agents determine what action is best for them to perform in concrete situations? Here, Kant's remarks on leeway (*latitudo*) contained in the *Doctrine of Virtue* incites them to grant that moral agents have a margin of maneuver when they seek to fulfill their obligations (e.g., "I will develop my natural talents," "I will promote the happiness of others," etc.). Specifically, we can conceive of situations in which there is no single best way of accomplishing a moral end, but many equally commendable actions that are available to us. After all, there are myriad ways of promoting the happiness of others, and how one should precisely do so depends on their desires, strengths, and weaknesses. Unlike my friend Walter, I will not attempt to make other people laugh in the face of adversity; he is much better at that than I am, and I must find my own way of cheering up my loved ones.

In light of these remarks, we can represent a model of moral judgement which synthesizes Kantian and neo-Aristotelian insights discussed throughout this book:

1. Before making a moral judgement, the agent first conceives of the situation in which they find themself as one which requires them to engage in deliberation.
2. They then determine which moral requirements apply to the case at hand. For instance, our agent might think that the situation is one in which they risk flouting their duties of fidelity (e.g., "I promised my friend that I would always be honest with her, but disclosing to her that her comment hurt me would make her uncomfortable").
3. The agent sets the general end of her action by formulating the first premise of a practical syllogism. Such a premise can express a desire to meet multiple obligations at the same time (e.g., "I wish to promote the happiness of my friend without lying to her").
4. The agent must now determine what particular action will best allow them to meet this end by formulating the second premise of the practical syllogism (e.g., "All things considered, telling my friend that her comment hurt me best allows me to promote her happiness without lying to her"). In other words, the agent engages in deliberation *per se* and makes a judgement about how they will act.
5. Moral judgement ends with the performance of the action identified in step 4.

When agents envision the situation in which they find themselves as one which requires deliberation and determine which moral requirements apply to the case at hand, *Urteilskraft* is at play. Whether agents possess virtues will also influence both the selection of a general end and the choice of a particular action which will be performed to meet this end. For instance, there are many ways in which an agent who lacks moderation might make moral mistakes: they might not formulate the desire to behave moderately, fail to find the moral strength to do so or, alternatively, fail to identify actions which count as courageous.

We can conceive of at least two objections against this model of moral judgement. A first objection amounts to the claim that it does violence to our everyday experience by excessively intellectualizing the way in which we make moral decisions. Admittedly, we make many judgements in a non-reflective manner, that is, without following these five steps in order. In fact, we frequently fulfill our moral obligations without conceiving of the situations in which we find ourselves as ones that require us to deliberate. Often, we act spontaneously. Accordingly, we can envision the model of moral judgement described above as primarily applying to hard cases, ones in which moral agents face an ethical dilemma or, at least, are uncertain of the best way to act. This model is also *normative* insofar as it reconstructs the mental operations in which agents *should* engage to take good moral decisions according to contemporary Kantians and neo-Aristotelians (or, at least, according to my interpretation of their work). Above all else, it provides us with historiographical insight as reflection on conflicting duties, *Urteilskraft* and virtues was at the forefront of Kantian and neo-Aristotelian moral theory in the second half of the twentieth century. Throughout this book, I also hope to have shown that contemporary Kantians developed this model of judgement *in response* to the neo-Aristotelian critique.

A second objection to the model of moral judgement sketched above amounts to the claim that concepts like *Urteilskraft* or *phronesis* introduce a kind of mysticism in philosophical discourse. This is an important objection to discuss considering that I directed it myself against McDowell's practical philosophy.[2] In many ways, the idea that wise agents simply "see" how they ought to act in particular situations is vague and frustrating. In my view, part of this frustration comes from the fact that such a claim is not action-guiding. When people decide to read or discuss moral theory, they are often motivated by the desire to live well from an ethical point of view. For instance, they want to learn whether it is morally acceptable for them to eat meat, lie to others, not give part of their salary to charity, and so on. When they raise questions about these issues, it would be obnoxious to tell them that, once they have become virtuous, they will find answers to their questions and "see" how they ought to behave. If we do, they might reasonably respond that our philosophical "wisdom" is quite shallow. Undoubtedly, we should accept to engage in discussion about the issues which concern them. That said, one charitable way to envision the neo-Aristotelian discourse on practical wisdom is to interpret it as one that places limits on philosophers' ambitions. Oftentimes, moral situations are better judged by those who face them than by philosophers who try to anticipate them or look at them retrospectively. Let us say that a student of mine asks me an embarrassing and inappropriate question in the middle of a lecture. Ultimately, the way I should reply to them depends on many things. Certainly, I should reflect upon the content of the question, but I should also consider the intent behind it: was it meant to humiliate me or to make me laugh? This itself will require me to observe the body language of the student who asked it, and to listen to the tone of their voice. Before I respond, I should also ask myself how different kinds of responses would affect the relationship I have forged with my students, one that is singular and difficult to fully understand for people who have not observed my teaching.

Here, the important point is that the best response to the student's embarrassing question depends on many details that are unavailable to people who are external to the situation. Now, let us say that I let this one go. Without answering the inappropriate question, I give it a laugh and continue with my lecture. Then, when recounting the events to a colleague of mine, this colleague tells me that I should have responded more hardly to the student to avoid letting them undermine my authority. In response, I tell my colleague that responding hardly was not the right thing to do and that, if they had been there, they would probably agree with me. Is this response obnoxious? I would argue that it is not. After all, my colleague was not there to grasp the mood of the class, and they also do not understand the pedagogical relationship that I have created with my students as much as I do. In this situation, it seems that I am *practically wise* relative to them. This is not because I am a better moral agent than them *in general*, but simply because I possess a stronger situational knowledge of the case at hand.[3] Surely, this is an unorthodox interpretation of practical wisdom, one that portrays it as a kind of situational knowledge which depends on circumstances as opposed to a skill possessed by agents who make good judgements about all cases regardless of their level of involvement in them. When they must make difficult moral decisions, *agents* have an edge over external *observers* for the situation in which they find themselves is always a singular one. By way of contrast, moral theorists often discuss simplified hypothetical examples. In the eye of the agent, however, there might be a morally relevant difference between the moral theorist's hypothetical example and the case at hand. Ultimately, no one can spare them of relying on their own judgement. Of course, this does not entail that we should give a free pass to moral agents; regardless of the decisions they take, it seems fair for others to ask them for a justification of their actions.

Let me now return to the philosophical question on which the lengthiest part of this book focuses: if good moral judgement is essentially a matter of respecting myriad moral obligations, where do these obligations ultimately come from? In chapters 4, 5 and 6, I have discussed three philosophical attempts to ground moral judgement in our identity as (i) sincere discussants (Habermas), (ii) rational human beings (Korsgaard) and (iii) members of the human specie (Foot). One common idea which undergirds these attempts is that moral obligations stem from the multiple dimensions of our practical identity. As a professor, for instance, I ought to care for my students and try my best to help them learn. As a friend, I ought to offer help to those with whom I have forged friendships when they face difficult life events. Simply put, this is what good professors and good friends do.

As we have seen, however, attempts to ground moral obligations in the normativity of practical identities face what I name the problem of reflexivity. Certainly, practical identities give rise to moral obligations, but our rational powers provide us with the capacity to question the value of these identities. While I know how good professors behave, what reasons do I have to value this identity in the first place or, at least, to prioritize the obligations which stem from it over those which relate to other dimensions of my practical identity? Ultimately, it seems that I remain free to prioritize certain practical identities over others, to abandon some of them, and to acquire new ones. If this is so, am I not—like all other agents—in control of the moral obligations which fall upon me? For instance, can I not freely decide to stop being a good professor and choose to become a good scoundrel instead? To avoid this conclusion, Kantian constructivists and neo-Aristotelian naturalists argue that moral agents *must* value some practical identities. As we have seen, the most sophisticated attempt to do so has been made by Christine Korsgaard, who contends that we must value our identity as rational human beings if we are to value anything at all. Yet even if we grant her this claim, it does not entail that the obligations which stem from our identity as rational human being necessarily trump those that relate to other dimensions of our practical identity. In my view, this objection generalizes to philosophical attempts to ground moral judgement in other practical identities like those made by Habermas and Foot. Instead of being a good rational being, a good discussant or a good member of the human specie, I can always choose to be a good x (where the content of x is fixed by an act of my own free will).

Can we conceive of solutions to the problem of the reflexivity? I see at least three, but only the third one seems convincing to me. A first solution amounts to embracing an existentialist position by accepting the view that no moral obligation truly binds us unless we freely choose to recognize it as binding. According to this perspective, agents ground the authority of moral reasons through free acts of their will. This is the position defended by French Kantian Alain Renaut, who argues that the moral law only binds us if we freely choose to recognize it as authoritative. This amounts to recognizing the problem of reflexivity without truly solving it. If I am free to reject the authority of the moral law through a free act of my will, then nothing prevents me from considering that I have no moral reason to show consideration for others. In fact, I can argue that this decision is not irrational in any sense of the term as moral reflection ultimately rests on a groundless choice to become *this* or *this* person.

A second solution to the problem of reflexivity amounts to rejecting the philosophical picture painted by Renaut and argue that it is based on a mistaken appreciation of the nature of moral reasons. In this view, moral reasons bind us regardless of what we think about them. Now, philosophers who defend this position often disagree about the source of moral obligations. According to moral realists like Charles Larmore, there exists an objective order of moral reasons, and the central task of moral judgement amounts to grasping these reasons. For instance, the reason to care for others exists independently of our will, and not recognizing it would amount to making a moral mistake. That we should care for others is a moral fact. In contrast, traditionalist neo-Aristotelians reject the view that there exist universal moral reasons and obligations. Instead, they argue that moral reasons ultimately derive from social norms and traditions. Regardless of who you are, you were born in a particular community at a specific point in time. In Heideggerian terms, we can say that you were "thrown" (*geworfen*) in a socio-historical context in which you have not chosen to live. Yet it falls upon you to comply with the traditional norms which make collective life in this community possible. According to this perspective, traditions are the ultimate repository of moral duties. As we have seen, however, moral traditionalism comes with an important danger. Throughout history, communal norms have given rise to inequalities and injustices, many of which persist to the present day. As a result, traditionalist ethics can easily lead to moral conformism, that is, incite people to accept the status quo instead of actively working to dismantle it. To avoid being complicit in injustice, we might have to look elsewhere. Still, the neo-Aristotelian critique of moral universalism poses a problem for moral realists. Indeed, Gadamer's claim that our appreciation of moral reasons is always filtered by a traditional worldview suggests that universalists might mistake their subjective preferences for universal moral standards.

Interestingly, this objection has long been pushed against European and American moral philosophers by proponents of postcolonial theory. By taking this objection seriously, I propose to sketch a third way out of the problem of reflexivity. In 1958, French philosopher Maurice Merleau-Ponty gave a conference at the Collège de France in which he distinguished between two concepts of the universal.[4] According to Merleau-Ponty (2008, 52), a well-known form of universalism is based on a concept that he names the "overarching universal" (*universel de surplomb*). In a nutshell, this is the universal of which philosophers are in search when they attempt to formulate moral principles through armchair reflection. The methodology they use to do so involves an examination of everyday moral intuitions, thought experiments, close readings of the Western philosophical canon and argumentation. For his part, Merleau-Ponty is sceptical that this methodology can help philosophers—who, like all of us, live at a very specific point in space and time—grasp truly universal moral principles. Here, his criticism of the overarching universal is similar to the one we examined in chapters 1 and 2 when discussing the works of MacIntyre and that of German neo-Aristotelians. Philosophical reflection on moral universalism is necessarily influenced by cultural prejudices and, as a result, people from different cultures have incompatible views about what human practices are morally good. Fortunately, Merleau-Ponty tells us (2008, 52), there is "a second way to the universal: no longer the overarching universal of a strictly objective method, but a sort of lateral universal which we acquire through ethnological experience."

When speaking of ethnological experience, Merleau-Ponty is primarily thinking of the work done by anthropologists who engage in the empirical study of other cultures, worldviews and ways of life. In fact, his conference was given to mark to creation of a research chair in social anthropology at the Collège de France. The fundamental idea behind Merleau-Ponty's concept of the "lateral universal" is quite simple: philosophers cannot solely rely on their own subjective intuitions if they hope to formulate universal moral principles. Instead, they must actively engage with the empirical work of sociologists and anthropologist and study the moral codes of a wide range of human societies. If they do not, then they risk formulating principles which only reflect the moral intuitions of members of their own society, not those of a diverse group of human beings. As Senegalese philosopher Souleymane Bachir Diagne underlines, arguing that these principles are universal would amount to arrogantly declaring, "I have the particularity of being universal" (Bachir Diagne and Amselle 2018, 68–69). In contrast, constructing the lateral universal requires philosophers to search for points of moral convergence between cultural worldviews, ones that Merleau-Ponty call "universal invariants" (2008, 51). By relying on social scientific work and engaging in dialogue with diverse groups of thinkers, philosophers can identify rules and practical identities that a wide range of human cultures value. For instance, one reason to take my duties as a professor seriously derives from the fact that all human cultures value education in one way or another. Perhaps more than transcendental arguments, *this* is the sign that the obligations which stem from this identity are truly universal.

Borrowing vocabulary from Kant, Merleau-Ponty argues that constructing the lateral universal requires scholars to engage in "enlarged thinking" and establish a "general system of reference" which reflects myriad cultural points of view.[5] Contrary to Kant, however, he explicitly ties enlarged thinking to the use of the empirical method. In his view, studying the moral codes of other human societies can lead us to see our own in a new light. For instance, it can help us realize that, from a global perspective, parenting practices which have become mainstream in Europe and America—repeatedly praising children, buying several toys, attempting to help children reach developmental milestones early, and so on—are the exception, not the rule (Doucleff 2021).[6] When we reinterpret our putatively universal intuitions and practices as peculiar cultural products, Merleau-Ponty argues, we become "ethnologists of our own society." Specifically, we learn "to see as foreign what is ours, and as ours what was foreign to us." Yet doing so requires a serious methodological shift in perspective from academic philosophers, who have been quite reluctant to engage with both social scientific work and less frequently taught philosophical traditions (Van Norden 2017). Building on the ideas contained in Merleau-Ponty's 1958 conference, Bachir Diagne contends that this shift in methodology has important postcolonial implications. From a historical point of view, the search for an overarching (as opposed to lateral) universal has led European and American philosophers to impose their preferred moral rules on other societies, without any attempt to learn from them in return. In a 1935 lecture on *Philosophy and the Crisis of European Man*, for instance, German philosopher Edmund Husserl commented on the British colonization of India by celebrating European culture. In his view, there lies something unique in Europe which leads Indians to "constantly Europeanize themselves, whereas we (Europeans), if we understand ourselves properly, will never, for instance, Indianize ourselves."[7] These remarks symbolize Europe's contempt for other cultures as well as the tendency of European and American philosophers to conceive of a peculiar moral universalism which, ironically, pays no attention to cultural variation.

Unlike Merleau-Ponty, however, the methodology that Bachir Diagne primarily associates with the lateral universal is that used by *translators* instead of sociologists and anthropologists. As he writes (2013, 15), "The language of the universal is translation." By learning to speak other languages and translating philosophical works into our native one, we create reciprocity between cultures. Specifically, Bachir Diagne suggests that translation instantly puts languages on a plane of equality. Indeed, translators must reconstruct the mental lives of both their audiences and authors to find terms which reflect the richness of the latter's reflection, but will also be understood by the former. When they successfully do so, they build bridges between cultural *psyches*. If we are to avoid unfairly privileging a culture over others, translations should also flow in multiple directions. Works of African or Asian philosophy should be translated into European languages and vice versa—but works of Africana philosophy should also be translated into Asian languages (and vice versa). If we only translate works of European philosophy into African and Asian languages, then we create the mistaken impression that only European philosophical concepts are worth translating. Yet even more dangerous than unilateral translations is the temptation *not to translate at all* as it mistakenly leads us to believe that we can reach moral universalism without engaging with more than one philosophical tradition. According to Bachir Diagne (2013, 16), this is impossible: "The Universal is not any more the prerogative of a language, it is to be experimented and maybe 'acquired' through the lateral process of translation."

In many ways, these remarks relate to the central themes of this book. First, Bachir Diagne's discussion of translation as the language of the universal is strongly reminiscent of MacIntyre's views on conflicts between traditions. As we have seen, traditions come into dialogue throughout history. When they do, philosophers who belong to a particular tradition sometimes come to realize that a rival one possesses moral resources which they themselves lack.

By integrating these resources to their own traditional worldview, these philosophers can—like anthropologists and translators—contribute to the construction of a lateral universal. Second, like discourse ethicists, Kantian constructivists and neo-Aristotelian naturalists, philosophers interested in building lateral universality sincerely attempt to identify moral principles by which *all* humans ought to live. In fact, all these philosophers reject the view that traditional standards are intrinsically authoritative from a moral point of view. In a Merleau-Pontian perspective, the fact that a traditional standard is strongly at odds with that of other human societies should incite us to critically examine it. Third, we have seen that, according to Jürgen Habermas, the validity of moral rules can only be assessed in the context of real discussions between all people who are—or would be—affected by their implementation. Such a regulative ideal is perfectly compatible with the claim that working towards the lateral universal requires human cultures to actively engage with one another through social scientific study, translation or other means. Following in Habermas's footsteps, we should commit to the view that no *a priori* thought experiment involving hypothetical subjects can replace real engagement with the discourses, literary works and cultural practices of others. Fourth, and lastly, building a lateral universal incites us to pay attention to the various ways in which members of the human specie structure collective life to *live well* with one another. In fact, cross-cultural dialogue can lead us to formulate truly universal Aristotelian categoricals similar to those that Anscombe has in mind (e.g., "In all human cultures, people keep their promises as this facilitates complex forms of social cooperation").

Admittedly, Merleau-Ponty's concept of the universal does not provide us with a perfect solution to the problem of reflexivity. Ultimately, nothing guarantees that philosophers and other scholars will successfully identify cultural invariants and, if they do, that these will allow us to revise current ethical frameworks. If we present them with transcultural practical identities or moral principles, moral agents will also still have the capacity to raise questions such as "Why should *I* value this particular identity?" or "Why should *I* comply with this rule?" In other words, the search for a lateral universal will not be the end of philosophical reflection, but it can bring philosophy closer to the social sciences and open new avenues of ethical inquiry. Even if attempts to ground moral judgement in *a priori* reflection are unsuccessful, we can attempt to formulate universal moral principles by looking for common grounds in the diverse ways humans live together and justify their practices to one another in myriad cultural contexts. Philosophers certainly like questioning assumptions, and using the tools of anthropology, sociology and translation seems to me like a fruitful way to do so.[8]

Perhaps most importantly, Merleau-Ponty's remarks should incite readers to be deeply suspicious of the conclusions I have attempted to draw in this book. Throughout my reflection, I have deliberately attempted to live up to Bachir Diagne's suggestion that translation is the language of the universal. My choice of introducing readers to philosophical perspectives on moral judgement stemming from France, Germany and the Anglo-American world is not arbitrary, but it is contingent on my life circumstances: it depends on the languages that I can read, and also on the traditions that I have been encouraged to study during my philosophical training. Yet this choice has not allowed me to look beyond Europe and North America, which means that my philosophical ideas should be taken with a grain of salt. In the end, I hope that this book will be a point of departure for its readers. If some of them choose to compare my claims to that of philosophers working outside of the French, German and Anglo-American philosophical traditions, they too will have attempted to contribute to a truly universal reflection on the nature and foundations of moral judgement.

Notes

INTRODUCTION

1. As I learned while reading *Normal People*, the Debs is the formal ball organized for graduating high school students in the Republic of Ireland.

2. I borrow the expression "acting on principle" from Onora O'Neill (2013).

3. Throughout this book, I mostly use the expression "Anglo-American philosophy" to refer to works of analytic philosophy written in English coming from the United Kingdom and the United States.

4. For a detailed discussion of Kant's categorical imperative, see chapter 1, "Rawls on Duty, Desire and the Categorical Imperative."

5. In several counties (such as Canada), this moral duty is also a legal one (i.e., one that is enforced by the State).

6. For a different account of the relationship between reason and desire, see Schroeder (2007).

7. The most influential defense of utilitarianism remains Mill (2002).

8. Bachir Diagne is a Senegalese philosopher who has been trained in France and currently works in the United States. I turn to his view of the relationship between translation and moral universalism in the conclusion of this book.

9. See Canto-Sperber (2001, 527). My translation.

10. It is likely that at least some philosophers I call "neo-Aristotelians" would prefer to be called "contemporary Aristotelians" as neo-Aristotelianism is often associated with communitarianism for reasons that will become obvious in the next two chapters. Throughout this book, I use "neo-Aristotelian" as a neutral umbrella term to refer to philosophers who were heavily influenced by Aristotle's views. In what follows, it will become apparent that many neo-Aristotelians are *not* communitarians. Moreover, I deliberately avoid using the term "neo-Kantian" as it customarily refers to the late-nineteenth- and early-twentieth-century German philosophical movement that formed around Hermann Cohen at Marburg University and Wilhelm Windelband in the province of Baden.

CHAPTER 1

1. See my description of the original position—the thought experiment which is meant to ground the validity of Rawls's principles of justice—below.
2. Kant's *Critique of Practical Reason* is divided into the "Doctrine of Elements" and the "Doctrine of Method." The "Doctrine of Elements" is itself divided into the "Analytic of Pure Practical Reason" and the "Dialectic of Pure Practical Reason."
3. W. M. Sibley (1953) already distinguished between the "Rational" and the "Reasonable."
4. The temptation of evil is a central theme in Kant's philosophy of religion. See Kant (2001) and Brown (2020) for a discussion.
5. Such an interpretation is also present in Rawls's *Lectures on the History of Moral Philosophy* (2000). See, for instance, the chapter titled "The Categorical Imperative: The First Formulation."
6. The verifiability principle—according to which statements are only meaningful if they are empirically verifiable or tautological—was famously defended by logical positivists. The kind of prescriptive statements I am considering here are of neither kind.
7. For a discussion of Sartrian existentialism and its influence on contemporary French Kantianism, see chapter 5 "Moral Agency and Radical Freedom."
8. It is worth noting that MacIntyre's criticism of the categorical imperative is different from Sartre's own, which focuses on its second formulation—the formula of humanity—according to which rational beings must act "so that they treat humanity, whether in their own person or in the person of any other, never merely as means, but always at the same time as an end" (Kant 1996, 80). Specifically, Sartre argues that his pupil would have treated his compatriots merely as means if he chose to stay with his mother. Yet he would also have treated his mother merely as means if he left her. No possible course of action would hence have satisfied the formula of humanity in this case.
9. When commenting on Aristotle's practical syllogism, MacIntyre is indebted to Anscombe, who argued that the conclusion of such syllogism is not a *belief*, but an *action*. See Anscombe (1957, 60).
10. I will return to the concept of moral salience when examining the Kantian-inspired theory of moral education put forward by Barbara Herman. See chapter 8, "Moral Literacy and Autonomous Judgement."
11. Some chefs are likely to object that this is an oversimplification of what good cooking entails! This may be true, but my point here is simply that cooking is a relatively simple practice *in comparison with* more complex ones (say, bringing up a child and helping her develop into a well-functioning adult).

CHAPTER 2

1. Gadamer's relationship with Nazism remains a point of contention between contemporary historians of philosophy. As Richard Wolin (2000) explains, in 1940,

Gadamer gave a conference titled "Volk and History in Herder's Thought" to French prisoners of war at the German Institute in Paris. In this conference, he criticized French rationalism and celebrated the depth of the German concept of *Volk* (which translates as "people"). Racist *Völkisch* rhetoric—in which a racially defined and agrarian German people is depicted as a living organism—was a key element in Nazi "blood and soil" propaganda. Whether or not Gadamer intended to contribute to Nazi propaganda, it seems reasonable to hold him accountable for deciding not to shy away from a language that unmistakeably evoked it.

2. The debate between Habermas and Bubner was originally published in German. See Habermas (1984) and Bubner (1984).

3. Unless otherwise specified, quotes from philosophical works in German contained in the references section are translated by me.

4. Odo Marquard, one of Ritter's most prolific pupils, explains that the critique of left-wing protest movements was a focal point of Ritter's circle. He summarizes the intellectual attitude of its members in a provocative slogan: "The opposite of right-wing totalitarianism is not left-wing totalitarianism, but liberal democracy." See Marquard (2003, 456).

5. For a description of Aristotle's practical syllogism, see chapter 1, "*Phronesis* and the Practical Syllogism."

6. Here, I am relying on Richard D. Winfield's translation of this passage. See Ritter (1982).

7. With the publication of *Truth and Method*, Gadamer became the father of contemporary hermeneutics, the branch of philosophical reflection that is concerned with methodology in the interpretation of texts.

8. Kant famously argued that lying is not warranted even when doing so would allow us to save the life of an innocent person. For a more thorough discussion of the case of the murderer at the door, see chapter 3, "An Intentionalist Account of Practical Reasoning." See also "On a Supposed Right to Lie from Philanthropy" in Kant (1996). I take it that most readers would disagree with Kant on that matter.

9. This is a claim that Arendt contests in her own interpretation of Kant's philosophy. See chapter 7, "Kantian *Urteilskraft* in Hannah Arendt's Philosophy."

10. See Fuller (1958, 663) for a more detailed discussion of this example.

11. See Heidegger (2010, 169–73) for a discussion.

12. I return to Habermassian discourse ethics in the second part of this book.

13. It is worth noting that discourse ethics says nothing about the *content* of the moral norms we ought to live by; it merely aims to define a discussion procedure through which the validity of *any* moral norm can be assessed.

14. As we have seen in chapter 1, this is traditionally known as the problem of the "tailoring of maxims."

15. This remark is heavily reminiscent of Ludwig Wittgenstein's (2009, 87e) rule-following paradox, according to which "no course of action could be determined by a rule, because any course of action can be made out to accord with the rule."

16. For a discussion of this point, see chapter 4, "Overcoming Neo-Aristotelianism."

CHAPTER 3

1. Books on contemporary French philosophy which discuss post-structuralist thinkers include Williams (2001), Gutting (2001), James (2012) and Somers-Hall (2021). Few books on French philosophy written in English focus on moral and political philosophy. One notable exception is a book of collected essays edited by Mark Lilla (1994) which includes contributions from Luc Ferry, Jean-Marc Ferry, Marcel Gauchet, Pierre Manent, Bernard Manin, Philippe Raynaud, Anne Godignon, Blandine Kriegel and Alain Renaut (amongst others).

2. See Descombes (1981) for this history of twentieth-century French philosophy. Descombes's book includes discussions of thinkers such as Alexandre Kojève, Maurice Merleau-Ponty, Jean-Paul Sartre, Louis Althusser, Jacques Derrida, Michel Foucault and Gilles Deleuze. One cannot help but notice that no section of the book is devoted to the work of a woman philosopher, and that a more exhaustive treatment of the subject would have included discussions of the work of Simone Weil and Simone de Beauvoir.

3. In formulating this objection, Descombes is indebted to the work of Pierre Aubenque, a French specialist of Aristotle's philosophy. Aubenque underlines that "the pretension of the 'practical syllogism' understood, in the scholastic manner, as the application of the universal principle to the particular case of my action, is to determine what action it is good to perform *without recourse to deliberation*" (Descombes 2007b, 126). See Aubenque (1963) for a more detailed discussion.

4. Unless otherwise specified, quotes from philosophical works in French contained in the references section of this book are translated by me.

5. These claims are part of what is commonly known as Aristotle's *ergon* argument, which he develops in the first book of his *Nicomachean Ethics*. This argument aims to demonstrate that the function of all human beings consists in activity of the rational part of the soul in accordance with virtue.

CHAPTER 4

1. More specifically, chapter 6 retraces a debate between Philippa Foot—the main proponent of contemporary neo-Aristotelian naturalism—and John McDowell.

2. Kant famously made a distinction between the public and private use of reason in a 1784 essay titled "An Answer to the Question: What Is Enlightenment?" See Kant (1996).

3. For a discussion of German neo-Aristotelianism and its pitfalls, see chapter 2.

4. A second important contributor to discourse ethics as a dialogical approach to the foundations of moral judgement is Karl-Otto. See Apel (1998) for an overview of his most important contributions. Unfortunately, I do not have the space to consider his work in this book.

5. As we will see in the conclusion of this book, this objection can also serve as the point of departure of a postcolonial critique of contemporary analytic moral philosophy. Analytic moral philosophers—who typically belong to a similar social class

and often share a similar cultural background—sometimes pretend to have identified universally valid principles of morality through philosophical reflection without engaging in dialogue with people whose identity is radically different from theirs.

6. Ultimately, it seems that Habermas assumes that *no one* can indefinitely resist argumentative discourse. Sooner or later, people attempt to justify their behavior by discussing with others. Interestingly, this claim was the object of a debate between Habermas and French post-structuralist philosopher Jacques Derrida. See Borradori (2003) for a discussion.

7. Bubner (1976, 232) appears to share this view when he writes: "The primary weakness [of discourse ethics] arises because situations of discussion *potentially* but never *factually* include all relevant subjects."

CHAPTER 5

1. Throughout this chapter, I sometimes refer to this philosophical thesis by speaking of the obligations that stem from the multiple dimensions of our practical "identity" (singular). Other times, I speak of the obligations that stem from our practical "identities" (plural). I take both phrasings to refer to the same fundamental idea, which is that we have obligations qua x, where x may refer to a profession (physician, school teacher, lawyer, etc.), a familial relationship (brother, mother, cousin, etc.), friendships, religious affiliations, political affiliations, and so on.

2. For a discussion, see chapter 3, "Vincent Descombes's Critique of Kantian 'Foundationism.'"

3. Here, I summarize what Korsgaard calls the "argument against particularistic willing."

4. In philosophy, a transcendental argument is an argument which begins with an accepted statement and then establishes the conditions which must be met in order for this statement to be true. Consider the following example. For the statement "Étienne is currently speaking" to be true, then it must be the case that the statement "Étienne is alive" is also true (assuming that dead people cannot speak).

5. In what follows, I use "the standpoint of rational human agency" and "the standpoint of humanity" interchangeably.

6. For the sake of discussion, I am assuming that Korsgaard's argument according to which valuing my humanity necessarily entails that I also value the humanity of others is successful.

7. It is possible that Renaut would disagree with my claim that his Kantianism was heavily influenced by French existentialism. In a book devoted to phenomenology and existentialism, Renaut (1993b) criticizes Sartre for his inability to build a moral philosophy out of the theses contained in *Being and Nothingness*. Yet philosophers often underestimate the impact that their intellectual adversaries' views have on their own. I know Renaut quite well—both philosophically and personally—as he was my doctoral supervisor. I remain convinced that his views on valuing and the nature of reasons bear some resemblance to Sartre's own. Fortunately, the reader need not take my word for it; this is the claim that the remainder of this chapter is meant to illustrate.

8. Moral philosophers express this idea in different ways. Instead of saying that my reason to help my brother is "weightier" than my reason to help my friend move, some would write that my reason to spend time with my brother "overrides" my reason to help my friend move or that, "all things considered," I should spend time with my brother instead of helping my friend move.

9. This does not mean that reasons for action are physical entities. In fact, according to Larmore, reasons are neither physical nor psychological, but of a third metaphysical kind. See Renaut and Larmore (2004) for a discussion.

10. The possibility that ethics rest on a fundamentally irrational free decision is one that Renaut takes very seriously. An entire book of his is devoted to a philosophical discussion of this claim. See Renaut and Mesure (1996).

CHAPTER 6

1. For discussion of this claim, see Heidegger, *The Fundamental Concepts of Metaphysics*, §§ 49–50. This book contains notes from a course taught by Heidegger at the University of Freiburg im Breisgau in 1929–1930.

2. As he himself emphasizes, MacIntyre's account of vulnerability and dependence share many similarities with the phenomenology of the human body developed by French philosopher Maurice Merleau-Ponty. As Merleau-Ponty explains in *Phénoménologie de la perception* (1945, 231), philosophers tend to forget that "I am [. . .] my body" (i.e., that is, that human existence is not solely characterized by rational thought, but also by bodily needs). In MacIntyre's perspective, the very fact that I am my body entails that I am a fundamentally vulnerable being.

3. For a discussion of the relationship between Thomas Aquinas's philosophy and MacIntyre's own, see chapter 4, "Overcoming Neo-Aristotelianism."

4. When neo-Aristotelian naturalists speak of "life-forms," they are thinking of natural species, which is not the same as what German neo-Aristotelians have in mind when they discuss "forms of life" (*Lebensformen*). As we have seen, *Lebensformen* essentially refer to historical communities (which, of course, all belong to the same specie).

5. For a detailed discussion of this idea, see chapter 5, "Two Objections Against Korsgaard's Transcendental Argument."

6. Foot borrows the idea that we should derive reasons for action from a representation of the good (and not vice versa) from the late Warren Quinn. See "Putting Rationality in its Place" in Quinn (1993).

7. In his introduction to his French translation of *Natural Goodness*, Jean-Marc Tétaz (2014, 13) opposes the foundationalist interpretation of Foot's philosophical project put forward by McDowell. In Tétaz's view, Foot rejects foundationalism to the extent that she believes, like McDowell, that moral agents come to value certain forms of behaviour by being socialized in a given community. For instance, the main reason I tend to keep my promises is that I am a socialized member of a community which encourages people to keep their promises. To believe that I should, I need not be explained that the keeping of promises contributes to the flourishing of the

human specie. Keeping promises has become part of my "second nature," a concept of McDowell's practical philosophy that I discuss below. Yet it seems to me that McDowell is right and Tétaz is wrong. Although Tétaz is right that moral agents might come to act virtuously without understanding that doing so contributes to the flourishing of the human species, Foot's philosophy still contains an explanation of *why virtuous behaviour is valuable* (i.e., because it contributes to natural goodness). In this sense, it remains foundationalist. By way of contrast, McDowell believes that foundationalist explanations of this kind are unnecessary.

CHAPTER 7

1. For a discussion, see chapter 6, "Rational Wolves and Reasons for Action: McDowell's Critique of Natural Goodness."
2. Kant most clearly defines the duties that fall upon all rational beings in his *Metaphysics of Morals*, which is itself divided into the "Doctrine of Right" and the "Doctrine of Virtue." While the former focuses on legal duties, the latter discusses moral duties.
3. In mathematics, an axiom is a self-evident statement that is not proven (i.e., derived from other rules), but from which other statements are derived.
4. This assertion runs contrary to Kant's claim, in the *Metaphysics of Morals*, that "a *collision of duties* and obligations is inconceivable." See Kant (1996, 379).
5. In contemporary moral philosophy, philosophers often use the expression "*pro tanto* duty" to refer to an obligation which might be overridden by other moral considerations. What they mean by this is no different than what Ross names prima facie duty, which translates as "duty at first sight."
6. For a discussion of these principles, see chapter 1, "Rawls on Duty, Desire and the Categorical Imperative." Rawls also argues that the equal opportunity principle takes precedence over the difference principle.
7. Translators typically translate "*Urtheilkraft*" as "judgement" or "power of judgement." The original title of Kant's third *Critique—Kritik der Urtheilskraft—*thus translates as *Critique of Judgement* or *Critique of the Power of Judgement*. Throughout this section, I use the modern German spelling, which drops the "h" in *Urtheilskfraft*.
8. In Kant's philosophy, the sublime refers to the feeling of our reason's own superiority over nature, and teleology refers to appeals to ends or purposes in our understanding of nature. See Ginsborg (2015) for a discussion.
9. This is known as the "banality of evil" thesis. By defending it, Arendt isolated herself from the postwar Jewish community, the intellectual leaders of which tended to portray men like Eichmann as having deliberately sought to do evil instead of unreflectively following directives. By way of contrast, Arendt is committed to the view that what Eichmann primarily lacked was a capacity for critical thinking. For a discussion, see Arendt (2006).
10. Interestingly, Singer might disagree with this point. The purpose of the drowning child scenario is to convince us that we should devote a significant portion of

our assets to charitable giving. As Singer argues, you have a moral duty to save lives through charitable giving just like you have a moral duty to save the drowning child. Ultimately, there are no morally relevant differences between these two cases. Right now, while sitting alone at home, you could take decisions that would save lives.

11. For a discussion of this problem, see chapter 1, "The Critique of Kantianism in MacIntyre's Communitarian Aristotelianism."

12. I discuss rules of moral salience in greater detail in the next chapter. See chapter 8, "Moral Literacy and Autonomous Judgement."

13. Here, my remarks are influenced by Rawls's interpretation of Kant's practical philosophy according to which the categorical imperative is a heuristic device which allows us to compare possible worlds. Arguably, a world in which all people prioritize the avoidance of embarrassment over the preservation of friendships would be worse than a world in which they do the opposite.

14. For a discussion, see chapter 3, "Vincent Descombes' Critique of Kantian 'Foundationism.'"

CHAPTER 8

1. As the apartheid example demonstrates, traditional norms are sometimes unjust. For a discussion of this problem, see chapter 2.

2. Habermas's own philosophy of education clearly contains this idea. Relying on Lawrence Kohlberg's theory of moral development, he argues that agents must learn to respect authority. Yet Habermas also emphasizes that the two final stages of moral development should bring agents to question authority. Specifically, agents should wonder whether socially dominant norms are compatible with individual rights and universal ethical principles. For a discussion of this point, see Habermas (1993), "Lawrence Kohlberg and Neo-Aristotelianism."

3. Neo-Aristotelians can avoid this objection by arguing that they only defend the second of these two theses, not the first. As Aristotle explains in the *Nicomachean Ethics*, virtuous agents do not act for the sake of happiness, but for the sake of the noble (*to kalon*). While acting for the sake of the noble does make virtuous agents happy, happiness need not be the *aim* of their actions.

4. See O'Neill (1996, 100–6) for a detailed discussion of these three assumptions.

5. One way in which moral agents can non-arbitrarily and justifiably injure others is through acts of self-defence.

6. In O'Neill's perspective, all human beings fall within the relevant domain of ethical concern. For a discussion of this claim, see O'Neill (1996, 97–100).

7. Considering the level of political polarization which currently plagues democracies, the contemporary relevance of this virtue seems obvious to me. For an interesting discussion of political polarization and possible responses to it, see Talisse (2019).

8. Here, I use "co-citizens" in a broad sense. In my view, this term refers to all people who live within the boundaries of a political territory. That some of them are not legal citizens but documented or undocumented migrants does not exclude them from citizenship in the philosophical sense.

9. The insurrectionists who violently stormed the Capitol Building on January 6, 2021, to overthrow the U.S. government have demonstrated that hatred for one's political opponents can also incite people to violate the principle of non-injury. Accordingly, we can envision tolerance as a virtue that helps moral agents respect both the principle of non-injury and the principle of non-indifference.

(A MERLEAU-PONTIAN) CONCLUSION

1. *Astheneia* and *propeteia* are two forms of what Aristotle (1984, 100–14) names *akrasia*, or weakness of will. For a discussion of *akrasia*, see Book VII of the *Nicomachean Ethics*. See also Kraut (2018).

2. For a discussion of this objection, see chapter 6, "Rational Wolves and Reasons for Action: McDowell's Critique of Natural Goodness."

3. Borrowing language from epistemologists, we can say that I possess "weak" expertise in this case. Individuals possess strong expertise when they possess superior epistemic skills over others and, as a result, can fulfill cognitive tasks better than others when presented with the same body of evidence. If an obstetrician and a layperson are presented with the same ultrasound, for example, the obstetrician will be in a better position to tell if a foetus is developing normally. By way of contrast, individuals possess weak expertise when they have access to evidence that is unavailable to others. There are many types of situations in which it is uncontroversial to claim that a person S will "at that time be epistemically expert relative to person H regarding some subject W" (Fricker 2006: 234).

4. The Collège de France is a prestigious public research institution created by François I in 1530. Its constitutive chairs are usually attributed to well-respected scholars who near the end of their career and then provide the public with free lectures. Merleau-Ponty held the Chair of Philosophy from 1952 until his death in 1961.

5. Admittedly, Merleau-Ponty's conference is not devoid of racist terminology. For instance, he contrasts the point of view of "civilized" people with that of "primitive" people. Like Bachir Diagne, I make the philosophical gamble that Merleau-Ponty's concept of the lateral universal can nonetheless serve anti-racist ends.

6. This is the fundamental idea defended by Michaeleen Doucleff in her best-selling book *Hunt, Gather, Parent*. Doucleff contrasts American parenting practices with those of Mayan, Inuit and Hadzabe families. Her reflection builds on the psychological research of Joseph Henrich (2020), who argues that Western, educated, industrialized, rich and democratic (WEIRD) societies consistently underestimate how peculiar their cultural practices are.

7. The passage is quoted in Bachir Diagne (2013, 9).

8. One philosophical subdiscipline which actively uses the tools of social science to inform philosophical reflection is experimental philosophy. See Knobe and Nichols (2016) for an introduction.

References

al-Attar, Mariam. 2017. "Meta-ethics: A Quest for an Epistemological Basis of Morality in Classical Islamic Thought." *Journal of Islamic Ethics* 1 (1/2): 29–50.
Anscombe, Elizabeth. 1957. *Intention*. Cambridge: Harvard University Press.
———. 1958. "Modern Moral Philosophy." *Philosophy* 33 (124): 1–19.
———. 1969. "On Promising and Its Justice, and Whether It Needs Be Respected *In Foro Interno*." *Critica* 3 (7/8): 61–83.
Apel, Karl-Otto. 1998. *Towards a Transformation of Philosophy*, translated by Glyn Adey and David Fisby. Milwaukee, WI: Marquette University Press.
Arendt, Hannah. 1961. *Between Past and Future: Six Exercises in Political Thought*. New York: The Viking Press.
———. 1992. *Lectures on Kant's Political Philosophy*, edited by Ronald Beiner. Chicago: The University of Chicago press.
———. 2006. *Eichmann in Jerusalem: A Report on the Banality of Evil*. London: Penguin Classics.
Aristotle. 1984a. *Complete Works. The Revised Oxford Translation. Volume One*, edited by Jonathan Barnes. Princeton: Princeton University Press.
———. 1984b. *Complete Works. The Revised Oxford Translation. Volume Two*, edited by Jonathan Barnes. Princeton: Princeton University Press.
Aubenque, Pierre. 1963. *La prudence chez Aristote*. Paris: Presses universitaires de France.
Ayer, Alfred J. 1936. *Language, Truth and Logic*. London: Gollancz.
Bachir Diagne, Souleyman. 2013. "On the Postcolonial and the Universal?" *Rue Descartes* 78 (2): 7–18.
Bachir Diagne, Souleyman, and Jean-Loup Amselle. 2018. *En quête d'Afrique(s): Universalisme et pensée décoloniale*. Paris: Albin Michel.
Beiner, Ronald. 1997. "Rereading Hannah Arendt's Kant Lectures." *Philosophy and Social Criticism* 23 (1): 21–32.
Bodéüs, Richard. 1989. "Deux propositions aristotéliciennes sur le droit naturel chez les continentaux d'Amérique." *Revue de Métaphysique et de Morale* 94 (3): 369–89.
Borradori, Giovanna. 2003. *Philosophy in a Time of Terror: Dialogues with Jürgen Habermas and Jacques Derrida*. Chicago: The University of Chicago Press.

Brown, Étienne. 2020. "Kant's Doctrine of the Highest Good: A Theologico-Political Interpretation." *Kantian Review* 25 (2): 193–217.

Bubner, Rüdiger. 1973. "Action and Reason." *Ethics* 83 (3): 224–36.

———. 1976. *Handlung, Sprache und Vernunft*. Frankfurt am Main: Suhrkamp.

———. 1984. "Rationalität, Lebensform und Geschichte." In *Rationalität. Philosophische Beiträge*, edited by Herbert Schnädelbach, 198–217. Frankfurt am Main: Suhrkamp Verlag.

Canto-Sperber, Monique. 2001. *Éthiques Grecques*. Paris: Presses Universitaires de France.

Carson, Thomas L. 2006. "The Definition of Lying." *Noûs* 40 (2): 284–306.

Cohen, G. A. 1996. "Reason, Humanity and the Moral Law." In *The Sources of Normativity*, by Christine Korsgaard, 167–88. Cambridge: Cambridge University Press.

Coulthard, Glen S. 2014. *Red Skin, White Masks: Rejecting the Colonial Politics of Recognition*. Minneapolis: University of Minnesota Press.

Descombes, Vincent. 1981. *Modern French Philosophy*. Cambridge: Cambridge University Press.

———. 1994. *Philosophie du jugement politique*. Paris: Points.

———. 2007a. *Questions disputées*, edited by Bruno Gnassouou and Cyrille Michon. Nantes: Éditions Cécile Defaut.

———. 2007b. *Le raisonnement de l'ours et autres essais de philosophie pratique*. Paris: Éditions du Seuil.

Doucleff, Michaeleen. 2021. *Hunt, Gather, Parent: What Ancient Cultures Can Teach Us about the Lost Art of Raising Happy Helpful Little Humans*. New York: Avid Reader Press.

Ferry, Jean-Marc. 1994a. *Philosophie de la communication. 1. De l'antinomie de la vérité à la fondation ultime de la raison*. Paris: Éditions du Cerf.

———. 1994b. *Philosophie de la communication. 2. Justice politique et démocratie procédurale*. Paris: Éditions du Cerf.

Finlayson, James Gordon. 2019. *The Rawls-Habermas Debate*. New York: Columbia University Press.

Foot, Philippa. 2001. *Natural Goodness*. New York: Oxford University Press.

Freeman, Samuel. 2019. "Original Position." In *The Stanford Encyclopedia of Philosophy*, edited by Edward N. Zalta.

Fricker, Elizabeth. 2006. "Testimony and Epistemic Autonomy." In *The Epistemology of Testimony*, edited by Jennifer Lackey and Ernest Sosoa, 225–53. New York: Oxford University Press.

Fuller, Lon. 1958. "Positivism and Fidelity to Law." *Harvard Law Review* 71 (4): 630–72.

Gadamer, Hans-Georg. 2004. *Truth and Method, Second, Revised Edition*. London: Continuum.

———. 2007. *The Gadamer Reader. A Bouquet of the Later Writings*, edited by Richard E. Palmer. Evanston, IL: Northwestern University Press.

Geach, Peter T. 1956. "Good and Evil." *Analysis* 17 (2): 33–42.

———. 1972. *Logic Matters*. Berkeley: University of California Press.

———. 1977. *The Virtues*. Cambridge: Cambridge University Press.
Ginsborg, Hannah. 2015. *The Normativity of Nature: Essays on Kant's* Critique of Judgement. Oxford: Oxford University Press.
Günther, Klaus. 1993. *The Sense of Appropriateness: Application Discourses in Law and Morality*. Albany: SUNY Press.
Gutting, Gary. 2001. *French Philosophy in the Twentieth Century*. Cambridge: Cambridge University Press.
Habermas, Jürgen. 1984. "Über Moralität und Sittlichkeit—Was macht eine Lebensform 'rational'?" In *Rationalität. Philosophische Beiträge*, edited by Herbert Schnädelbach, 218–35. Frankfurt am Main: Suhrkamp Verlag.
———. 1990. *Moral Consciousness and Communicative Action*, translated by Christian Lenhardt and Shierry Weber Nicholsen. Oxford: Polity Press.
———. 1993. *Justification and Application: Remarks on Discourse Ethics*, translated by Ciaran Cronin. Cambridge, MA: MIT Press.
Heidegger, Martin. 1995. *The Fundamental Concepts of Metaphysics: World, Finitude, Solitude*. Bloomington: Indiana University Press.
———. 2010. *Being and Time*, translated by Joan Stambaugh. Albany: SUNY Press.
Herman, Barbara. 1993. *The Practice of Moral Judgment*. Cambridge, MA: Harvard University Press.
———. 2007. *Moral Literacy*. Cambridge, MA: Harvard University Press.
Henrich, Joseph. 2020. *The WEIRDest People in the World: How the West Became Psychologically Peculiar and Particularly Prosperous*. New York: Farrar, Straus and Giroux.
Höffe, Otfried. 1990. "Universalistiche Ethik und Urteilskraft: Ein aristotelischer Blick auf Kant." *Zeitschrift für philosophische Forschung* 44 (4): 537–63.
Hume, David. 1888. *A Treatise of Human Nature*, edited by L. A. Selby-Bigge. Oxford: Clarendon.
Hursthouse, Rosalind. 2001. *On Virtue Ethics*. New York: Oxford University Press.
James, Ian. 2012. *The New French Philosophy*. Cambridge: Polity Press.
Kant, Immanuel. 1996. *Practical Philosophy*, edited by Paul Guyer and Allen W. Wood. Cambridge: Cambridge University Press.
———. 1998. *Critique of Pure Reason*, edited by Paul Guyer and Allen W. Wood. Cambridge: Cambridge University Press.
———. 2000. *Critique of the Power of Judgment*, edited by Paul Guyer. Cambridge: Cambridge University Press.
———. 2001. *Religion and Rational Theology*, edited and translated Allen W. Wood and George di Giovanni. Cambridge: Cambridge University Press.
———. 2007. *Anthropology, History, and Education*, edited by Günther Zöller and Robert B. Louden. Cambridge: Cambridge University Press.
Knobe, Joshua, and Shaun Nichols. 2018. *Experimental Philosophy*. New York: Oxford University Press.
Korsgaard, Christine. 1996. *The Sources of Normativity*. Cambridge: Cambridge University Press.
———. 2008. *The Constitution of Agency: Essays on Practical Reason and Moral Psychology*. Oxford: Oxford University Press.

———. 2009. *Self-Constitution: Agency, Identity and Integrity*. Oxford: Oxford University Press.

Kraut, Richard. 2018. "Aristotle's Ethics." In *The Stanford Encyclopedia of Philosophy*, edited by Edward N. Zalta.

Lai, Karyn L. 2009. "Judgment in Confucian Ethics." *Sophia* 48 (1): 77–84.

Langton, Rae. 1993. "Speech Acts and Unspeakable Acts." *Philosophy & Public Affairs* 22 (4): 392–30.

Lilla, Mark. 1994. *New French Thought: Political Philosophy*. Princeton, NJ: Princeton University Press.

MacIntyre, Alasdair. 1957. "What Morality Is Not." *Philosophy* 32 (123): 325–35.

———. 1988. *Whose Justice? Which Rationality?* Notre Dame, IN: University of Notre Dame Press.

———. 1999. *Dependent Rational Animals*. Chicago: Open Court Publishing.

———. 2006. *The Tasks of Philosophy: Selected Essays. Volume 1*. Cambridge: Cambridge University Press.

———. 2007. *After Virtue: A Study in Moral Theory, Third Edition*. Notre Dame, IN: University of Notre Dame Press.

Mandeville, Bernard. 1989. *The Fable of the Bees*. London: Penguin Books.

Marquard, Odo. 2003. "Positivierte Entzweiung. Joachim Ritters Philosopher der bürgerlichen Welt." In *Metaphysik und Politik. Erweiterte Neuausgabe*, by Joachim Ritter, 442–56. Frankfurt am Main: Suhrkamp Verlag.

McDowell, John. 1979. "Virtue and Reason." *The Monist* 62 (3): 331–50.

———. 1998. *Mind, Value and Reality*. Cambridge, MA: Harvard University Press.

———. 2009. *The Engaged Intellect: Philosophical Essays*. Cambridge, MA: Harvard University Press.

Menkiti, Ifeanyi A. 1984. "Person and Community in African Traditional Thought." In *African Philosophy: An Introduction. Third Edition*, edited by R. A. Wright, 171–81. New York: University Press of America.

Merleau-Ponty, Maurice. 1945. *Phénoménologie de la perception*. Paris: Gallimard.

———. 2008. "Rapport pour la création d'une chaire d'Anthropologie sociale." *La lettre du Collège de France* Hors-Série 2: 49–53.

Metz, Thaddeus. 2007. "Toward an African Moral Theory." *Journal of Political Philosophy* 15 (3): 321–341.

Milkman, Katherine L., Modupe Akinola and Dolly Chugh. 2015. "What Happens Before? A Field Experiment Exploring How Pay and Representation Differentially Shape Bias on the Pathway into Organizations." *Journal of Applied Psychology* 100 (6): 1678–1712.

Mill, John S. 2002. *On Liberty, Utilitarianism and Other Essays*, edited by Mark Philip and Frederick Rosen. New York: Oxford University Press.

Mills, Charles W. 2017. *Black Rights/White Wrongs: The Critique of Racial Liberalism*. New York: Oxford University Press.

Mulla, Zubin R., and Venkat R. Krishnan. 2014. "Karma-Yoga: The Indian Model of Moral Development." *Journal of Business Ethics* 123 (2): 339–51.

O'Neill, Onora. 1996. *Toward Justice and Virtue: A Constructive Account of Moral Reasoning*. Cambridge: Cambridge University Press.

———. 2001. "Practical Principles & Practical Judgment." *The Hastings Center Report* 31 (4): 15–23.

———. 2007. "Normativity and Practical Judgement." *Journal of Moral Philosophy* 4 (3): 393–405.

———. 2013. *Acting on Principle: An Essay on Kantian Ethics*. Cambridge: Cambridge University Press.

Quinn, Warren. 1993. *Morality and Action*. Cambridge: Cambridge University Press.

Rawls, John. 1980. "Kantian Constructivism in Moral Theory." *Journal of Philosophy* 77 (9): 515–72.

———. 1993. *Political Liberalism*. New York: Columbia University Press.

———. 1999a. *A Theory of Justice, Revised Edition*. Cambridge, MA: Harvard University Press.

———. 1999b. *Collected Papers*, edited by Samuel Freeman. Cambridge, MA: Harvard University Press.

———. 2000. *Lectures on the History of Moral Philosophy*, edited by Barbara Herman. Cambridge, MA: Harvard University Press.

Renaut, Alain. 1993a. "Habermas ou Rawls?" *Réseaux* 11 (60): 123–36.

———. 1993b. *Sartre: Le dernier philosophe*. Paris: Grasset.

———. 2003. "L'éthique de la discussion. Questions et réponses." In *L'éthique de la discussion et la question de la vérité*, by Jürgen Habermas, 11–15. Paris: Grasset.

Renaut, Alain, and Charles Larmore. 2004. *Débat sur l'éthique*. Paris: Grasset.

Renaut, Alain, and Sylvie Mesure. 1996. *La guerre des dieux: Essai sur la querelle des valeurs*. Paris: Grasset.

Ritter, Joachim. 1982. "Morality and Ethical Life: Hegel's Controversy with Kantian Ethics." In *Hegel and the French Revolution*, translated by Richard D. Winfield, 151–82. Cambridge, MA: MIT Press.

———. 2003. *Metaphysik und Politik*. Frankfurt am Main: Suhrkamp Verlag.

Ross, David. *The Right and the Good*, edited by Philip Stratton-Lake. New York: Oxford University Press.

Sartre, Jean-Paul. 1969. *Being and Nothingness*, translated by Hazel E. Barnes. London: Methuen Press.

———. 2007. *Existentialism Is a Humanism*, translated by Carl Macomber and edited by John Kulka. New Haven, CT: Yale University Press.

Schroeder, Mark. 2007. *Slave of the Passions*. New York: Oxford University Press.

Sherman, Nancy. 1997. *Making a Necessity of Virtue: Aristotle and Kant on Virtue*. Cambridge: Cambridge University Press.

Sibley, W. M. 1953. "The Rational versus the Reasonable." *Philosophical Review* 62 (4): 554–60.

Singer, Peter. 1972. "Famine, Influence and Morality." *Philosophy and Public Affairs* 1 (3): 229–43.

Somers-Hall, Henry. 2021. *Judgement and Sense in Modern French Philosophy: A New Reading of Six Thinkers*. Cambridge: Cambridge University Press.

Sticker, Martin. 2015. "Educating the Common Agent: Kant on the Varieties of Moral Education." *Archiv für Geschichte der Philosophie* 97 (3): 358–87.

Talisse, Robert. 2019. *Overdoing Democracy: Why We Must Put Politics in Its Place*. New York: Oxford University Press.

Tétaz, Jean-Marc. 2014. *Le bien naturel*. Geneva: Labor et Fides.

Thompson, Michael. 2008. *Life and Action: Elementary Structures of Practice and Practical Thought*. Cambridge, MA: Harvard University Press.

Tugendhat, Ernst. 1992. *Philosophische Aufsätze*. Frankfurt am Main: Suhrkamp.

Van Norden, Bryan W. 2017. *Taking Back Philosophy: A Multicultural Manifesto*. New York: Columbia University Press.

Varden, Helga. 2010. "Kant and Lying to the Murderer at the Door . . . One More Time: Kant's Legal Philosophy and Lies to Murderers and Nazis." *Journal of Social Philosophy* 41 (4): 403–21.

Werner-Müller, Jan. 2003. *A Dangerous Mind: Carl Schmitt in Post-War European Thought*. New Haven, CT: Yale University Press.

Wiggins, David. 1975–1976. "Deliberation and Practical Reason." *Proceedings of the Aristotelian Society* 76: 29–51+viii.

Williams, Bernard. 2011. *Ethics and the Limits of Philosophy*. London: Routledge.

Williams, Caroline. 2001. *Contemporary French Philosophy: Modernity and the Persistence of the Subject*. London: The Athlone Press.

Wittgenstein, Ludwig. 2009. *Philosophical Investigations*, edited by P. M. S. Hacker and Joachim Schulte. West-Sussex: Wiley-Blackwell.

Wolin, Richard. 2000. "Untruth and Method: Nazism and the Complicities of Hans-Georg Gadamer." *New Republic* 222 (20): 36–45.

Wood, Allen. 2011. "Kant and Agent-Oriented Ethics." In *Perfecting Virtue: New Essays on Kantian Ethics and Virtue Ethics*, edited by Lawrence Jost and Julian Wuerth,

Wynes, Seth, and Kimberly A. Nicholas. 2017. "The Climate Mitigation Gap: Education and Government Recommendations Miss the Most Effective Individual Actions." *Environmental Research Letter* 12 (7): article id. 074024.

Index

acting according to one's own law, 100–102
active gratitude, 185
adjusted social world, 23
aesthetic judgements, 46, 153–156
affective gratitude, 185
affects, 183
After Virtue (MacIntyre), 60, 121
akrasia, 213n1
analytic moral philosophy, 208–209n5
"Analytic of Pure Practical Reason" (Kant), 20
Anscombe, Elizabeth, 8, 26, 57, 60–63, 118, 120, 128, 135–136, 206n9, 209n7
"Answer to the Question: What Is Enlightenment? An" (Kant), 208n2
Anthropology (Kant), 183–184
apathy, 183–184
Aquinas, Thomas of, 78, 125
Arendt, Hannah, 9, 10, 71, 147, 152–162, 163–164, 207n9
argumentation, rules of, 51
Aristotelian categoricals, 131–132, 135, 137
Aristotle: animal behaviour and, 131; Descombes and, 58, 59–60; Gadamer and, 45, 49; *History of Animals*, 131; influence of, 4–7; Kant and, 180, 191; MacIntyre and, 26, 27; *Metaphysics*, 132; nature and, 121; *Nicomachean Ethics*, 5, 31, 42, 43, 45, 59–60, 121, 123, 140, 179, 191, 208n5; perception and, 148; *Politics*, 42; on practical wisdom, 144, 168; racist elements of, 13; Ritter and, 42, 43; syllogisms and, 31–32; unity of virtue and, 33–34, 78; on virtuous action, 140–143, 212n31n
astheneia, 194
attributive adjectives, 128–129
Aubenque, Pierre, 208n3
authoritarianism, 39–40, 44
autonomous judgement, 174–178
autonomy, 21, 100–102, 115–116, 119

Bachir Diagne, Souleymane, 10, 201, 201–204, 213n5
bad faith, acting in, 113–114
"banality of evil" thesis, 211n9
"Bear and the Gardener, The" (La Fontaine), 68
Beiner, Ronald, 155–156
Being and Nothingness (Sartre), 112–113
Bentham, Jeremy, 6
"blood and soil" propaganda, 207n1
Bodéüs, Richard, 39

Bubner, Rüdiger, 8, 10, 40, 52–56, 75, 82–84, 114, 209n7

Canto-Sperber, Monique, 11
Capitol insurrection, 213n9
Carson, Thomas, 55
categorical imperative, 5, 7–8, 18–25, 53, 101–102, 117, 166–167
charity (*caritas*), 78
CI-Procedure, 23–25
cognitive function of virtues, 193–194
Cohen, G. A., 108
Cohen, Hermann, 205n10
Collegium philosophicum, 41
collision of duties, 65–66
communal norms, 43, 47–48, 54–55
communitarianism, 205n10
conceptual thought, animals and, 123–124
Constant, Benjamin, 64, 171
critical theory, 49
Critique of Practical Reason (Kant), 46
Critique of Pure Reason (Kant), 46, 101
Critique of the Power of Judgement (Kant), 45–46, 71, 153, 161

Dasein, 47
Davidson, Donald, 123
decisionism, 59
deductive theoretical reasoning, 67
deliberation, 66–69, 171–172
deliberative presumptions, 166–168, 171
Dependent Rational Animal (MacIntyre), 122–123, 126, 127–128, 136
Derrida, Jacques, 209n6
Descombes, Vincent, 8, 10, 11, 57–72, 76, 98–100, 110, 118, 120
determining judgement, 153, 161–162
dialogical approaches to moral judgement, 84–88
difference principle, 150
discernment, 68
discourse ethics, 8, 50–52, 54–55, 76, 89–95

Doctrine of Rights (Kant), 52, 186, 211n2
Doctrine of Virtue (Kant), 9, 65, 161–172, 179, 181–182, 183, 185, 186, 188, 195, 211n2
Doucleff, Michealeen, 213n6
drowning child scenario, 162–163
duty/duties: collision of, 65–66; imperfect, 147–148, 162–172; moral, 17; natural, 18–19; negative, 18–19, 65; perfect, 171–172; positive, 18–19, 65; prima facie, 149–150; Samaritan, 5

Eichmann in Jerusalem (Arendt), 156
empathy, 193–194
empirical practical reason, 22
enlarged mentality, 154–157, 161, 201
Enlightenment, 26, 27
equal opportunity principle, 150
ergon argument, 208n5
ethical naturalism, 9, 128–136
ethos, 8, 40, 41–45, 47, 49
evil, temptation of, 206n4
excellence, internal standards of, 35
excellency of reason, 134
excellency of will, 134
exemplars/exemplary validity, 157–161
existentialism, 112, 114–116, 119
Existentialism Is a Humanism (Sartre), 29–30

Fable of the Bees (Mandeville), 126
Ferry, Jean-Marc, 75–76, 87–88, 92
Finlayson, James Gordon, 86
first-person reasoning, 68
Flaubert, Gustave, 137
Foot, Philippa, 9, 10, 11, 122, 128, 129–134, 139–140, 208n1
formalism, 165
forms of life (*Lebensformen*), 8, 53, 82–83, 210n4
Formula of Humanity, 102, 103, 105, 108–109
Formula of Universal Law, 51, 53, 102

foundationists, 58–59
free acts of will in moral judgement, 100–101, 115–117
freedom to prioritize, 112
Fuller, Lon, 47
Fundamental Concepts of Metaphysics, The (Heidegger), 210n1

Gadamer, Hans-Georg, 8, 40, 45–49, 56, 200
Geach, Peter, 8, 57, 66–67, 128–129, 135–136
Geworfenheit, 47
"Good and Evil" (Geach), 128–129
gratitude, 185–186
greatest equal liberty principle, 150
Greek Ethics (Canto-Sperber), 11
grounding of moral judgement, 5, 7–9, 56, 69, 70, 75, 94, 120
Groundwork for the Metaphysics of Morals (Kant), 102, 159, 178–179, 181, 183
Günther, Klaus, 42

Habermas, Jürgen, 8, 10, 39–40, 44, 49–56, 71, 75, 82–92, 203
happiness (*eudaimonia*), 179
Hart, H. L. A., 47
Hegel, 42, 43
Heidegger, Martin, 47, 123, 210n1
Henrich, Joseph, 213n6
Herman, Barbara, 9, 10, 161, 165–168, 171–172, 173, 174–178
hermeneutics, 45, 47, 207n7
heteronomy, 21
historical relativism, 34–35, 37, 52–53, 56, 75, 76, 77–80, 121–122
History of Animals (Aristotle), 131
Höffe, Otfried, 162
Homer, 157–158
Humanity, Formula of, 102, 103, 105, 108–109
Hume, David, 27, 79
Hunt, Gather, Parent (Doucleff), 213n6
Hursthouse, Rosalind, 130, 173

Husserl, Edmund, 202

"idealized Mafioso," 108
ignorance, veil of, 86–87
Iliad (Homer), 157–158
imagination, 153–154
imperfect duty, 147–148, 162–172
indeterminacy, problem of, 9
instrumental rationality, 21–22
intentionalist account of practical reasoning, 8, 57, 63–69
internal standards of excellence, 35

judgement, faculty of (*Urteilskraft*), 45–46, 147, 152–161, 162, 163–164, 195–197
justice, Rawls on, 18–19

Kant, Immanuel: aesthetic judgements and, 153–156; "Analytic of Pure Practical Reason," 20; "An Answer to the Question: What Is Enlightenment?" 208n2; *Anthropology*, 183–184; Bubner and, 52–53; *Critique of Practical Reason*, 46; *Critique of Pure Reason*, 46, 101; *Critique of the Power of Judgement*, 46, 71, 153, 161; Descombes and, 58–63; *Doctrine of Rights*, 52, 186, 211n2; *Doctrine of Virtue*, 9, 65, 161–172, 179, 181–182, 183, 185, 186, 188, 195, 211n2; exemplary validity and, 159; free will and, 101–102; *Groundwork for the Metaphysics of Morals*, 102, 159, 178–179, 181, 183; on imperfect duty, 170; influence of, 4–7; *Lectures on Pedagogy*, 174–175, 191; on leeway in judgement, 168–169; MacIntyre and, 25–31; *Metaphysics of Morals*, 46, 72, 161, 169, 170, 171, 180, 183, 184, 186, 211n2, 211n4; moral deliberation and, 161; on moral education, 173–174; on moral maxims, 175; "murderer at the door" case and, 64–65; neo-Aristotelian critique of, 70–72; *Pedagogy*, 9; on private use of reason, 81–82; racists elements of, 12–13; Rawls and, 19–21; *Religion within the Bounds of Mere Reason*, 182; Ritter and, 43; universal law and, 165–166; *Urteilskraft* model and, 45–46, 147; on virtue, 178–182

"Kantian Constructivism in Moral Theory" (Rawls), 22

Kantian models, overview of objections to, 7, 70–72

Kantian virtues, 182–191

Karl-Otto, 208n4

Kohlberg, Lawrence, 212n2

Korsgaard, Christine, 8–10, 63, 71, 75, 85, 97–99, 100–102, 103–112, 119, 199

La Fontaine, Jean de, 68

language, philosophy of ordinary, 128–129

Larmore, Charles, 115, 117–118, 199

lateral universal, 10, 200, 203–204

laws of nature, 24

Lectures on Kant's Political Philosophy (Arendt), 152–153, 157–158

Lectures on Pedagogy (Kant), 174–175, 191

Lectures on the History of Moral Philosophy (Rawls), 206n5

leeway (*latitudo*), 170–171, 175, 195

lexical ordering, 19, 147, 148–152

liberalism, 187

Life of the Mind, The (Arendt), 152

Logic Matters (Geach), 66–67

logical positivism, 206n6

logos, 136–137, 141, 143

Lübbe, Herman, 41

lying example, 46, 55, 143

MacIntyre, Alasdair: analytic philosophers and, 10; on animal behaviour, 133; critique of Kantianism in, 25–31; historical relativism and, 56, 77–80, 121–122; identities and, 60; illusion of self-sufficiency and, 123–126; narrative conception of self and, 76; neo-Aristotelianism and, 11; neutral philosophical standpoint and, 127–128; O'Neill and, 83; as particularist, 81; *phronesis* and, 71; practical identities and, 103, 110; practical wisdom and, 32–36; rational grounding and, 9; Rawls and, 7–8, 17; on reflection, 136; summary of, 75; traditional norms and, 114

Madame Bovary (Flaubert), 137

Mandeville, Barnard, 126

margin of tolerance (*Toleranzmarge*), 55

Marquard, Odo, 41, 207n4

McDowell, John, 10, 47, 122, 136–144, 149, 197, 208n1, 210–211n7

Menkiti, Ifeanyi, 36

mercy, 125–126

Merleau-Ponty, Maurice, 10, 200–204, 210n2

Metaphysics (Aristotle), 132

Metaphysics of Morals (Kant), 46, 72, 161, 169, 170, 171, 180, 183, 184, 186, 211n2, 211n4

military actions, 2–3

Mill, John Stuart, 6

Mills, Charles, 12–13

"Modern Moral Philosophy" (Anscombe), 26

Modernity, 25–28

monological approaches to moral judgement, 75, 84–88

moral duty, 17

moral education, 173–174, 178

moral faults, examination of, 2

moral improvisation, 177

Moral Law, 102

moral literacy, 174–178

moral perception, 166–167

moral reasoning, instrumental rationality and, 21–22

moral salience, rules of, 166
moral sensation (*aisthesis*), 5
moral universalism, 40
Moralität, 42–43
"murderer at the door" case, 64–65, 171

narrative conception of self, 35–36, 76–77
natural duties, 18–19
natural goodness: critique of, 136–144; neo-Aristotelianism and, 122; overview of argument of, 128–136
Natural Goodness, 210–211n7
natural law, 43
nature: Aristotle's conception of, 121; laws of, 24
Nazism, 39–40, 44, 52
negative duties, 18–19, 65
neo-Aristotelian, use of term, 11
neo-Aristotelianism: critique of Kantian judgement and, 70–72; overcoming, 76–84. *See also individual thinkers*
Nicomachean Ethics (Aristotle), 5, 31, 42, 43, 45, 59–60, 121, 123, 140, 179, 191, 208n5
non-indifference, principle of, 189
non-injury, principle of, 188–189
Normal People (Rooney), 1, 3
normativist account of moral reasoning, 63–69
normativity of practical identities thesis, 97, 99–100, 102–106
norms/social norms: communal, 43, 47–48, 54–55; dominant, 40–41, 82–83; questioning of, 111–112; traditional, 114–115
"North American Continentals," 39

obligations, 18
"On the Possibility of a Philosophical Ethics" (Gadamer), 49
O'Neill, Onora, 10, 72, 75, 80–81, 83, 91, 161, 163–164, 178, 186–191, 212n6
original position, 85–88

overarching universal, 200–201, 202

particularists, Aristotelian, 81. *See also* tradition/traditionalism
passions, 183
Pedagogy (Kant), 9
perfect duties, 171–172
perfect virtue, 181
"Person and Community in African Traditional Thought" (Menkiti), 36
Phénoménologie de la perception (Merleau-Ponty), 210n2
phenomenology, 10
phronesis, 5–6, 8, 31–37, 68, 71, 147, 155, 163, 168, 169, 197–198
policy-making, example of, 66
Politics (Aristotle), 42
pornography example, 176–177
positive duties, 18–19, 65
practical identities, 59–63, 97–98, 102–108, 109–112, 118–120, 198–199
practical reasoning, 66–68
practical syllogism, 31–37, 208n3
practical wisdom (*phronesis*), 5–6, 8, 31–37, 147, 155, 163, 168, 169, 197–198
pre-deliberative moral knowledge, 166–167
predicative adjectives, 128–129
"prejudice" (*Vorurteil*), 47–48
prima facie duties, 149–150
principle of discourse ethics, 51–52, 54–55, 89–95
principle of universalization (U), 51, 89–95
principles, moral faults and, 2
principles for individuals, 18
prioritize, freedom to, 112
priority of the right over the good, 20
priority problem, 149–152
promising, 135, 140–141
propeteia, 194
pure practical reason, 22

Quinn, Warren, 210n6

racism in the history of philosophy, 12–13
ranking of human goods, 76–78
rational agency, 63
rational forms of life, 82–83
rational grounding of moral judgements, 8, 94–95
rational human agents, practical identities and, 103–108
"rational Nazi" thought experiment, 60–63, 99–100, 110
Rational versus Reasonable, 22
rational wolf experiment, 136–138
Rawls, John: analytic philosophers and, 10; on duty, desire, and categorical imperative, 18–25; Habermas and, 51–52; "Kantian Constructivism in Moral Theory," 22; *Lectures on the History of Moral Philosophy*, 206n5; lexical ordering and, 148; MacIntyre and, 7–8, 17, 29; original position and, 85–87; priority problem and, 149–152; rational grounding of moral judgements and, 95; *Themes in Kant's Moral Philosophy*, 23; *A Theory of Justice*, 18, 19, 21–22, 95, 149–151; universal and, 70; virtue and, 31, 186
Rawls-MacIntyre debate, 7–8
reason, private use of, 81–82
rebellious teenagers, 111–112
reflection, 154
reflective judgement, 9, 153, 162–164
reflexivity, problem of, 9, 111, 122, 133, 139, 198–200
Religion within the Bounds of Mere Reason (Kant), 182
Renaut, Alain, 9, 10, 11, 75–76, 86–87, 99, 115–119, 199
rigorism, 165, 167, 171
Ritter, Joachim, 8, 39–40, 41–45, 83, 84
Rooney, Sally, 1, 3
Ross, David, 148–150
Rousseau, Jean-Jacques, 52
rule-following paradox, 207n15

rules-based reasoning, 17, 31

safety, 85
Samaritan duty, 5
Sartre, Jean-Paul, 9, 10, 29–30, 99, 112–120
Schadenfreude, 184–185
scholasticism, 58
self, narrative conception of, 35–36, 76–77
self-defence, 212n5
self-sufficiency, illusion of, 123–126
sensitivity, 185–186
sensus communis, 154–156, 161
sentimentality, 185–186
Sherman, Nancy, 9, 10, 72, 161, 168, 170, 171–172, 178, 182–186
Sibley, W. M., 206n3
Singer, Peter, 162
Sittlichkeit (ethical life), 42–43
social conservatism, 56
social norms/norms: communal, 43, 47–48, 54–55; dominant, 40–41, 82–83; questioning of, 111–112; traditional, 114–115
soldiers, 2–3
solicitude, 189–190
solidarity, 190
Sources of Normativity (Korsgaard), 98
South Africa, 176, 177
Spaemann, Robert, 41
Stagirite's perspective, 140, 179
syllogisms, 31–32
sympathy, 184–185
syntheses of traditions, 78–80

teleological moral theories, 20
Tétaz, Jean-Marc, 210–211n7
Themes in Kant's Moral Philosophy (Rawls), 23
theoretical reasoning, 66–67
Theory of Justice, A (Rawls), 18, 19, 21–22, 95, 149–151
Thomas of Aquinas, 78, 125
Thompson, Michael, 131–132

tolerance, 55, 190
tradition/traditionalism, 36–37, 46, 200, 202–203
transcendental conditions, 51
translation, 202–204
Truth and Method (Gadamer), 45, 47
Truth and Reconciliation Commission, 176, 177

unity of virtue, 33, 78
universal: conception of, 28; lateral, 10, 201, 203–204
universal invariants, 201
universal law, 23, 29–30, 53
Universal Law, Formula of, 51, 53, 102
universalism, 200–204
universalists, Aristotelian, 80–81
universalization, principle of, 51
universalization tests, 17, 23–25, 30–31, 53–54, 165–167
Urteilskraft model, 46, 147, 152–161, 161–162, 163–164, 195–197
utilitarians, 6

Varden, Helga, 171
veil of ignorance, 86–87

verifiability principle, 206n6
vice, 194
virtue ethics, 58, 126–127
virtues, 31, 32–33, 45, 47, 78, 178–182, 193–194
virtues, Kantian, 182–191
virtuous action, 140–143, 212n3
"Volk and History in Herders Thought" (Gadamer), 207n1
Vow of allegiance of the Professors of the Germany University and High Schools to Adolf Hitler and the National Socialist State, 39–40

waiter example, 112–114
Werner-Müller, Jan, 41
"What Morality Is Not" (MacIntyre), 29–30
Whose Justice? Which Rationality? (MacIntyre), 25, 121
Wiggins, David, 12, 47
Williams, Bernard, 121, 139–140
Windelband, Wilhelm, 205n10
Wittgenstein, Ludwig, 58, 128, 207n15
Wolin, Richard, 206–207n1

www.ingramcontent.com/pod-product-compliance
Lightning Source LLC
Chambersburg PA
CBHW020117010526
44115CB00008B/868